UNDERSTANDING AND USING

ENGLISH GRAMMAR

Third Edition   Volume B

UNDERSTANDING AND USING

ENGLISH GRAMMAR

Third Edition

Volume B

Betty Schrampfer Azar

PRENTICE HALL REGENTS
A VIACOM COMPANY
Upper Saddle River, NJ 07458

Azar, Betty Schrampfer
    Understanding and using English grammar / Betty Schrampfer Azar
    - - 3rd ed.
            p.   cm.
    Includes index.
    ISBN 0-13-0-13-958752-7
    1. English language– –Textbooks for foreign speakers.   2. English
    language– –Grammar– –Problems, exercises, etc.   I. Title.
    PE1128.A97   1998   97-47425
    428.2'4– –dc21   CIP

Publisher: *Mary Jane Peluso*
Development Editor: *Janet Johnston*
AVP/Director of Production and Manufacturing: *Aliza Greenblatt*
Executive Managing Editor: *Dominick Mosco*
Managing Editor: *Shelley Hartle*
Electronic Production Editors: *Christine Mann, Rachel Baumann*
Electronic Art Production Supervisor: *Ken Liao*
Electronic Publishing Specialist: *Steven Greydanus*
Art Director: *Merle Krumper*
Cover & Interior Design: *Eric Dawson*
Manufacturing Manager: *Ray Keating*
Illustrator: *Don Martinetti*

Published by PRENTICE HALL REGENTS
Prentice-Hall, Inc.
A Simon & Schuster Company
PRENTICE HALL REGENTS
A VIACOM COMPANY Upper Saddle River, New Jersey 07458

Printed in the United States of America
10 9 8 7 6 5 4 3 2 1

0-13-958752-7

0-13-958729-2   (Volume A)
0-13-958661-X   (full)

Prentice-Hall International (UK) Limited, *London*
Prentice-Hall of Australia Pty. Limited, *Sydney*
Prentice-Hall Canada Inc., *Toronto*
Prentice-Hall Hispanoamericana, S.A., *Mexico*
Prentice-Hall of India Private Limited, *New Delhi*
Prentice-Hall of Japan, Inc., *Tokyo*
Simon & Schuster Asia Pte. Ltd., *Singapore*
Editora Prentice-Hall do Brasil, Ltda., *Rio de Janeiro*

In memoriam

To my wonderful parents,
Frances Nies Schrampfer
and
William H. Schrampfer,
who set me on my path.

CONTENTS

Preface to the Third Edition

Understanding and Using English Grammar is a developmental skills text for intermediate to advanced students of English as a second or foreign language. While focusing on grammar, it promotes the development of all language skills in a variety of ways. It functions principally as a classroom teaching text but also serves as a comprehensive reference text for students.

The eclectic approach and abundant variety of exercise material remain the same as in the earlier editions, but each new edition incorporates new ways and means. In particular:

- The communicative aspects of *Understanding and Using English Grammar* are more fully developed and explicit in the third edition. There are numerous "real communication" opportunities for the teacher to exploit. The text often uses the students' own life experiences as context and regularly introduces topics of interest to stimulate the free expression of ideas in structured as well as open discussions. The text supports the view of many experienced teachers that grammar-based and communicative approaches are not mutually exclusive, but rather mutually supportive, and can advantageously co-exist in the same language program, even in the same class, even in the same lesson.

- Similarly, the interactive aspects of the text receive greater emphasis in the third edition. Many of the exercises formerly designated ORAL or ORAL (BOOKS CLOSED) are now reformatted to be more clearly available for pair work or group work, in addition to still being viable as class work led by a teacher. This edition encourages interactivity but leaves it open for the users to decide what degree of interactivity best suits their needs.

- There is now an even wider variety of exercise types. This edition has a larger number of free-response exercises and open-ended communicative tasks, while still providing ample controlled-response exercises to aid initial understanding of the form, meaning, and usage of the target structures. It also includes more writing topics, more speaking activities, expanded error analysis exercises, and additional extended-context exercises.

- Long chapters have been broken into shorter units, and certain grammar units have been reorganized.

The bird soaring upward and forward on the cover of this new edition is a swallow. Found throughout the world, swallows are joyful, playful, energetic birds whose comings and goings announce changes in the seasons. Like the butterfly on the second edition, the swallow on this edition signals new beginnings—as student, teacher, and text writer come together in our shared journey toward the learning of a new language.

Understanding and Using English Grammar is accompanied by

- a *Workbook,* consisting principally of selfstudy exercises for independent work.
- a *Chartbook,* a reference book consisting of only the grammar charts.
- an *Answer Key,* with the answers to the exercises.
- a *Teacher's Guide,* with teaching suggestions and additional notes on grammar, as well as the answers to the exercises.

The *Azar Grammar Series* consists of

- *Understanding and Using English Grammar* (blue cover) for upper-level students.
- *Fundamentals of English Grammar* (black) for mid-level students.
- *Basic English Grammar* (red) for lower or beginning levels.

Supplementary works by other authors

- *Fun with Grammar,* a teacher resource text by Suzanne Woodward
- *Azar Interactive,* a CD-ROM program by Howard Beckerman

Acknowledgments

The second edition of *UUEG* was thoroughly reviewed by twenty-five ESL/EFL professionals. Their reviews were outstandingly helpful in their insights and suggestions. I studied the reviews with great care, and they greatly influenced the revision in matters large and small. I could not, unfortunately, make every change and addition that every reviewer sought (not without writing a 1000-page book—which my publisher would definitely frown upon!). I wish to express my heartfelt thanks for the care and thought these colleagues put into their reviews. They are Catherine Sajna, Hawaii Pacific University, English Foundations Program; Brian White, Lakeview Learning Center/ALSP; Anne Albarelli-Siegfried, North Harris Community College; Akabi Danielan, Glendale Career College; M. Cristina Parsons, Pueblo High School; Peter Jarvis, Pace University; Cheri Boyer, University of Arizona, CESL; Molly Burns, Wisconsin ESL Language Institute; Molly McGrath, Hunter College, IELI; James Burke, El Paso Community College; Deborah Healey, Oregon State University, ELI; Dan Manolescu, Adelphi University, Berlitz on Campus Language Institute for English; Gerald Lee Boyd, Northern Virginia Community College; Karen Richelli-Kolbert, Manhattanville College, School of Education; Marjorie Friedman, Eckerd College, ELS Language Center; Natalie Gast, Customized Language Skills Training; Anna Krauthammer, Touro College; Russell Hirsch, Touro College; Stacy Hagen, Edmond's Community College, Intensive ESL; Lida Baker, University of California, Los-Angeles; Susan Kash-Brown, Southeast Community College.

I have a topnotch professional support team. They allow me to do what I do with enjoyment and ease. Chief among them are Shelley Hartle, my managing editor, whose wide-ranging skills make her my indispensable right hand in all matters; Janet Johnston, publishing and wordsmithery expert par excellence, who cheerfully holds me to account for every dot and letter; Barbara Matthies, the teacher's guide co-author, who is my most splendid (i.e., toughest) critic; and our publisher, Mary Jane Peluso, who smooths our paths in myriad, much appreciated ways. In addition I wish to thank Robin Baliszewski, who as the new president of Prentice Hall Regents has brought a breath of fresh air and renewed dedication to quality in ESL/EFL publication; Stella Reilly, especially for the superb job she did in collating the reviews; Christine Mann, who transformed our disk into a beautifully and precisely formatted text; her colleague, Rachel Baumann; and also Julie Alexander, Aliza Greenblatt, Dom Mosco, Merle Krumper, and Eric Dawson.

I also once again thank Don Martinetti, the illustrator, whose touches of whimsy are so delightful. My appreciation also goes to graphic designer Christine Shrader, creator of the swallow that heralds this third edition.

I wish to express special acknowledgment of the contributing writers for the *Understanding and Using English Grammar Workbook,* Second Edition: Rachel Spack Koch, Susan Jamieson, Barbara Andrews, and Jeanie Francis. Some of the exercise material originally created for the workbook has been woven into this third edition of the student book, and I thank them for the ways in which this material has enrichened the text.

In addition, my thanks go to Tina Carver, Stacy Hagen, Mary Barratt, Ayse Stromsdorfer, Bonnie Arndt, Chelsea Azar, Rachel Flaherty, Nick Harris, Joy Edwards, Carolyn Cliff, Sue Van Etten, Patti Gulledge-White, R.T. Steltz, Buffy Cribbs, Bruce Morrow, and in loving memory, Holly Turner. And finally, very special thanks to Larry Harris for his support, his strength, his *joie de vivre* — and for opening doors.

UNDERSTANDING
AND USING

ENGLISH
GRAMMAR

Third Edition   Volume B

John is going to school ← subject

who?

CHAPTER 12
Noun Clauses

CONTENTS

12-1 INTRODUCTION

independent clause (a) Sue lives in Tokyo. independent clause (b) Where does Sue live?	A clause is a group of words containing a subject and a verb.★ An *independent clause* (or *main clause)* is a complete sentence. It contains the main subject and verb of a sentence. Examples (a) and (b) are complete sentences. (a) is a statement, and (b) is a question.
dependent clause (c) where Sue lives	A *dependent clause* (or *subordinate clause*) is not a complete sentence. It must be connected to an independent clause. Example (c) is a dependent clause.
indep. cl. dependent cl. (d) I know *where Sue lives.*	Example (d) is a complete sentence. It has an independent clause with the main subject **(I)** and verb **(know)** of the sentence. **Where Sue lives** is a dependent clause connected to an independent clause. **Where Sue lives** is called a *noun clause.*
noun phrase (e) **His story** was interesting. noun clause (f) **What he said** was interesting.	A *noun phrase* is used as a subject or an object. A *noun clause* is used as a subject or an object. In other words, a noun clause is used in the same ways as a noun phrase. In (e): **His story** is a noun phrase. It is used as the subject of the sentence. In (f): **What he said** is a noun clause. It is used as the subject of the sentence. The noun clause has its own subject **(he)** and verb **(said)**.
noun phrase (g) I heard **his story**. noun clause (h) I heard **what he said**.	In (g): **his story** is a noun phrase. It is used as the object of the verb **heard**. In (h): **what he said** is a noun clause. It is used as the object of the verb **heard**.
noun phrase (i) I listened to **his story**. noun clause (j) I listened to **what he said**.	In (i): **his story** is a noun phrase. It is used as the object of the preposition **to**. In (j): **what he said** is a noun clause. It is used as the object of the preposition **to**.

★A *phrase* is a group of words that does NOT contain a subject and a verb.

★★See Appendix Unit B for more information about question words and question forms.

☐ EXERCISE 1. Noun clauses. (Chart 12-1)

Directions: Add the necessary punctuation and capitalization to the following. <u>Underline</u> the noun clauses.

1. I couldn't hear the teacher what did she say

   → *I couldn't hear the teacher.* ***What did she say?***

2. I couldn't hear <u>what the teacher said.</u>

3. Where did Tom go no one knows. *where*

4. No one knows <u>where Tom went.</u> *when*

5. <u>Where Tom went</u> is a secret.

6. What does Anna want we need to know.

7. We need to know <u>what Anna wants.</u>

8. What does Alex need do you know

9. Do you know <u>what Alex needs.</u>

10. <u>What Alex needs</u> is a new job.

11. We talked about <u>what Alex needs.</u>

12. What do you need did you talk to your parents about what you need

---

12-2 NOUN CLAUSES BEGINNING WITH A QUESTION WORD

QUESTION	NOUN CLAUSE	
Where does she live? What did he say? When do they arrive?	(a) I don't know *where she lives.* (b) I couldn't hear *what he said.* (c) Do you know *when they arrive?*	In (a): *where she lives* is the object of the verb *know*. In a noun clause, the subject precedes the verb. Do not use question word order in a noun clause. Notice: *does, did*, and *do* are used in questions, but not in noun clauses. See Appendix Unit B for more information about question words and question forms.
S V Who lives there? What happened? Who is at the door?	**S V** (d) I don't know *who lives there.* (e) Please tell me *what happened.* (f) I wonder *who is at the door.*	In (d): The word order is the same in both the question and the noun clause because *who* is the subject in both.
V S Who is she? Who are those men? Whose house is that?	**S V** (g) I don't know *who she is.* (h) I don't know *who those men are.* (i) I wonder *whose house that is.*	In (g): *she* is the subject of the question, so it is placed in front of the verb *be* in the noun clause.*
What did she say? What should they do?	(j) *What she said* surprised me. (k) *What they should do* is obvious.	In (j): *What she said* is the subject of the sentence. Notice in (k): A noun clause subject takes a singular verb (e.g., *is*).

*COMPARE: *Who is at the door?* = *who* is the subject of the question.

         Who are those men? = *those men* is the subject of the question, so *be* is plural.

□ EXERCISE 2. Noun clauses beginning with a question word. (Chart 12-2)

Directions: Change the question in parentheses to a noun clause.

1. (How old is he?) I don't know _how old he is_ ✓ .

2. (What was he talking about?) _What he was talking about_

was interesting.

3. (Where do you live?) Please tell me _where you live._ ✓ .

4. (What did she say?) _what she said_ wasn't true. ✓

5. (When are they coming?) Do you know _when they are comming_ ✓

6. (How much does it cost?) I can't remember _How much it cost._ ✓

7. (Which one does he want?) Let's ask him _which one he wants_ ✓

8. (Who is coming to the party?) I don't know _who is comming to the Party._ ✓

9. (Who are those people?) I don't know _I don't know who are those People._ are

10. (Whose pen is this?) Do you know _whose pen this is_ ✓ ?

11. (Why did they leave the country?) _Why they left the cauntry,_ is a secret.

12. (What are we doing in class?) _what we are doing in class_ is easy.

13. (Where did she go?) _Where she went_ is none of your business.

14. (How many letters are there in the English alphabet?) I don't remember _how many letters there are in the English alphabet._

15. (Who is the mayor of New York City?) I don't know _who is the major of New York city._

16. (How old does a person have to be to get a driver's license?) I need to find out _to get drivers License how old a person have to be._

17. (What happened?) I don't know _what happened_ .

18. (Who opened the door?) I don't know _who opened the door_ .

Noun word not include.
Nor
Does, DD.

☐ **EXERCISE 3. Noun clauses beginning with a question word. (Chart 12-2)**
Directions: Work in pairs, in groups, or as a class.
Speaker A: Your book is open. Ask the question.
Speaker B: Your book is closed. Begin your response with "I don't know . . . ."

Example:
SPEAKER A *(book open):* What time is it?
SPEAKER B *(book closed):* I don't know what time it is.

(Switch roles if working in pairs.)

1. Where does (. . .) live?
2. What country is (. . .) from?
3. How long has (. . .) been living here?
4. What is (. . .)'s telephone number?
5. Where is the post office?
6. How far is it to (Kansas City)?
7. Why is (. . .) absent?
8. Where is my book?
9. What kind of watch does (. . .) have?
10. Why was (. . .) absent yesterday?
11. Where did (. . .) go yesterday?
12. What kind of government does (Italy) have?

13. What is (. . .)'s favorite color?
14. How long has (. . .) been married?
15. Why are we doing this exercise?
16. Who turned off the lights?
17. Where is (. . .) going to eat lunch/dinner?
18. When does (the semester) end?
19. Where did (. . .) go after class yesterday?
20. Why is (. . .) smiling?
21. How often does (. . .) go to the library?
22. Whose book is that?
23. How much did that book cost?
24. Who took my book?

☐ **EXERCISE 4. Noun clauses beginning with a question word.**
(Chart 12-2 and Appendix Unit B)
Directions: Make a question from the given sentence. The words in parentheses should be the answer to the question you make. Use a question word (***who, what, how,*** etc.).★ Then change the question to a noun clause.

1. Tom will be here *(next week)*.

   QUESTION: _____ When will Tom be here?_____

   NOUN CLAUSE: Please tell me ___ when Tom will be here._____

2. He is coming *(because he wants to visit his friends)*.

   QUESTION: ___ Why is he coming?_____

   NOUN CLAUSE: Please tell me ___ when he is coming_____
   friends

3. He'll be on flight *(645, not flight 742)*.

   QUESTION: ___ Which flight will he be on?_____

   NOUN CLAUSE: Please tell me ___ which flight he will be on._____
   Flight 742.
   which flight he will be on

★See Appendix Unit B for information about forming questions.

4. *(Jim Hunter)* is going to meet him at the airport.

QUESTION: _who is going to meet him at the Airport?_

NOUN CLAUSE: Please tell me _whether who ~~ter~~ is going to meet him at the Airport_

5. Jim Hunter is *(his roommate)*.

QUESTION: _who is Jim Hunter?_

NOUN CLAUSE: Please tell me _who Jim Hunter is + his roommate_

6. Tom's address is *(4149 Riverside Road)*.

QUESTION: _what is Tom's address?_

NOUN CLAUSE: Please tell me _what Tom's address is. Road_

7. He lives *(on Riverside Road in Columbus, Ohio, USA)*.

QUESTION: _Where does he live?_

NOUN CLAUSE: Please tell me _where he lives_

8. He was *(in Chicago)* last week.

QUESTION: _where he was last week?_

NOUN CLAUSE: Please tell me _where he was last week_

9. He has been working for IBM* *(since 1998)*.

QUESTION: _How long has been working for IBM?_

NOUN CLAUSE: Do you know _How long has been working for IBM_

10. He has *(an IBM)* computer at home.

QUESTION: _what kind of computer has he at home_

NOUN CLAUSE: Do you know _what kind of computer has at home._

☐ EXERCISE 5. Noun clauses beginning with a question word.
    (Chart 12-2 and Appendix Unit B)
Directions: Use the words in parentheses to complete the sentences. Use any appropriate verb tense. Some of the completions contain noun clauses, and some contain questions.

1. A: Where *(Ruth, go)* _did Ruth go_ ? She's not in her room.

   B: I don't know. Ask her friend Tina. She might know where *(Ruth, go)*
   Ruth went .

2. A: Oops! I made a mistake. Where *(my eraser, be)* _is my eraser_ ?
   Didn't I lend it to you?

   ✔ B: I don't have it. Ask Sally where *(it, be)* _it is_ . I think I saw
   her using it.

―――――――――
*IBM = the name of a corporation (**I**nternational **B**usiness **M**achines)

✓ 3. A: The door isn't locked! Why (Fred, lock, not) _didn't Fred lock_ it before he left?*

   ✓ B: Why ask me? How am I supposed to know why (he, lock, not) _he didn't lock._ it? Maybe he just forgot.

✓ 4. A: Mr. Lee is a recent immigrant, isn't he? How long (he, be) _has he been_ in this country?

   ✓ B: I have no idea, but I'll be seeing Mr. Lee this afternoon. Would you like me to ask him how long (he, live) _he has lived_ _been living_ here? / he has been living

✓ 5. A: Are you a student here? I'm a student here, too. Tell me what classes (you, take) _you are taking_ this term. Maybe we're in some of the same classes.

   B: Math 4, English 2, History 6, and Chemistry 101. What classes (you, take) _are you taking._ ?

✓ 6. A: Help! Quick! Look at that road sign! Which road (we, be supposed) _are we supposed_ to take?

   B: You're the driver! Don't look at me! I don't know which road (we, be supposed) _we are supposed_ to take. I've never been here before in my entire life.

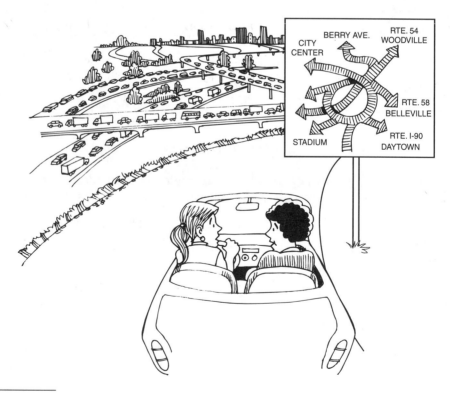

*Word order in negative questions:
  Usual: *Why didn't you call me?* (with *did* + *not* contracted)
  Very formal: *Why did you not call me?*

□ EXERCISE 6. Information questions and noun clauses.
    (Charts 12-1 and 12-2; Appendix Unit B)
    Directions: Work in pairs. Switch roles after every group of five items.
    Speaker A: Your book is open. Ask any question using the given words.
    Speaker B: Your book is closed. To make sure you understood Speaker A correctly, repeat
        what s/he said, using a noun clause. Begin by saying "You want to know . . . ."
    Listen to each other's grammar carefully, especially word order.

Example: who \ roommate

SPEAKER A *(book open):* Who is your roommate?

SPEAKER B *(book closed):* You want to know who my roommate is.

Example: where \ go

SPEAKER A *(book open):* Where did you go after class yesterday?

SPEAKER B *(book closed):* You want to know where I went after class yesterday.

Example: how far \ it

SPEAKER A *(book open):* How far is it from Bangkok to Rangoon?

SPEAKER B *(book closed):* You want to know how far it is from Bangkok to Rangoon.

1. whose \ that
2. how much \ cost
3. what time \ get
4. how long \ you
5. what kind \ have

6. when \ you
7. where \ last night
8. why \ didn't
9. what \ like
10. where \ the teacher

11. who \ prime minister
12. which \ want
13. why \ blue
14. what \ after
15. from whom \ borrow

16. where \ born
17. what color \ eyes
18. whose \ is
19. which \ you
20. why \ ask

21. when \ get
22. where \ located
23. who \ is
24. who \ talk
25. how many \ go

26. what \ tomorrow
27. how far \ it
28. what kind \ buy
29. how often \ you
30. to whom \ give

12-3 NOUN CLAUSES BEGINNING WITH *WHETHER* OR *IF*

YES/NO QUESTION	NOUN CLAUSE	

Will she come?
 	
Does he need help?
	(a) I don't know *whether she will come.*
	    I don't know *if she will come.*
	(b) I wonder *whether he needs help.*
	    I wonder *if he needs help.*
		When a yes/no question is changed to a noun clause, ***whether*** or ***if*** is used to introduce the clause.
		(Note: ***Whether*** is more acceptable in formal English, but ***if*** is quite commonly used, especially in speaking.)

	(c) I wonder *whether or not* she will come. (d) I wonder *whether* she will come *or not.* (e) I wonder *if* she will come *or not.*	In (c), (d), and (e): Notice the patterns when ***or not*** is used.
	(f) ***Whether she comes or not*** is unimportant to me.	In (f): Notice that the noun clause is in the subject position.

☐ **EXERCISE 7. Noun clauses beginning with WHETHER or IF. (Chart 12-3)**
   Directions: Work in pairs, in groups, or as a class. Begin all responses with "I wonder . . . ."

   Examples:
   SPEAKER A *(book open):* Does (. . .) need any help?
   SPEAKER B *(book closed):* I wonder whether/if (. . .) needs any help.

   SPEAKER A *(book open):* Where is (. . .)?
   SPEAKER B *(book closed):* I wonder where (. . .) is.

   1. Where is your friend?
   2. Should we wait for him?
   3. Should you call him?
   4. Where is your dictionary?
   5. Who took your dictionary?
   6. Did (. . .) borrow your dictionary?
   7. Who is that woman?
   8. Does she need any help?
   9. Why is the sky blue?
   10. How long does a butterfly live?
   11. What causes earthquakes?
   12. When was the first book written?
   13. Who is that man?
   14. What is he doing?
   15. Is he having trouble?
   16. Should you offer to help him?
   17. How far is it to (Florida)?
   18. Do we have enough time to go to (Florida) over vacation?
   19. Whose book is this?
   20. Does it belong to (. . .)?
   21. Why did dinosaurs become extinct?
   22. Is there life on other planets?
   23. How did life begin?
   24. Will people live on the moon someday?

☐ **EXERCISE 8. Noun clauses. (Charts 12-2 and 12-3)**
   Directions: Work in pairs, in groups, or as a class. Begin all responses with "Could you please tell me . . . ."

   Example:
   SPEAKER A *(book open):* What is this?
   SPEAKER B *(book closed):* Could you please tell me what this is?

   1. Does this bus go downtown?
   2. How much does this book cost?
   3. When is Flight 62 expected to arrive?
   4. Where is the nearest phone?
   5. Is this word spelled correctly?
   6. What time is it?
   7. Is this information correct?
   8. How much does it cost to fly from (Chicago) to (New York)?
   9. Where is the bus station?
   10. Whose pen is this?

☐ EXERCISE 9. Error analysis: noun clauses. (Charts 12-1 → 12-3)
　　　Directions: Correct the errors.

　　1. Please tell me what is your name. → *Please tell me what **your name is.***

　✓2. No one seems to know when will Maria arrive.

　✓3. I wonder why was Bob late for class.

　✓4. I don't know what ~~does~~ that word means.

　✓5. I wonder ~~does~~ the teacher knows the answer?.

　✓6. What should they do about the hole in their roof is their most pressing problem.

　✓7. I'll ask her would she like some coffee or not.

　✓8. Be sure to tell the doctor where ~~does~~ it hurts.

　✓9. Why am I unhappy is something I can't explain.

　　　　　　　If / whether,
　✓10. I wonder ~~does~~ Tom knows about the meeting or not.

　✓11. I need to know who ~~is~~ your teacher. *is*

　✓12. I don't understand why is the car not running properly.

　✓13. My young son wants to know where ~~do~~ the stars go in the daytime?.

12-4　QUESTION WORDS FOLLOWED BY INFINITIVES

(a) I don't know *what I should do*. (b) I don't know ***what to do***. (c) Pam can't decide *whether she should go or stay home*. (d) Pam can't decide ***whether to go or (to) stay home***. (e) Please tell me *how I can get to the bus station*. (f) Please tell me ***how to get to the bus station***. (g) Jim told us *where we could find it*. (h) Jim told us ***where to find it***.	Question words (***when, where, how, who, whom, whose, what, which***) and ***whether*** may be followed by an infinitive. Each pair of sentences in the examples has the same meaning. Notice that the meaning expressed by the infinitive is either ***should*** or ***can/could***.

☐ EXERCISE 10. Question words followed by infinitives. (Chart 12-4)
　　　Directions: Create sentences with the same meaning by using infinitives.

　　1. He told me when I should come. → *He told me when to come.*
　　2. The plumber told me how I could fix the leak in the sink.　*to fix the leak in the sink.*
　　3. Please tell me where I should meet you.　*to meet you*
　　4. Don had an elaborate excuse for being late for their date, but Sandy didn't know whether she should believe him or not.
　　5. Jim found two shirts he liked, but he had trouble deciding which one ~~he should~~ buy.　*to*
　　6. I've done everything I can think of to help Andy get his life straightened out. I don't know what else ~~I can~~ do.　*to*

Complete the following; use infinitives in your completions.

✓ 7. I was tongue-tied. I didn't know what ___to ~~do~~ say___.

✓ 8. A: I can't decide ___what to wear~~it~~___ to the reception.

B: How about your green suit?

✓ 9. A: Where are you going to live when you go to the university?

B: I'm not sure. I can't decide whether ___to live in the room or home___

✓ 10. A: Do you know how ___to speak English.___?

B: No, but I'd like to learn.

✓ 11. A: I don't know what ___to buy___ for her birthday. Got any suggestions?

B: How about a book? *un plesent choise.*

12. My cousin has a dilemma. He can't decide whether ___to go___ or ___✓to stay___. What do you think he should do?

13. Before you leave on your trip, read this tour book. It tells you where ___to go___ and how ___to get___.

12-5 NOUN CLAUSES BEGINNING WITH *THAT*

STATEMENT	NOUN CLAUSE	
He is a good actor.	(a) I think *that he is a good actor.* (b) I think *he is a good actor.*	In (a): *that he is a good actor* is a noun clause. It is used as the object of the verb *think*.
The world is round.	(c) We know *(that) the world is round.*	The word *that,* when it introduces a noun clause, has no meaning in itself. It simply marks the beginning of the clause. Frequently it is omitted, as in (b), especially in speaking. (If used in speaking, it is unstressed.)
She doesn't understand spoken English.	(d) *That* she doesn't understand spoken English is obvious. (e) *It* is obvious *(that)* she doesn't understand spoken English.	In (d): The noun clause (*That she doesn't understand spoken English*) is the subject of the sentence. The word *that* is not omitted when it introduces a noun clause used as the subject of a sentence, as in (d) and (f).
The world is round.	(f) *That* the world is round is a fact. (g) *It* is a fact *that* the world is round.	More commonly, the word *it* functions as the subject and the noun clause is placed at the end of the sentence, as in (e) and (g).

☐ EXERCISE 11. Noun clauses beginning with THAT. (Chart 12-5)

Directions: Work in pairs, in groups, or as a class.

Speaker A: Change the given sentence into a noun clause. Use *it* + any appropriate expression from the list.

Speaker B: Give the equivalent sentence by using a *that*-clause as the subject.

Example: The world is round.

SPEAKER A *(book open):* It is a fact that the world is round.

SPEAKER B *(book closed):* That the world is round is a fact.

a fact	*obvious*	*surprising*	*unfair*	*a shame*
a well-known fact	*apparent*	*strange*	*too bad*	*a pity*
true	*clear*		*unfortunate*	

1. Tim hasn't been able to make any friends. It is a shame b

2. Drug abuse can ruin one's health. It is obvious.

3. Some women do not earn equal pay for equal work. it is unfair

4. The earth revolves around the sun. It is a well known fact

5. Irene, who is an excellent student, failed her entrance examination. It is suprising

6. Smoking can cause cancer. it is true.

7. English is the principal language of the business community throughout much of the world. it is true.

☐ EXERCISE 12. Noun clauses beginning with THAT. (Chart 12-5)

Directions: Work in pairs or as a class.

Speaker A: Make an original sentence by using *it* and the given expression.

Speaker B: Give the equivalent sentence by using a *that*-clause as the subject.

Example: true

SPEAKER A: It is true that plants need water in order to grow.

SPEAKER B: That plants need water in order to grow is true.

(Switch roles if working in pairs)

1. a fact
2. surprising
3. obvious
4. too bad
5. a well-known fact

6. unfortunate
7. true
8. strange
9. unlikely
10. undeniable

☐ EXERCISE 13. Noun clauses beginning with THAT. (Chart 12-5)

Directions: Complete the sentences.

1. It is my belief that . . . *the war between those two countries will end soon.*

2. It seems to me that . . . .

3. It is my impression that . . . .

4. It is my theory that . . . .

5. It is widely believed that . . . .

6. It is thought that . . . .

7. It has been said that . . . .

8. It is a miracle that . . . .

□ EXERCISE 14. Noun clauses beginning with THAT. (Chart 12-5)
Directions: *That*-clauses may follow **be** + certain adjectives that express feelings or attitudes. Complete the following with your own words.

1. I'm sorry (that) ... *I was late for class.*
2. I'm glad (that) ....
3. I'm disappointed (that) ....
4. I'm pleased (that) ....
5. I'm surprised (that) ....
6. I'm sure (that) ....
7. I'm amazed (that) ....
8. I'm happy (that) ....
9. Yesterday I was annoyed (that) ....
10. I'm afraid (that)★ ....

□ EXERCISE 15. Noun clauses beginning with THAT. (Chart 12-5)
Directions: A *that*-clause may follow **be** directly. Complete the sentences with your own ideas by using *that*-clauses.

1. He says he is twenty-one, but the truth is ... *that he is only eighteen.*
2. There are two reasons why I do not want to go out tonight.
   The first reason is ... *that I have to study.*
   The second reason is ... *that I do not have enough money.*★★
3. There are several reasons why I am studying English.
   One reason is ....
   Another reason is ....
   A third reason is ....
4. I have had three problems since I came here.
   One problem is that ....
   Another problem is that ....
   The third problem I have had is that ....
5. One advantage of owning your own car is ....
   Another advantage is ....
   One disadvantage, however, of owning your own car is ....

□ EXERCISE 16. Noun clauses beginning with THAT. (Chart 12-5)
Directions: A *that*-clause is frequently used with **the fact**. Combine the sentences using "the fact that" to introduce a noun clause.

1. Ann was late. That didn't surprise me.

   → *The fact that Ann was late didn't surprise me.*

2. Rosa didn't come. *That* made me angry.
3. I'm a little tired. I feel fine except for *that*.
4. Natasha didn't pass the entrance examination. She was not admitted to the university due to *that*.
5. Many people in the world live in intolerable poverty. *That* must concern all of us.

★*To be afraid* has two possible meanings:
  (1) It can express fear: *I'm afraid of dogs. I'm afraid that his dog will bite me.*
  (2) In informal English, it often expresses a meaning similar to "*to be sorry*":
      I'm afraid that I can't accept your invitation.
      I'm afraid you have the wrong number.
★★NOTE: *That* is used, not **because**, to introduce the clause. (**Because** might occur only in very informal spoken English: *The first reason is because I have to study.*)

6. Surasuk is frequently absent from class. *That* indicates his lack of interest in school.

7. I was supposed to bring my passport to the examination for identification. I was not aware of *that*.

8. The people of the town were given no warning of the approaching tornado. Due to *that*, there were many casualties.

12-6 QUOTED SPEECH

Quoted speech refers to reproducing words exactly as they were originally spoken.*
Quotation marks ("...") are used.**

QUOTING ONE SENTENCE (a) She said, *"M*y brother is a student*."* (b) "My brother is a student," she said. (c) "My brother," she said, *"i*s a student."	In (a): Use a comma after *she said*. Capitalize the first word of the quoted sentence. Put the final quotation marks outside the period at the end of the sentence. In (b): Use a comma, not a period, at the end of the quoted sentence when it precedes *she said*. In (c): If the quoted sentence is divided by *she said*, use a comma after the first part of the quote. Do not capitalize the first word after *she said*.
QUOTING MORE THAN ONE SENTENCE (d) "My brother is a student. He is attending a university," she said. (e) "My brother is a student," she said. *"H*e is attending a university."	In (d): Quotation marks are placed at the beginning and end of the complete quote. Notice: There are no quotation marks after **student**. In (e): If *she said* comes between two quoted sentences, the second sentence begins with quotation marks and a capital letter.
QUOTING A QUESTION OR AN EXCLAMATION (f) She asked, "When will you be here?" (g) "When will you be here?" she asked. (h) She said, "Watch out*!*"	In (f): The question mark is inside the quotation marks. In (g): If a question mark is used, no comma is used before *she asked*. In (h): The exclamation point is inside the quotation marks.
(i) "My brother is a student," *said Anna*. "My brother," *said Anna*, "is a student."	In (i): The noun subject (**Anna**) follows **said**. A noun subject often follows the verb when the subject and verb come in the middle or at the end of a quoted sentence. (Note: A pronoun subject almost always precedes the verb. Very rare: *"My brother's a student," said she.*)
(j) "Let's leave," *whispered* Dave. (k) "Please help me," *begged* the unfortunate man. (l) "Well," Jack *began*, "it's a long story."	*Say* and *ask* are the most commonly used quote verbs. Some others: *add, agree, announce, answer, beg, begin, comment, complain, confess, continue, explain, inquire, promise, remark, reply, respond, shout, suggest, whisper.*

*Quoted speech is also called "direct speech." *Reported speech* (discussed in Chart 12-7, p. 254) is also called "indirect speech."

**In British English, quotation marks are called "inverted commas" and can consist of either double marks (") or a single mark ('): She said, 'My brother is a student.'

□ EXERCISE 17. Quoted speech. (Chart 12-6)

Directions: Add the necessary punctuation and capitalization.

✓ 1. Henry said, "There is a phone call for you."

✓ 2. "There is a phone call for you," he said.

✓ 3. "There is," said Henry, "a phone call for you."

✓ 4. "There is a phone call for you. It's your sister," said Henry.

✓ 5. "There is a phone call for you," he said. "It's your sister."

✓ 6. I asked him, "Where is the phone?"

✓ 7. "Where is the phone?" she asked.

✓ 8. "Stop the clock!" shouted the referee. "We have an injured player."

✓ 9. "Who won the game?" asked the spectator.

10. "I'm going to rest for the next three hours," she said. "I don't want to be disturbed."

"That's fine. I replied, "You get some rest. I'll make sure no one disturbs you."

□ EXERCISE 18. Quoted speech. (Chart 12-6)

Directions: Add the necessary punctuation and capitalization. Notice that a new paragraph begins each time the speaker changes.

When the police officer came over to my car, he said, "Let me see your driver's license, please."

"What's wrong, Officer? I asked. "Was I speeding?"

"No, you weren't speeding," he replied. "You went through a red light at the corner of Fifth Avenue and Main Street." You almost caused an accident.

"Did I really do that?" I said. "I didn't see a red light."

☐ EXERCISE 19. Activity: quoted speech. (Chart 12-6)

Directions: Choose two of your classmates to have a brief conversation in front of the class, and decide upon a topic for them (what they did last night, what they are doing right now, sports, music, books, etc.). Give them a few minutes to practice their conversation. Then, while they are speaking, take notes so that you can write their exact conversation. Use quoted speech in your written report. Be sure to start a new paragraph each time the speaker changes.

☐ EXERCISE 20. Activity: quoted speech. (Chart 12-6)

Directions: Write fables using quoted speech.

   1. In fables, animals have the power of speech. Discuss what is happening in the illustrations of the grasshopper and the ants. Then write a fable based on the illustrations. Use quoted speech in your fable.

   2. Write a fable that is well known in your country. Use quoted speech.

12-7 REPORTED SPEECH: VERB FORMS IN NOUN CLAUSES

QUOTED SPEECH	REPORTED SPEECH	
(a) "I *watch* TV every day."	→ She said she *watched* TV every day.	*Reported speech* refers to using a noun clause to report what someone has said. No quotation marks are used.
(b) "I *am watching* TV."	→ She said she *was watching* TV.	
(c) "I *have watched* TV."	→ She said she *had watched* TV.	
(d) "I *watched* TV."	→ She said she *had watched* TV.	If the reporting verb (the main verb of the sentence, e.g., *said*) is simple past, the verb in the noun clause will usually also be in a past form, as in the examples.
(e) "I *had watched* TV."	→ She said she *had watched* TV.	
(f) "I *will watch* TV."	→ She said she *would watch* TV.	
(g) "I *am going to watch* TV."	→ She said she *was going to watch* TV.	
(h) "I *can watch* TV."	→ She said she *could watch* TV.	
(i) "I *may watch* TV."	→ She said she *might watch* TV.	
(j) "I *must watch* TV."	→ She said she *had to watch* TV.	
(k) "I *have to watch* TV."	→ She said she *had to watch* TV.	
(l) "I *should watch* TV." "I *ought to watch* TV." "I *might watch* TV."	→ She said she *should watch* TV. → She said she *ought to watch* TV. → She said she *might watch* TV.	In (l): *should*, *ought to*, and *might* do not change to a past form.
(m) Immediate reporting: —What did the teacher just say? I didn't hear him. —He said he *wants* us to read Chapter Six. (n) Later reporting: —I didn't go to class yesterday. Did Mr. Jones make any assignments? —Yes. He said he *wanted* us to read Chapter Six.		Changing verbs to past forms in reported speech is common in both speaking and writing. However, sometimes in spoken English, no change is made in the noun clause verb, especially if the speaker is reporting something immediately or soon after it was said.
(o) "The world *is* round."	→ She said the world *is* round.	Also, sometimes the present tense is retained even in formal English when the reported sentence deals with a general truth, as in (o).
(p) "I *watch* TV every day."	→ She *says* she *watches* TV every day.	When the reporting verb is simple present, present perfect, or future, the noun clause verb is not changed.
(q) "I *watch* TV every day."	→ She *has said* that she *watches* TV every day.	
(r) "I *watch* TV every day."	→ She *will say* that she *watches* TV every day.	
(s) "*Watch* TV."	→ She *told* me *to watch* TV.★	In reported speech, an imperative sentence is changed to an infinitive. *Tell* is used instead of *say* as the reporting verb. See Chart 14-7, p. 307, for other verbs followed by an infinitive that are used to report speech.

*NOTE: *Tell* is immediately followed by a (pro)noun object, but *say* is not: *He told **me** he would be late. He said he would be late.* Also possible: *He said **to me** he would be late.*

☐ EXERCISE 21. Reported speech. (Chart 12-7)
   Directions: Complete the sentences by reporting the speaker's words in a noun clause. Use past verb forms in noun clauses if appropriate.

   1. Pedro said, "I will help you."

      Pedro said _____(that) he would help me._____

   2. "Do you need a pen?" Annie asked.

      Annie asked me _____if I needed a pen._____

3. Jennifer asked, "What do you want?"

Jennifer asked me ___what I wanted.___

4. Talal asked, "Are you hungry?"

Talal wanted to know ___If I was hungary.___

5. "I want a sandwich," Elena said.

Elena said ___she wanted a sandwich.___

6. "I'm going to move to Ohio," said Bruce.

Bruce informed me ___he was moving to ohio___

7. "Did you enjoy your trip?" asked Kim.

Kim asked me ___If i had enjoyed my trip.___

8. Oscar asked, "What are you talking about?"

Oscar asked me ___what I was talking about___

9. Maria asked, "Have you seen my grammar book?"

Maria wanted to know ___if I have seen her grammar book.___

10. Yuko said, "I don't want to go."

Yuko said ___she didn't want to go.___

11. Sam asked, "Where is Nadia?"

Sam wanted to know ___where Nadia was.___

12. "Can you help me with my report?" asked David.

David asked me ___whether I could help___

13. "I may be late," said Mike.

Mike told me ___he might be late___

14. Felix said, "You should work harder."

Felix told me ___that I should work harder.___

15. Rosa said, "I have to go downtown."

Rosa said ___she had to go downt___

16. "Why is the sky blue?" my young daughter often asks.

My young daughter often asks me ___why the sky is blue.___

17. My mother asked, "Why are you tired?"

My mother wondered ___that I was tired___

18. "I will come to the meeting," said Pedro.

Pedro told me ___he would come to the meeting___

19. Ms. Adams just asked Ms. Chang, "Will you be in class tomorrow?"

Ms. Adams wanted to know ___if Ms chang___

20. "The sun rises in the east," said Mr. Clark.

Mr. Clark, an elementary school teacher, explained to his students _____ the sun rises in the east.

21. "Someday we'll be in contact with beings from outer space."

The scientist predicted _____ some day we would be

22. "I think I'll go to the library to study."

Joe said _____ he thought he would go to library

23. "Does Omar know what he's doing?"

I wondered _____ Omar knew what he was doing.

24. "Is what I've heard true?"

I wondered _____ what I have heard was true.

25. "Sentences with noun clauses are a little complicated."

Olga thinks _____

☐ **EXERCISE 22. Activity: reported speech. (Chart 12-7)**

Directions: Form groups of three and choose a leader. Only the leader's book is open.
Speaker A: You are the leader. Your book is open. Whisper a question to Speaker B.
Speaker B: Your book is closed. Make sure you understand the question.
Speaker C: Your book is closed. Ask Speaker B something like "What did Speaker A want
        to know/say/ask you?"
Speaker B: Begin your response with "He (She) asked me . . . ."

Example:

SPEAKER A to B *(whispered):* Where is your friend?

SPEAKER C to B *(aloud):* What did (Speaker A) want to know?

SPEAKER B to C *(aloud):* He (She) asked me where my friend was (OR is).

1. What time is it?
2. Can you speak Arabic?
3. Have you seen *(title of a movie)*?
4. Will you be here tomorrow?
5. What kind of camera do you have?
6. What courses are you taking?
7. Did you finish your assignment?
8. *(Make up your own question.)*

Switch roles.

9. Have you read any good books lately?
10. How do you like living here?
11. May I borrow your dictionary?
12. Where will you be tomorrow around
    three o'clock?
13. What are you going to do during
    vacation?

14. Did you go to a party last night?
15. Can I use your pen?
16. *(Make up your own question.)*

Switch roles.

17. How many people have you met in the
    last couple of months?
18. Where should I meet you after class?
19. Do you understand what I am saying?
20. Did you go to class yesterday?
21. Is what you said really true?
22. Is what you want to talk to me about
    important?
23. How do you know that what you said
    is true?
24. *(Make up your own question.)*

□ **EXERCISE 23. Activity: reported speech. (Chart 12-7)**
Directions: With books closed, report to the class at least one question you were asked in the previous exercise and who asked it. Use a past verb form in the noun clause.

Example: Roberto asked me if I'd read any good books lately.

□ **EXERCISE 24. Reported speech: verb forms in noun clauses. (Chart 12-7)**
Directions: Complete the sentences, using the information in the dialogue. Change the verbs to a past form as appropriate.

1. *Fred asked me, "Can we still get tickets to the game?"*
I said, "I've already bought them."

   When Fred asked me if we __could still get__

   tickets to the game, I told him that I

   __had already bought__ them.

2. *Mrs. White said, "Janice, you have to clean up*
your room and empty the dishwasher before
you leave for the game."
   Janice said, "Okay, Mom. I will."

   Mrs. White told Janice that she __had to clean up__

   her room and empty the dishwasher before she __could leave__

   for the game. Janice promised her mom that she __would__ .

3. *I asked the ticket seller, "Is the concert going to be rescheduled?"*
The ticket seller said, "I don't know, Ma'am. I just work here."

   When I asked the ticket seller if the concert _____ to be

   rescheduled, she told me that she _____ and said that she just

   _____ there.

4. *I asked Boris, "Where will the next chess match take place?"*
Boris replied, "It hasn't been decided yet."

   When I asked Boris _____ place, he replied that it

   __hadn't been decided__ yet.

5. *I said to Alan, "I'm very discouraged. I don't think I'll ever speak English well."*
   Alan said, "Your English is getting better every day. In another year, you'll be speaking
English with the greatest of ease."

   I complained that I _____ very discouraged. I said that I

   _____ I _____ ever _____ English

   well. Alan told me that my English _____ better every day. He

   assured me that in another year, I _____ English with the

   greatest of ease.

6.   *A person in the audience asked the speaker, "Are the necessary means to increase the world's food supply presently available?"*
The agronomy professor said, "It might be possible to grow 50 percent of the world's food in underwater cultivation if we can develop inexpensive methods."

A person in the audience asked the agronomy professor if the necessary means to increase the world's food supply ___were___ presently available. The professor stated that it ___might be___ possible to grow 50 percent of the world's food under water if we _____ inexpensive methods.

□ EXERCISE 25. Reported speech. (Chart 12-7)
   Directions: Change the quoted speech to reported speech. Study the example carefully and use the same pattern: ***said that . . . and that*** OR ***said that . . . but that***.

1. "My father is a businessman. My mother is an engineer."
   He said that ___his father was a businessman and that his mother was an engineer.___

2. "I'm excited about my new job. I've found a nice apartment."
   I got a letter from my sister yesterday. She said ___she was excited about her new job and that she had found a nice___

3. "Your Uncle Harry is in the hospital. Your Aunt Sally ~~is~~ *was* very worried about him."
   The last time my mother wrote to me, she said ___her uncle harry was in the hospital and that s___

4. "I expect you to be in class every day. Unexcused absences ~~may~~ *might* affect your grades."
   Our sociology professor said ___That I___
   _____

5. "Highway 66 ~~will~~ *would* be closed for two months. *and that* Commuters should seek alternate routes."
   The newspaper said _____
   _____

6. "~~I'm~~ *he was* getting good grades, *and that had.* but I ~~have~~ difficulty understanding lectures."
   My brother is a junior at a state university. In his last letter, he wrote _____
   _____

7. "Every obstacle ~~is~~ *was* a steppingstone to success. *and that my* ~~You~~ *I* should view problems in ~~your~~ life as opportunities to prove yourself."
   My father often told me _____
   _____

8. "I'll come to the meeting, but I can't stay for more than an hour."

would   *couldn't*

✓ Julia told me <u>That she would come.</u>

_____

☐ **EXERCISE 26. Activity: reported speech. (Charts 12-1 → 12-7)**

Directions: Work in groups or as a class.
Speaker A: Ask a question on the given topic—whatever comes into your mind. Use a
              question word (***when, how, where, what, why,*** *etc.*).
Speaker B: Answer the question in a complete sentence.
Speaker C: Report what Speaker A and Speaker B said.

Example: tonight
SPEAKER A (ROSA):   What are you going to do tonight?
SPEAKER B (ALI):   I'm going to study.
SPEAKER C (YUNG):   Rosa asked Ali what he was going to do tonight, and Ali replied that
                     he was going to study.

1. tonight	5. book	9. television
2. music	6. this city	10. dinner
3. courses	7. population	11. next year
4. tomorrow	8. last year	12. vacation

☐ **EXERCISE 27. Review: noun clauses. (Charts 12-1 → 12-7)**

Directions: Complete the sentences.

1. I cannot understand why . . . .
2. One of the students remarked that . . . .
3. I was not sure whose . . . .
4. What . . . surprised me.
5. That she . . . surprised me.
6. One of the students stated that . . . .
7. I could not . . . due to the fact that . . . .
8. What he said was that . . . .
9. No one knows who . . . .
10. The instructor announced that . . . .
11. What I want to know is why . . . .
12. What . . . is not important.
13. We discussed the fact that . . . .
14. I wonder whether . . . .

☐ **EXERCISE 28. Activity: noun clauses. (Charts 12-1 → 12-7)**

Directions: Read each dialogue and then write a report about it. The report should include
an accurate idea of the speakers' words, but doesn't have to use their exact words.

Example: Jack said, "I can't go to the game."
          Tom said, "Oh? Why not?"
          "I don't have enough money for a ticket," replied Jack.

Possible written reports of the above dialogue:

a. Jack told Tom that he couldn't go to the game because he didn't have enough
   money for a ticket.
b. When Tom asked Jack why he couldn't go to the game, Jack said he didn't have
   enough money for a ticket.
c. Jack said he couldn't go to the game. When Tom asked him why not, Jack replied
   that he didn't have enough money for a ticket.

Write reports of the following dialogues:

1. "What are you doing?" Alex asked.
   "I'm drawing a picture," I said.

2. Ann said, "Do you want to go to a movie Sunday night?"
   Sue said, "I'd like to, but I have to study."

3. "How old are you, Mrs. Robinson?" the little boy asked.
   Mrs. Robinson said, "It's not polite to ask people their age."

4. "Is there anything you especially want to watch on TV tonight?" my sister asked.
   "Yes," I replied. "There's a show at eight that I've been waiting to see for a long time."
   "What is it?" she asked.
   "It's a documentary on green sea turtles," I said.
   "Why do you want to see that?"
   "I'm doing a research paper on sea turtles. I think I might be able to get some good information from the documentary. Why don't you watch it with me?"
   "No, thanks," she said. "I'm not especially interested in green sea turtles."

□ EXERCISE 29. Activity: noun clauses. (Charts 12-1 → 12-7)
   Directions: Make up a dialogue for the two characters waiting in the supermarket line, and then write a story about the picture. The events in the picture happened yesterday.

Directions: Correct the errors.

✓ 1. Tell the taxi driver where ~~do~~ you want to go.

✓ 2. My roommate came into the room and asked me ~~"~~why aren't you in class~~?~~ I said I am

waiting for a telephone call from my family~~.~~"

— ✓ 3. It was my first day at the university, and I ~~am~~ *was* on my way to my first class. I wondered

who else will be in the class~~.~~ *and* ~~What~~ the teacher would be like?

✓ 4. He asked me that what ~~did~~ I intend ~~to~~ *ed* do after I graduate~~?~~ ~~?~~

✓ 5. Many of the people in the United States *don't* ~~doesn't~~ know much about geography. For

example, people will ask you where *is* ~~is~~ Japan located.

✓ 6. What ~~does~~ a patient tell*s* a doctor ~~it~~ is confidential.

7. What my friend and I did ~~it~~ was our secret. We didn't even tell our parents what ~~did~~ *we*

~~we~~ do.

8. The doctor asked ~~that~~ *if* I felt okay. I told him that I ~~don't~~ *didn't* feel well.

✓ 9. *It* ~~Is~~ clear that the ability to use a computer ~~it~~ is an important skill in the modern world.

10. I asked him what kind of movies ~~does~~ *d* he like~~,~~ he ~~said~~ *told* me *^* I like romantic movies~~.~~"

11. *^* Is true you almost drowned? my friend asked me. Yes, I said. I'm really glad to be

alive. It was really frightening.

12. It is a fact that I almost drowned makes me very careful about water safety whenever I

go swimming.

13. I didn't know where am I supposed to get off the bus, so I asked the driver where is

the science museum. She tell me the name of the street. She said she will tell me

when should I get off the bus.

14. My mother did not live with us. When other children asked me where was my mother,

I told them she is going to come to visit me very soon.

15. When I asked the taxi driver to drive faster he said I will drive faster if you pay me

more. At that time I didn't care how much would it cost, so I told him to go as fast as

he can.

16. We looked back to see where are we and how far are we from camp. We don't know, so we decided to turn back. We are afraid that we wander too far.

17. After the accident, I opened my eyes slowly and realize that I am still alive.

18. My country is prospering due to it is a fact that it has become a leading producer of oil.

19. Is true that one must to know english in order to study at an american university.

20. My mother told me what it was the purpose of our visit.

☐ EXERCISE 31. Activity: noun clauses. (Charts 12-1 → 12-7)
Directions: Choose one of the following.

1. Think of a letter written in English that you have received recently. In a short paragraph, summarize some of the news or information in this letter. (If you have not recently received a letter written in English, invent one.) Include at least two sentences that use the pattern *said that . . . and that* OR *said that . . . but that*.

2. Student A: Write a letter to a classmate (Student B). Give it to Student B.
   Student B: Write a report summarizing Student A's letter.

☐ EXERCISE 32. Activity: noun clauses. (Charts 12-1 → 12-7)
Directions: Form small groups and discuss one (or more) of the following topics. Then write a report of the main points made by each speaker in your group. (Do not attempt to report every word that was spoken.)

In your report, use words such as *think, believe, say, remark,* and *state* to introduce noun clauses. When you use *think* or *believe,* you will probably use present tenses (e.g., *Omar thinks that money is the most important thing in life.*). When you use *say, remark,* or *state,* you will probably use past tenses (e.g., *Olga said that many other things were more important than money.*).

Do you agree with the given statements? Why or why not?

1. Money is the most important thing in life.
2. A woman can do any job a man can do.
3. When a person decides to get married, his or her love for the other person is the only important consideration.
4. A world government is both desirable and necessary. Countries should simply become the states of one nation, the Earth. In this way, wars could be eliminated and wealth could be equally distributed.

☐ EXERCISE 33. Activity: noun clauses. (Charts 12-1 → 12-7)
Directions: Give a one-minute impromptu speech on any topic that comes to mind (pollution, insects, soccer, dogs, etc.). Your classmates will take notes as you speak. Then, in a short paragraph or orally, they will report what you said.

☐ EXERCISE 34. Activity: noun clauses. (Charts 12-1 → 12-7)

Directions: You and your classmates are newspaper reporters at a press conference. You will all interview your teacher or a person whom your teacher invites to class. Your assignment is to write a newspaper article about the person whom you interviewed.

Take notes during the interview. Write down some of the important sentences so that you can use them for quotations in your article. Ask for clarification if you do not understand something the interviewee has said. It is important to report information accurately.

In your article, try to organize your information into related topics. For example, if you interview your teacher:

I. General introductory information

II. Professional life
   A. Present teaching duties
   B. Academic duties and activities outside of teaching
   C. Past teaching experience
   D. Educational background

III. Personal life
   A. Basic biographical information (e.g., place of birth, family background, places of residence)
   B. Spare-time activities and interests
   C. Travel experiences

The above outline only suggests a possible method of organization. You must organize your own article, depending upon the information you have gained from your interview.

When you write your report, most of your information will be presented in reported speech; use quoted speech only for the most important or memorable sentences. When you use quoted speech, be sure you are presenting the interviewee's *exact words.* If you are simply paraphrasing what the interviewee said, do not use quotation marks.

12-8 USING THE SUBJUNCTIVE IN NOUN CLAUSES

(a) The teacher *demands* that we *be* on time. (b) I *insisted* that he *pay* me the money. (c) I *recommended* that she *not go* to the concert. (d) *It is important* that they *be told* the truth.	A subjunctive verb uses the simple form of a verb. It does not have present, past, or future forms; it is neither singular nor plural. Sentences with subjunctive verbs generally *stress importance or urgency.* A subjunctive verb is used in *that*-clauses that follow the verbs and expressions listed below. In (a): *be* is a subjunctive verb; its subject is *we.* In (b): *pay* (not *pays*, not *paid*) is a subjunctive verb; it is in its simple form, even though its subject (*he*) is singular. Negative: *not + simple form,* as in (c). Passive: *simple form of **be** + past participle,* as in (d).
(e) I *suggested* that she *see* a doctor. (f) I *suggested* that she *should see* a doctor.	***Should*** is also possible after ***suggest*** and ***recommend.***

COMMON VERBS AND EXPRESSIONS FOLLOWED BY THE SUBJUNCTIVE IN A NOUN CLAUSE			
advise (that) *ask (that)* *demand (that)* *insist (that)*	*propose (that)* *recommend (that)* *request (that)* *suggest (that)*	*it is essential (that)* *it is imperative (that)* *it is important (that)*	*it is critical (that)* *it is necessary (that)* *it is vital (that)*

*The subjunctive is more common in American English than British English. In British English, ***should*** + *simple form* is more usual than the subjunctive: *The teacher **insists** that we **should be** on time.*

☐ EXERCISE 35. Using the subjunctive in noun clauses. (Chart 12-8)
  Directions: Complete the sentences. There is often more than one possible completion.

  1. Mr. Adams insists that we _____ *be* _____ careful in our writing.

  2. They requested that we not _____ *go* _____ after midnight.

  3. She demanded that I _____ *should tell* _____ her the truth.

  4. I recommended that Jane _____ *is* _____ to the head of the department.

  5. I suggest that everyone _____ *should write* _____ a letter to the governor.

  6. It is essential that I _____ *should see* _____ you tomorrow.

  7. It is important that he _____ *should speak to* _____ the director of the English program.

  8. It is necessary that everyone _____ *be* _____ here on time.

☐ EXERCISE 36. Using the subjunctive in noun clauses. (Chart 12-8)
  Directions: Give the correct form of the verb in parentheses. Some of the verbs are passive.

  1. Her advisor recommended that she *(take)* _____ *should take* _____ five courses.

  2. Roberto insisted that the new baby *(name)* _____ after his grandfather.

  3. The doctor recommended that she *(stay)* _____ *should stay* _____ in bed for a few days.

  4. The students requested that the test *(postpone)* _____ *should postpone* _____, but the instructor decided against a postponement.

  5. It is essential that no one *(admit)* _____ *should admit* _____ to the room without proper identification.

  6. It is critical that pollution *(control)*
     _____ *control.* _____ and eventually
     (eliminate) _____ *should eliminate* _____

  7. It was such a beautiful day that one of the students suggested we *(have)*
     _____ *should have* _____. class outside.

  8. The movie director insisted that everything about his productions *(be)* *should be*. authentic.

  9. It is vital that no one else *(know)* _____ *be know* _____ about the secret government operation.

  10. Mrs. Wah asked that we *(be)* _____ sure to lock the door behind us.

  11. I requested that I *(permit)* _____ to change my class.

12. It is important that you *(be, not)* _____ late.

13. It is imperative that he *(return)* _____ home immediately.

14. The governor proposed that a new highway *(build)* _____.

15. Fumiko specifically asked that I *(tell, not)* _____ anyone else about it.

    She said it was important that no one else *(tell)* _____ about it.

12-9 USING -*EVER* WORDS

The following -*ever* words give the idea of "any." Each pair of sentences in the examples has the same meaning.

whoever	(a)	***Whoever*** wants to come is welcome.
		Anyone who wants to come is welcome.
who(m)ever	(b)	He makes friends easily with ***who(m)ever*** he meets.*
		He makes friends easily with *anyone who(m)* he meets.
whatever	(c)	He always says ***whatever*** comes into his mind.
		He always says *anything that* comes into his mind.
whichever	(d)	There are four good programs on TV at eight o'clock. We can
		watch ***whichever program*** (***whichever one***) you prefer.
		We can watch *any of the four programs that* you prefer.
whenever	(e)	You may leave ***whenever*** you wish.
		You may leave *at any time that* you wish.
wherever	(f)	She can go ***wherever*** she wants to go.
		She can go *anyplace that* she wants to go.
however	(g)	The students may dress ***however*** they please.
		The students may dress *in any way that* they please.

*In (b): ***whomever*** is the object of the verb ***meets***. In American English, ***whomever*** is rare and very formal. In British English, ***whoever*** (not ***whomever***) is used as the object form: *He makes friends easily with whoever he meets.*

☐ **EXERCISE 37. Using -EVER words. (Chart 12-9)**
Directions: Complete the following by using -*ever* words.

1. Mustafa is free to go anyplace he wishes. He can go _____ **wherever** _____ he wants.

2. Mustafa is free to go anytime he wishes. He can go _____ *whenever* _____ he wants.

3. I don't know what you should do about that problem. Do _____ *whatever* _____
   seems best to you.

4. There are five flights to Chicago every day. I don't care which one we take. We can
   take _____ *whichever* _____ one fits in best with your schedule.

5. I want you to be honest. I hope you feel free to say _____ *whatever* _____ is on your
   mind.

6. _____ *Whatever* _____ leads a life full of love and happiness is rich.

7. No one can tell him what to do. He does _____whatever_____ he wants.

8. If you want to rearrange the furniture, go ahead. You can rearrange it _____whenever_____ you want. I don't care one way or the other.

9. Those children are wild! I feel sorry for _____whoever_____ has to be their babysitter.

10. I have a car. I can take you _____wherever_____ you want to go.

11. Scott likes to tell people about his problems. He will talk to _____whoever_____ will listen to him. But he bores _____whenever_____ he talks to.

12. To Ellen, the end justifies the means. She will do _____whatever_____ she has to do in order to accomplish her objective.

13. I have four. Take _____whichever_____ one pleases you most.

14. My wife and I are going to ride our bicycles across the country. We'll ride for six to seven hours every day, then stop for the night _____wherever_____ we happen to be.

15. Irene does _____whatever_____ she wants to do, goes _____wherever_____ she wants to go, gets up _____whenever_____ she wants to get up, makes friends with _____whoever_____ she meets, and dresses _____however_____ she pleases.

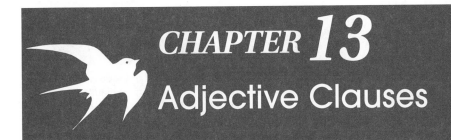

CHAPTER *13*
Adjective Clauses

CONTENTS

13-1   INTRODUCTION

CLAUSE:	*A clause* is a group of words containing a subject and a verb.
INDEPENDENT CLAUSE:	*An independent clause* is a complete sentence. It contains the main subject and verb of a sentence. (It is also called "a main clause.")
DEPENDENT CLAUSE:	*A dependent clause* is not a complete sentence. It must be connected to an independent clause.
ADJECTIVE CLAUSE:	*An adjective clause* is a dependent clause that modifies a noun. It describes, identifies, or gives further information about a noun. (An adjective clause is also called "a relative clause.")
ADJECTIVE CLAUSE PRONOUNS:	An adjective clause uses pronouns to connect the dependent clause to the independent clause. The *adjective clause pronouns* are *who, whom, which, that,* and *whose.* (Adjective clause pronouns are also called "relative pronouns.")

13-2 ADJECTIVE CLAUSE PRONOUNS USED AS THE SUBJECT

I thanked the woman. **She** helped me. ↓ (a) I thanked the woman **who** *helped me.* (b) I thanked the woman **that** *helped me.*	In (a): **I thanked the woman** = an independent clause; **who helped me** = an adjective clause. The adjective clause modifies the noun **woman**.
	In (a): **who** is the subject of the adjective clause. In (b): **that** is the subject of the adjective clause. Note: (a) and (b) have the same meaning. (c) and (d) have the same meaning.
The book is mine. **It** is on the table. ↓ (c) The book **which** *is on the table* is mine. (d) The book **that** *is on the table* is mine.	**who** = used for people **which** = used for things **that** = used for both people and things
(e) *INCORRECT:* *The book is mine that is on the table.*	An adjective clause closely follows the noun it modifies.

☐ EXERCISE 1. Adjective clause pronouns used as subjects. (Chart 13-2)
   Directions: Combine the two sentences. Use the second sentence as an adjective clause.

1. I saw the man. He closed the door. → *I saw the man* $\begin{Bmatrix} who \\ that \end{Bmatrix}$ *closed the door.*
2. The girl is happy. She won the race.
3. The student is from China. He sits next to me.
4. The students are from China. They sit in the front row.
5. We are studying sentences. They contain adjective clauses.
6. I am using a sentence. It contains an adjective clause.
7. Algebra problems contain letters. They stand for unknown numbers.
8. The taxi driver was friendly. He took me to the airport.

13-3 ADJECTIVE CLAUSE PRONOUNS USED AS THE OBJECT OF A VERB

The man was Mr. Jones. I saw **him**. ↓ (a) The man **who(m)** *I saw* was Mr. Jones. (b) The man **that** *I saw* was Mr. Jones. (c) The man **Ø** *I saw* was Mr. Jones.	Notice in the examples: The adjective clause pronouns are placed at the beginning of the clause.
	In (a): **who** is usually used instead of **whom**, especially in speaking. **Whom** is generally used only in very formal English.
The movie wasn't very good. We saw **it** last night. ↓ (d) The movie **which** *we saw last night* wasn't very good. (e) The movie **that** *we saw last night* wasn't very good. (f) The movie **Ø** *we saw last night* wasn't very good.	In (c) and (f): An object pronoun is often omitted from an adjective clause. (A subject pronoun, however, may not be omitted.)
	who(m) = used for people **which** = used for things **that** = used for both people and things
(g) *INCORRECT:* The man who(m) I saw *him* was Mr. Jones. The man that I saw *him* was Mr. Jones. The man I saw *him* was Mr. Jones.	In (g): The pronoun **him** must be removed. It is unnecessary because *who(m)*, *that*, or Ø functions as the object of the verb **saw**.

☐ **EXERCISE 2. Adjective clause pronouns used as the object of a verb. (Chart 13-3)**
    Directions: Combine the sentences, using the second sentence as an adjective clause. Give all the possible patterns.

1. The book was good. I read it.
2. I liked the woman. I met her at the party last night.
3. I liked the composition. You wrote it.
4. The people were very nice. We visited them yesterday.
5. The man is standing over there. I was telling you about him.

13-4 ADJECTIVE CLAUSE PRONOUNS USED AS THE OBJECT OF A PREPOSITION

<table>
<tr>
<td colspan="2">

She is the woman.
I told you ***about her***.

(a) She is the woman ***about whom*** *I told you.*
(b) She is the woman *who(m)*   *I told you **about**.*
(c) She is the woman ***that***   *I told you **about**.*
(d) She is the woman Ø   *I told you **about**.*

</td>
<td>

In very formal English, the preposition comes at the beginning of the adjective clause, as in (a) and (e). Usually, however, in everyday usage, the preposition comes after the subject and verb of the adjective clause, as in the other examples.

</td>
</tr>
<tr>
<td colspan="2">

The music was good.
We listened ***to it*** last night.

(e) The music ***to which*** *we listened*   *last night* was good.
(f) The music ***which***   *we listened **to** last night* was good.
(g) The music ***that***   *we listened **to** last night* was good.
(h) The music Ø   *we listened **to** last night* was good.

</td>
<td>

Note: If the preposition comes at the beginning of the adjective clause, only ***whom*** or ***which*** may be used. A preposition is never immediately followed by ***that*** or ***who***.★

</td>
</tr>
</table>

★*INCORRECT:* She is the woman *about who* I told you.
INCORRECT: The music *to that* we listened last night was good.

☐ **EXERCISE 3. Adjective clause pronouns used as the object of a preposition. (Chart 13-4)**
    Directions: Combine the sentences, using the second sentence as an adjective clause. Give all the possible patterns.

1. The meeting was interesting. I went to it.
2. The man was very kind. I talked to him yesterday.
3. I must thank the people. I got a present from them.
4. The picture was beautiful. She was looking at it.
5. The man is standing over there. I was telling you about him.
6. I ran into a woman. I had gone to elementary school with her.
7. The topic was interesting. Omar talked about it.
8. The people were friendly. I spoke to them.
9. Olga wrote on a topic. She knew nothing about it.
10. The candidate didn't win the election. I voted for her.

☐ **EXERCISE 4. Adjective clauses. (Charts 13-2 → 13-4)**

Directions: Identify the adjective clause in each sentence. Then give the other possible patterns.

Example: The dress which she is wearing is new.
→ Adjective clause: *which she is wearing.*

Other possible patterns: *The dress* $\begin{Bmatrix} that \\ \emptyset \end{Bmatrix}$ *she is wearing is new.*

1. Did I tell you about the woman I met last night?

2. The woman I was dancing with stepped on my toe.

3. The report Joe is writing must be finished by Friday.

4. The doctor who examined the sick child was gentle.

5. The people I was waiting for were late.

6. Did you hear about the earthquake that occurred in California?

13-5 USUAL PATTERNS OF ADJECTIVE CLAUSES

(a) USUAL: I like the people *who live next to me.* LESS USUAL: I like the people *that live next to me.*	In everyday informal usage, often one adjective clause pattern is used more commonly than another.* In (a): As a subject pronoun, *who* is more common than *that*.
(b) USUAL: I like books *that have good plots.* LESS USUAL: I like books *which have good plots.*	In (b): As a subject pronoun, *that* is more common than *which*.
(c) USUAL: I liked the people Ø *I met last night.* (d) USUAL: I liked the book Ø *I read last week.*	In (c) and (d): Object pronouns are commonly omitted, especially in speaking.

*See Chart 13-10, p. 281, for patterns of pronoun usage when an adjective clause requires commas.

☐ **EXERCISE 5. Adjective clauses. (Charts 13-2 → 13-5)**

Directions: Combine the sentences, using the second sentence as an adjective clause. Give all the possible adjective clause patterns. Discuss which patterns are used more commonly than others.

Example: The scientist is well known for her research. We met her yesterday.

→ *The scientist* $\begin{Bmatrix} \emptyset \\ who(m) \\ that \end{Bmatrix}$ *we met yesterday is well known for her research.*

1. She lectured on a topic. I know very little about it.

2. The students missed the assignment. They were absent from class.

3. Yesterday I ran into an old friend. I hadn't seen him for years.

4. The young women are all from Japan. We met them at the meeting last night.

5. I am reading a book. It was written by Jane Austen.

6. The man gave me good advice. I spoke to him.

7. I returned the money. I had borrowed it from my roommate.

8. The dogcatcher caught the dog. It had bitten my neighbor's daughter.

9. I read about a man. He keeps chickens in his apartment.

☐ EXERCISE 6. Adjective clauses. (Charts 13-2 → 13-5)
Directions: All of these sentences contain errors in adjective clause structures. Correct the errors.

1. In our village, there were many people didn't have much money.

2. I enjoyed the book that you told me to read it.

3. I still remember the man who he taught me to play the violin when I was a boy.

4. I showed my father a picture of the car I am going to buy it as soon as I save enough money.

5. The woman about who I was talking about suddenly walked into the room. I hope she didn't hear me.

6. Almost all of the people appear on television wear makeup.

7. I don't like to spend time with people which loses their temper easily.

8. The boy drew pictures of people at an airport which was waiting for their planes.

9. People who works in the hunger program they estimate that 3500 people in the world die from starvation every day of the year.

10. In one corner of the marketplace, an old man who was playing a violin.

☐ **EXERCISE 7. Adjective clauses. (Charts 13-2 → 13-5)**
Directions: Work in pairs (switching roles after item 6), in groups, or as a class.
Speaker A: Your book is open. Ask the questions. Use the names of classmates.
Speaker B: Your book is closed. Begin your answer with "Yes, she/he did. She/He told me about *the* . . . ." Use an adjective clause in the completion. Omit the object pronoun.

Example: Did (. . .) write a report?
SPEAKER A *(book open):* Did Carmen write a report?
SPEAKER B *(book closed):* Yes, she did. She told me about **the** report she wrote.

1. Did (. . .) get a letter from (her/his) brother yesterday?
2. Did (. . .) write a letter to *(name of a person)?*
3. Did (. . .) go to a party yesterday?
4. Did (. . .) meet some people at that party?
5. Did (. . .) take a trip to *(name of a country)* last summer?
6. Did (. . .) have some experiences in *(name of that country)?*
7. Did (. . .) use to live in a small town?
8. Did (. . .) watch a program on TV last night?
9. Did (. . .) interview for a job?
10. Did (. . .) have to write a report for (her/his) boss?
11. Did (. . .) talk to a person about health insurance?
12. Did (. . .) go to the meeting for new employees?

□ EXERCISE 8. Adjective clauses. (Charts 13-2 → 13-5)
   Directions: Work in pairs.
   Speaker A: Your book is open. Look at a cue briefly. Then, without looking at the text,
             say the cue sentence to Speaker B.
   Speaker B: Your book is closed. Begin your answer with "Yes."

Examples:

SPEAKER A: You read **a** book. Was it interesting?
SPEAKER B: Yes, **the** book I read was interesting.

SPEAKER A: You drank **some** tea. Did it taste good?
SPEAKER B: Yes, **the** tea I drank tasted good.

SPEAKER A: **A** stranger gave you directions to the post office. Did she speak too fast?
SPEAKER B: Yes, **the** stranger who gave me directions to the post office spoke too fast.

SPEAKER A: **A** police officer helped you. Did you thank her?
SPEAKER B: Yes, I thanked **the** police officer who helped me.

1. You are sitting in a chair. Is it comfortable?
2. You saw a man. Was he wearing a brown suit?
3. You talked to a woman. Did she answer your question?
4. A woman stepped on your toe. Did she apologize?
5. Some students took a test. Did most of them pass?
6. You had some meat for dinner last night. Was it good?
7. A woman shouted at you. Was she angry?
8. A person is sitting next to you. Do you know him/her?
9. A woman came into the room. Did you recognize her?
10. You bought a coat. Does it keep you warm?
11. You watched a TV program last night. Was it good?
12. You were reading a book. Did you finish it?

Switch roles.

13. You stayed at a hotel. Was it in the middle of the city?
14. We are doing an exercise. Is it easy?
15. A waiter served you at a restaurant. Was he polite?
16. A student stopped you in the hall. Did he ask you for the correct time?
17. Some students are sitting in this room. Can all of them speak English?
18. You were looking for a book. Did you find it?
19. You are wearing (boots/tennis shoes/loafers). Are they comfortable?
20. A taxi driver took you to the bus station. Did you have a conversation with her?
21. A man opened the door for you. Did you thank him?
22. A clerk cashed your check. Did he ask for identification?
23. You got a package in the mail. Was it from your parents?
24. A man stopped you on the street. Did he ask you for directions?

☐ EXERCISE 9. Adjective clauses. (Charts 13-4 → 13-5)

Directions: Work in pairs or as a class.

Speaker A: Your book is open. Give the cues from the text.

Speaker B: Your book is closed. Repeat the cue, changing "you" to "I" as necessary. Then make a second sentence with an adjective clause. The adjective clause should modify the noun at the end of the first sentence, as in the examples.

Examples:

SPEAKER A *(book open):* You're looking at a person.

SPEAKER B *(book closed):* I'm looking at **a person**. **The person** I'm looking at is Peter Lo.

SPEAKER A *(book open):* You're sitting at a desk.

SPEAKER B *(book closed):* I'm sitting at **a desk**. **The desk** I'm sitting at has many scratches on it.

(Switch roles if working in pairs.)

1. You're studying at a school.
2. You're living in a (city/town).
3. That book belongs to a student.*
4. (. . .) and you listened to some music.
5. (. . .) went to a movie last night.
6. You are sitting next to a person.

7. You're living with some people.
8. (. . .) was talking about a movie.
9. You're interested in a field of study.
10. That (bookbag/backpack/bag) belongs to a person.
11. You spoke to some people.
12. You went to a doctor to get some medicine.

13-6   USING *WHOSE*

I know the man.
 His bicycle was stolen.
 ↓
 (a) I know the man *whose bicycle was stolen.*
	Whose is used to show possession. It carries the same meaning as other possessive pronouns used as adjectives: *his, her, its,* and *their.* Like *his, her, its,* and *their,* ***whose*** is connected to a noun:
	   *his bicycle → **whose** bicycle*
	   *her composition → **whose** composition*
	 Both ***whose*** and the noun it is connected to are placed at the beginning of the adjective clause. ***Whose*** cannot be omitted.

The student writes well. I read ***her composition***. ↓ (b) The student *whose composition I read* writes well.	
Mr. Catt has a painting. ***Its value*** is inestimable. ↓ (c) Mr. Catt has a painting *whose value is inestimable.*	***Whose*** usually modifies people, but it may also be used to modify things, as in (c).

*Sometimes a sentence has "that that": *I've read the book that that man wrote.* In this example, the first **that** is an adjective clause pronoun. The second **that** is a demonstrative adjective, like *this* or *x*

Directions: Combine the sentences, using the second sentence as an adjective clause.

1. I know a man. His last name is Goose.
   → *I know a man whose last name is Goose.*
2. I apologized to the woman. I spilled her coffee.

3. The man called the police. His wallet was stolen.

4. I met the woman. Her husband is the president of the corporation.

5. The professor is excellent. I am taking her course.

6. Mr. North teaches a class for students. Their native language is not English.

7. The people were nice. We visited their house.

8. I live in a dormitory. Its residents come from many countries.

9. I have to call the man. I accidentally picked up his umbrella after the meeting.

10. The man poured a glass of water on his face. His beard caught on fire when he lit a cigarette.

☐ EXERCISE 11. Using WHOSE in adjective clauses. (Chart 13-6)

Directions: Work in pairs (switching roles after item 4), in groups, or as a class.
Speaker A: Your book is open. Give the cues from the text.
Speaker B: Your book is closed. Repeat the cue, changing "you" to "I" as necessary. Then combine the two sentences into one that contains an adjective clause with **whose**.

Example:
SPEAKER A *(book open):* Dr. Jones is a professor. You're taking his course.
SPEAKER B *(book closed):* Dr. Jones is **a** professor. I'm taking his course.
Dr. Jones is **the** professor whose course I'm taking.

1. Maria is a student. You found her book.
2. Omar is a student. You borrowed his dictionary.
3. You used a woman's phone. You thanked her.
4. You broke a child's toy. He started to cry.
5. You stayed at a family's house. They were very kind.
6. A woman's purse was stolen. She called the police.
7. *(Name of a famous singer)* is a singer. You like his/her music best.
8. Everyone tried to help a family. Their house had burned down.

□ EXERCISE 12. Using WHOSE in adjective clauses. (Chart 13-6)

Directions: Pair up. Pretend you are in a room full of people. You and your classmate are speaking. Together, you are identifying various people in the room. Begin each sentence with "There is . . . ." Alternate items, with Speaker A doing Item 1, Speaker B doing Item 2, Speaker A doing Item 3, etc.

1. That man's wife is your teacher.
   → SPEAKER A: *There is the man whose wife is my teacher.*

2. That woman's husband is a football player.
   → SPEAKER B: *There is the woman whose husband is a football player.*

3. That boy's father is a doctor.

4. That girl's mother is a dentist.

5. That person's picture was in the newspaper.

6. That woman's car was stolen.

7. That man's daughter won a gold medal at the Olympic Games.

8. You found that woman's keys.

9. You are in that teacher's class.

10. We met that man's wife.

11. You read that author's book.

12. You borrowed that student's lecture notes.

□ EXERCISE 13. Using WHOSE in adjective clauses. (Chart 13-6)

Directions: Combine the sentences, using *whose* in an adjective clause.

1. The man's wife had been admitted to the hospital. I spoke to him.
   → *I spoke to the man whose wife had been admitted to the hospital.*

2. I read about a child. Her life was saved by her pet dog.
   → *I read about a child whose life was saved by her pet dog.*

3. The students raised their hands. Their names were called.

4. Jack knows a man. The man's name is William Blueheart Duckbill, Jr.

5. The woman's purse was stolen outside the supermarket. The police came to question her.

6. The day care center was established to take care of children. These children's parents work during the day.

7. We couldn't find the person. His car was blocking the driveway.

8. Three students' reports were turned in late. The professor told them he would accept the papers this time but never again.

13-7 USING *WHERE* IN ADJECTIVE CLAUSES

					Where is used in an adjective clause to modify a place (*city, country, room, house, etc.*).
	The building is very old. He lives *there (in that building)*.				If *where* is used, a preposition is NOT included in the adjective clause, as in (a). If *where* is not used, the preposition must be included, as in (b).
(a)	The building	*where*	*he lives*	is very old.	
(b)	The building	*in which*	*he lives*	is very old.	
	The building	*which*	*he lives in*	is very old.	
	The building	*that*	*he lives in*	is very old.	
	The building	Ø	*he lives in*	is very old.	

□ EXERCISE 14. Using WHERE in adjective clauses. (Chart 13-7)
Directions: Combine the sentences, using the second sentence as an adjective clause.

1. The city was beautiful. We spent our vacation there (in that city).
2. That is the restaurant. I will meet you there (at that restaurant).
3. The town is small. I grew up there (in that town).
4. That is the drawer. I keep my jewelry there (in that drawer).

13-8 USING *WHEN* IN ADJECTIVE CLAUSES

				When is used in an adjective clause to modify a noun of time (*year, day, time, century, etc.*).
	I'll never forget the day. I met you *then (on that day)*.			The use of a preposition in an adjective clause that modifies a noun of time is somewhat different from that in other adjective clauses: a preposition is used preceding *which*, as in (b). Otherwise, the preposition is omitted.
(a)	I'll never forget the day	*when*	*I met you.*	
(b)	I'll never forget the day	*on which*	*I met you.*	
(c)	I'll never forget the day	*that*	*I met you.*	
(d)	I'll never forget the day	Ø	*I met you.*	

□ EXERCISE 15. Using WHEN in adjective clauses. (Chart 13-8)
Directions: Combine the sentences, using the second sentence as an adjective clause.

1. Monday is the day. We will come then (on that day).
2. 7:05 is the time. My plane arrives then (at that time).
3. July is the month. The weather is usually the hottest then (in that month).
4. 1960 is the year. The revolution took place then (in that year).

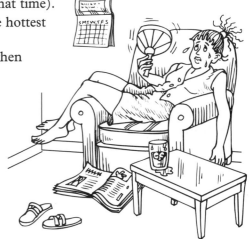

☐ **EXERCISE 16. Using WHERE and WHEN in adjective clauses. (Charts 13-7 and 13-8)**
   Directions: Combine the sentences by using either **where** or **when** to introduce an adjective clause.

   1. That is the place. The accident occurred there.
      → *That is the place* ***where*** *the accident occurred.*

   2. There was a time. Movies cost a dime then.
      → *There was a time* ***when*** *movies cost a dime.*

   3. A cafe is a small restaurant. People can get a light meal there.

   4. Every neighborhood in Brussels has small cafes. Customers drink coffee and eat pastries there.

   5. There was a time. Dinosaurs dominated the earth then.

   6. The house was destroyed in an earthquake ten years ago. I was born and grew up there.

   7. Summer is the time of year. The weather is the hottest then.

   8. The miser hid his money in a place. It was safe from robbers there.

   9. There came a time. The miser had to spend his money then.

   10. His new shirt didn't fit, so Dan took it back to the store. He'd bought it there.

☐ **EXERCISE 17. Adjective clauses. (Charts 13-2 → 13-8)**
   Directions: Work in pairs, in groups, or as a class. Begin your response to the cue with either "I'll never forget the . . . " or "I'll always remember the . . . ."

   Example: trip
   Response: I'll never forget the trip . . . *I took to France.*

   1. trip
   2. experiences
   3. day
   4. first day
   5. time
   6. first time
   7. person
   8. people
   9. woman
   10. man
   11. house
   12. story
   13. accident
   14. wonderful food
   15. room
   16. friends

□ EXERCISE 18. Activity: adjective clauses. (Charts 13-2 → 13-8)
Directions: Work in groups of four or as a class. Only the leader's book is open.

Leader: Direct the questions to the group as a whole, or sometimes to a particular student.

Speaker A: Answer the questions, inventing your answers if necessary.

Leader: Ask another student to summarize the information in Speaker A's responses in one sentence beginning with "The . . . ."

Speaker B: Begin with "The . . . ." Use an adjective clause.

Example:

LEADER TO GROUP: Who got a letter yesterday?
SPEAKER A: I did.
LEADER TO A: Who was it from?
SPEAKER A: My brother.
LEADER TO B: Can you summarize this information? Begin with "The."
SPEAKER B: The letter (Ali) got yesterday was from his brother.

1. Who got a letter last week?
   Where was it from?

2. Who is wearing earrings?
   What are they made of?

3. Who lives in an apartment?
   Is it close to school?

4. Pick up something that doesn't belong to you. What is it?
   Whose is it?

Change leaders.

5. Who grew up in a small town?
   In what part of the country is it located?

6. Who has bought something recently?
   What have you bought recently?
   Was it expensive?

7. Hold up a book.
   What is the title?

8. Who went to a bar/restaurant last night?
   Was it crowded?

Change leaders.

9. What did you have for dinner last night?
   Was it good?

10. Who watched a TV program last night?
    What was it about?

11. Who has borrowed something recently?
    What did you borrow?
    Who does it belong to?

12. Who shops for groceries?
    What is the name of the store?

Change leaders.

13. Who eats lunch away from home?
    Where do you usually eat?
    Does it have good food?

14. Who took the bus to class today?
    Was it late or on time?

15. Who read a newspaper today?
    Which newspaper?

16. Point at a person.
    Who are you pointing at?

13-9 USING ADJECTIVE CLAUSES TO MODIFY PRONOUNS

(a) There is *someone (whom) I want you to meet.* (b) *Everything he said* was pure nonsense. (c) *Anybody who wants to come* is welcome.	Adjective clauses can modify indefinite pronouns (e.g., *someone, everybody*). Object pronouns (e.g., *who(m)*, *that*, *which*) are usually omitted in the adjective clause.
(d) Paula was *the only one I knew at the party.* (e) Scholarships are available for *those who need financial assistance.*	Adjective clauses can modify *the one(s)* and *those.**
(f) INCORRECT: *I who am a student at this school* come from a country in Asia. (g) It is *I who am responsible.* (h) *He who laughs last* laughs best.	Adjective clauses are almost never used to modify personal pronouns. Native English speakers would not write the sentence in (f). (g) is possible, but very formal and uncommon. (h) is a well-known saying in which *he* is used as an indefinite pronoun (meaning "anyone," "any person").

*An adjective clause with *which* can also be used to modify the demonstrative pronoun *that*. For example:
We sometimes fear *that which* we do not understand.
The bread my mother makes is much better than *that which* you can buy at a store.

☐ **EXERCISE 19. Using adjective clauses to modify pronouns. (Chart 13-9)**
Directions: Complete the sentences with adjective clauses.

1. Ask Jack. He's the only one _____ who knows the answer. _____

2. I have a question. There is something _____

3. He can't trust anyone. There's no one _____

4. I'm powerless to help her. There's nothing _____

5. I know someone _____

6. Susan makes a good first impression. She charms everyone _____

7. What was Mrs. Wood talking about? I didn't understand anything _____

8. I listen to everything _____

9. You can believe him. Everything _____

10. All of the students are seated. The teacher is the only one _____

11. The test we took yesterday was easier than the one _____

12. The courses I'm taking this term are more difficult than the ones _____

13. The concert had already begun. Those _____
    had to wait until intermission to be seated.

14. The class was divided in half. Those _____
    were assigned to Section A. Those _____
    were assigned to Section B.

□ EXERCISE 20. Review: adjective clauses. (Charts 13-1 → 13-9)
Directions: Create sentences in which you use the given groups of words. Each sentence should contain an adjective clause.

Examples: the people that I
→ One of **the people that I** admire most in the history of the world is Gandhi.
the people with whom we
→ I enjoyed talking to **the people with whom we** had dinner last night.

1. the things I	7. the time my	13. everything you
2. the people who	8. a person whose	14. those who
3. a person who	9. a woman I	15. the only one who
4. the man to whom I	10. employees who	16. nothing I
5. the place I	11. the restaurant where	17. everyone she
6. a book that	12. someone that I	18. the doctor he

13-10 PUNCTUATING ADJECTIVE CLAUSES

General guidelines for the punctuation of adjective clauses:
(1) **DO NOT USE COMMAS IF** the adjective clause is necessary to identify the noun it modifies.*
(2) **USE COMMAS IF** the adjective clause simply gives additional information and is not necessary to identify the noun it modifies.**

(a) *The professor* who teaches Chemistry 101 is an excellent lecturer. (b) *Professor Wilson,* who teaches Chemistry 101, is an excellent lecturer.	In (a): No commas are used. The adjective clause is necessary to identify which professor is meant. In (b): Commas are used. The adjective clause is not necessary to identify Professor Wilson. We already know who he is: he has a name. The adjective clause simply gives additional information.
(c) *Hawaii,* which consists of eight principal islands, is a favorite vacation spot. (d) *Mrs. Smith,* who is a retired teacher, does volunteer work at the hospital.	Guideline: Use commas, as in (b), (c), and (d), if an adjective clause modifies a proper noun. (A proper noun begins with a capital letter.) Note: A comma reflects a pause in speech.
(e) *The man* { who(m) / that / Ø } *I met* teaches chemistry. (f) *Mr. Lee,* whom I met yesterday, teaches chemistry.	In (e): If no commas are used, any possible pronoun may be used in the adjective clause. Object pronouns may be omitted. In (f): When commas are necessary, the pronoun *that* may not be used (only *who, whom, which, whose, where,* and *when* may be used), and object pronouns cannot be omitted.
COMPARE THE MEANING (g) We took some children on a picnic. *The children, who wanted to play soccer,* ran to an open field as soon as we arrived at the park. (h) We took some children on a picnic. *The children who wanted to play soccer* ran to an open field as soon as we arrived at the park. The others played a different game.	In (g): The use of commas means that *all* of the children wanted to play soccer and *all* of the children ran to an open field. The adjective clause is used only to give additional information about the children. In (h): The lack of commas means that *only some* of the children wanted to play soccer. The adjective clause is used to identify which children ran to the open field.

*Adjective clauses that do not require commas are called "essential" or "restrictive" or "identifying."

**Adjective clauses that require commas are called "nonessential" or "nonrestrictive" or "nonidentifying."

NOTE: Nonessential adjective clauses are more common in writing than in speaking.

☐ **EXERCISE 21. Punctuating adjective clauses. (Chart 13-10)**

Directions: Add commas where necessary. Change the adjective clause pronoun to
that if possible.

1. Alan and Jackie, who did not come to class yesterday, explained their absence to the
   teacher. *("Who" cannot be changed to "that.")*

2. The students who did not come to class yesterday explained their absence to the
   teacher. *(No commas; "who" can be changed to "that.")*

3. Only people who speak Russian should apply for the job.

4. Matthew who speaks Russian applied for the job.

5. The rice which we had for dinner last night was very good.

6. Rice which is grown in many countries is a staple food throughout much of the world.

7. The newspaper article was about a man who died two years ago of a rare tropical disease.

8. Paul O'Grady, who died two years ago, was a kind and loving man.

9. I have fond memories of my hometown which is situated in a valley.

10. I live in a town which is situated in a valley.

11. The Mississippi River which flows south from Minnesota to the Gulf of Mexico is the
    major commercial river in the United States.

12. A river which is polluted is not safe for swimming.

13. Mr. Brown whose son won the spelling contest is very proud of his son's achievement.
    The man whose daughter won the science contest is also very pleased and proud.

14. Goats which were first tamed more than 9,000 years ago in Asia have provided people
    with milk, meat, and wool since prehistoric times.

15. Mrs. Clark has two goats. She's furious at the goat which got on the wrong side of the
    fence and is eating her flowers.

□ EXERCISE 22. Punctuating adjective clauses. (Chart 13-10)
   Directions: Circle the correct explanation (a. or b.) of the meaning of each sentence.

1. The teacher thanked the students, who had given her some flowers.
   a. The flowers were from *only some* of the students.
   (b.) The flowers were from *all* of the students.

2. The teacher thanked the students who had given her some flowers.
   (a.) The flowers were from *only some* of the students.
   b. The flowers were from *all* of the students.

3. There was a terrible flood. The villagers who had received a warning of the impending flood escaped to safety.
   a. *Only some* of the villagers had been warned; only some escaped.
   b. *All* of the villagers had been warned; all escaped.

4. There was a terrible flood. The villagers, who had received a warning of the impending flood, escaped to safety.
   a. *Only some* of the villagers had been warned; only some escaped.
   b. *All* of the villagers had been warned; all escaped.

5. Roberto reached down and picked up the grammar book, which was lying upside down on the floor.
   a. There was *only one* grammar book near Roberto.
   b. There was *more than one* grammar book near Roberto.

6. Roberto reached down and picked up the grammar book which was lying upside down on the floor.
   a. There was *only one* grammar book near Roberto.
   b. There was *more than one* grammar book near Roberto.

Discuss the differences in meaning in the following pairs of sentences.
7. He reached in the basket and threw away the apples that were rotten.
8. He reached in the basket and threw away the apples, which were rotten.

9. The students who had done well on the test were excused from class early.
10. The students, who had done well on the test, were excused from class early.

11. Cindy was delighted when she opened the present, which was from her grandmother.
12. Cindy was delighted when she opened the present that was from her grandmother.

13. The teacher pointed to the maps that were hanging on the rear wall of the classroom.
14. The teacher pointed to the maps, which were hanging on the rear wall of the classroom.

□ EXERCISE 23. Punctuating adjective clauses. (Chart 13-10)
   Directions: Add commas where necessary.

1. We enjoyed the city where we spent our vacation.

2. We enjoyed Mexico City where we spent our vacation.

3. An elephant which is the earth's largest land mammal has few natural enemies other than human beings.

4. One of the elephants which we saw at the zoo had only one tusk.

5. At the botanical gardens, you can see a Venus's-flytrap which is an insectivorous plant.

6. In Venezuela, there are plants that eat insects with their roots.

7. One of the most useful materials in the world is glass which is made chiefly from sand, soda, and lime.

8. Glaciers which are masses of ice that flow slowly over land form in the cold polar regions and in high mountains.

9. A rebel is a person who resists or fights against authority.

10. Petroleum which some people refer to as black gold is one of the most valuable resources in the world today.

11. You don't need to take heavy clothes when you go to Bangkok which has one of the highest average temperatures of any city in the world.

12. A political party is an organized group of people who control or seek to control a government.

13. Child labor was a social problem in late eighteenth-century England where employment in factories became virtual slavery for children.

14. We had to use a telephone, so we went to the nearest house. The woman who answered our knock listened cautiously to our request.

15. According to a newspaper article which I read, the police arrested the man who had robbed the First National Bank. The man who was wearing a plaid shirt and blue jeans was caught shortly after he had left the bank.

16. I watched a scientist conduct an experiment on bees. The research scientist who was well protected before she stepped into the special chamber holding the bees was not stung. A person who was unprotected by the special clothing could have gotten 300 to 400 bee stings within a minute.

13-11 USING EXPRESSIONS OF QUANTITY IN ADJECTIVE CLAUSES

In my class there are 20 students. *Most of **them** are from the Far East.* (a) In my class there are 20 students, *most of **whom*** are from Asia.	An adjective clause may contain an expression of quantity with ***of***: *some of, many of, most of, none of, two of, half of, both of, neither of, each of, all of, several of, a few of, little of, a number of,* etc.
He gave several reasons. *Only a few of **them** were valid.* (b) He gave several reasons, *only a few of **which*** were valid.	The expression of quantity precedes the pronoun. Only ***whom***, ***which***, and ***whose*** are used in this pattern.
The teachers discussed Jim. *One of **his** problems was poor study habits.* (c) The teachers discussed Jim, *one of **whose** problems* was poor study habits.	Adjective clauses that begin with an expression of quantity are more common in writing than speaking. Commas are used.

☐ **EXERCISE 24. Using expressions of quantity in adjective clauses. (Chart 13-11)**
Directions: Combine the two sentences. Use the second sentence as an adjective clause.

1. The city has sixteen schools. Two of them are junior colleges.

   → *The city has sixteen schools, two of which are junior colleges.*

2. Last night the orchestra played three symphonies. One of them was Beethoven's Seventh.
3. I tried on six pairs of shoes. I liked none of them.
4. The village has around 200 people. The majority of them are farmers.
5. That company currently has five employees. All of them are computer experts.
6. After the riot, over one hundred people were taken to the hospital. Many of them had been innocent bystanders.

☐ **EXERCISE 25. Using expressions of quantity in adjective clauses. (Chart 13-11)**
Directions: Complete the sentences.

1. Al introduced me to his roommates, both of ___whom are from California.___

2. The Paulsons own four automobiles, one of _____

3. I have three brothers, all of _____

4. I am taking four courses, one of _____

5. I have two roommates, neither of _____

6. This semester I had to buy fifteen books, most of _____

7. The company hired ten new employees, some of _____

8. In my apartment building, there are twenty apartments, several of _____

   _____

13-12 USING NOUN + *OF WHICH*

We have an antique table. *The top of it* has jade inlay. (a) We have an antique table, *the top of which* has jade inlay.	An adjective clause may include *a noun* + *of which* (e.g., *the top of which*). This pattern carries the meaning of *whose* (e.g., *We have an antique table whose top has jade inlay.*). This pattern is used in an adjective clause that modifies a thing and occurs primarily in formal written English. A comma is used.

☐ EXERCISE 26. Using noun + OF WHICH. (Chart 13-12)

Directions: Combine the two sentences. Use the second sentence as an adjective clause.

1. We toured a 300-year-old house. The exterior of the house consisted of logs cemented with clay.

    → *We toured a 300-year-old house, the exterior of which consisted of logs cemented with clay.*

2. They own an original Picasso painting. The value of the painting is more than a million dollars.

3. I bought a magazine. The title of the magazine is *Contemporary Architectural Styles*.

4. My country is dependent upon its income from coffee. The price of coffee varies according to fluctuations in the world market.

5. The genetic engineers are engaged in significant experiments. The results of the experiments will be published in the *Journal of Science*.

6. The professor has assigned the students a research paper. The purpose of the research paper is to acquaint them with methods of scholarly inquiry.

13-13 USING *WHICH* TO MODIFY A WHOLE SENTENCE

(a) Tom was late. (b) *That* surprised me. (c) Tom was late, *which surprised me.*	The pronouns *that* and *this* can refer to the idea of a whole sentence which comes before. In (b): The word *that* refers to the whole sentence "Tom was late."
(d) The elevator is out of order. (e) *This* is too bad. (f) The elevator is out of order, *which is too bad.*	Similarly, an adjective clause with *which* may modify the idea of a whole sentence. In (c): The word *which* refers to the whole sentence "Tom was late." Using *which* to modify a whole sentence is informal and occurs most frequently in spoken English. This structure is generally not appropriate in formal writing. Whenever it is written, however, it is preceded by a comma to reflect a pause in speech.

☐ EXERCISE 27. Using WHICH to modify a whole sentence. (Chart 13-13)

Directions: Use the second sentence as an adjective clause.

1. Max isn't home yet. That worries me.

    → *Max isn't home yet, which worries me.*

2. My roommate never picks up after herself. This irritates me.

3. Mrs. Anderson responded to my letter right away. I appreciated that very much.

4. There's been an accident on Highway 5. That means I'll be late to work this morning.
5. I shut the door on my necktie. That was really stupid of me.

6. Sally lost her job. That wasn't surprising.
7. She usually came to work late. That upset her boss.
8. So her boss fired her. That made her angry.
9. She hadn't saved any money. That was unfortunate.
10. So she had to borrow some money from me. I didn't like that.
11. She has found a new job. That is lucky.
12. So she has repaid the money she borrowed from me. I appreciate that.
13. She has promised herself to be on time to work every day. That is a good idea.

☐ EXERCISE 28. Using WHICH to modify a whole sentence. (Chart 13-13)
   Directions: Make up a sentence to precede the given sentence. Then combine the two sentences, using the second sentence as an adjective clause.

1. <u>The student next to me kept cracking his knuckles.</u> That bothered
   me a lot. → *The student next to me kept cracking his knuckles, which bothered me a lot.*

2. _____ That disappointed me.

3. _____ That made me nervous.

4. _____ That shocked all of us.

5. _____ That means he's probably in trouble.

6. _____ That was a pleasant surprise.

7. _____ That made her very unhappy.

8. _____ I appreciated that very much.

9. _____ That made it difficult for me to concentrate.

10. _____ That bothered me so much that I couldn't get to sleep.

□ EXERCISE 29. Special adjective clauses. (Charts 13-11 → 13-13)
   Directions: Create sentences that contain the following groups of words. Do not change the order of the words as they are given. Add words only before and after the group of words. Add punctuation as necessary.

   Examples: . . . yesterday which surprised . . . .
   → *Tom didn't come to class **yesterday, which surprised** me.*

   . . . people to my party some of whom . . . .
   → *I invited ten **people to my party, some of whom** are my classmates.*

   1. . . . brothers all of whom . . . .
   2. . . . early which was fortunate . . . .
   3. . . . students three of whom . . . .
   4. . . . ideas none of which . . . .
   5. . . . jewelry the value of which . . . .
   6. . . . teachers some of whom . . . .
   7. . . . mother which made me . . . .
   8. . . . a little money all of which . . . .
   9. . . . sisters each of whom . . . .
   10. . . . new car the inside of which . . . .
   11. . . . clothes some of which . . . .
   12. . . . two days ago which surprised . . . .

□ EXERCISE 30. Adjective clauses. (Charts 13-1 → 13-13)
   Directions: Combine the sentences. Use formal written English. Use (b) as an adjective clause. Punctuate carefully.

   1. (a) An antecedent is a word.
      (b) A pronoun refers to this word.
      → *An antecedent is a word to which a pronoun refers.*

   2. (a) The blue whale is considered the largest animal that has ever lived.
      (b) It can grow to 100 feet and 150 tons.

   3. (a) The plane was met by a crowd of three hundred people.
      (b) Some of them had been waiting for more than four hours.

   4. (a) In this paper, I will describe the basic process.
      (b) Raw cotton becomes cotton thread by this process.

   5. (a) The researchers are doing case studies of people to determine the importance of heredity in health and longevity.
      (b) These people's families have a history of high blood pressure and heart disease.

   6. (a) At the end of this month, scientists at the institute will conclude their AIDS research.
      (b) The results of this research will be published within six months.

   7. (a) According to many education officials, "math phobia" (that is, a fear of mathematics) is a widespread problem.
      (b) A solution to this problem must and can be found.

   8. (a) The art museum hopes to hire a new administrator.
      (b) Under this person's direction it will be able to purchase significant pieces of art.

9. (a) The giant anteater licks up ants for its dinner.
   (b) Its tongue is longer than 30 centimeters (12 inches).

10. (a) The anteater's tongue is sticky.
    (b) It can go in and out of its mouth 160 times a minute.

☐ EXERCISE 31. Activity: adjective clauses. (Charts 13-1 → 13-13)
Directions: Discuss and/or write definitions for one or more of these people. Include an adjective clause in your definition. Include several qualities of each person. If you are writing, expand your definition to a whole paragraph.

1. the ideal friend
2. the ideal mother
3. the ideal father
4. the ideal wife
5. the ideal husband

6. the ideal teacher
7. the ideal student
8. the ideal political leader
9. the ideal doctor
10. the ideal *(use your own words)*

☐ EXERCISE 32. Activity: adjective clauses. (Charts 13-1 → 13-13)
Directions: Discuss and/or write about one or more of these topics.

1. the ideal vacation
2. the ideal job
3. the ideal school
4. the ideal system of government

13-14 REDUCING ADJECTIVE CLAUSES TO ADJECTIVE PHRASES: INTRODUCTION

CLAUSE: *A clause is a group of related words that contains a subject and a verb.*
PHRASE: *A phrase is a group of related words that does not contain a subject and a verb.*

(a) ADJECTIVE CLAUSE: The girl *who is sitting next to me* is Maria. (b) ADJECTIVE PHRASE: The girl *sitting next to me* is Maria.	An adjective phrase is a reduction of an adjective clause. It modifies a noun. It does not contain a subject and verb. The adjective clause in (a) can be reduced to the adjective phrase in (b). (a) and (b) have the same meaning.
(c) CLAUSE: The boy *who is playing the piano* is Ben. (d) PHRASE: The boy *playing the piano* is Ben.	Only adjective clauses that have a subject pronoun—*who*, *which*, or *that*—are reduced to modifying adjective phrases.
(e) CLAUSE: The boy *(whom) I saw* was Tom. (f) PHRASE: *(none)*	The adjective clause in (e) cannot be reduced to an adjective phrase.

13-15 CHANGING AN ADJECTIVE CLAUSE TO AN ADJECTIVE PHRASE

(a) CLAUSE: The man *who is talking* to John is from Korea. PHRASE: The man Ø Ø *talking* to John is from Korea.	There are two ways in which an adjective clause is changed to an adjective phrase.
(b) CLAUSE: The ideas *which are presented* in that book are good. PHRASE: The ideas Ø Ø *presented* in that book are good. (c) CLAUSE: Ann is the woman *who is responsible* for the error. PHRASE: Ann is the woman Ø Ø *responsible* for the error. (d) CLAUSE: The books *that are on that shelf* are mine. PHRASE: The books Ø Ø *on that shelf* are mine.	1. If the adjective clause contains the *be* form of a verb, omit the pronoun and the *be* form, as in examples (a), (b), (c), and (d).
(e) CLAUSE: English has an alphabet *that consists* of 26 letters. PHRASE: English has an alphabet Ø *consisting* of 26 letters. (f) CLAUSE: Anyone *who wants* to come with us is welcome. PHRASE: Anyone Ø *wanting* to come with us is welcome.	2. If there is no *be* form of a verb in the adjective clause, it is sometimes possible to omit the subject pronoun and change the verb to its *-ing* form, as in (e) and (f).
(g) George Washington, *who was the first president of the United States,* was a wealthy colonist and a general in the army. (h) George Washington, *the first president of the United States,* was a wealthy colonist and a general in the army.	If the adjective clause requires commas, as in (g), the adjective phrase also requires commas, as in (h).
(i) *Paris, the capital of France,* is an exciting city. (j) I read a book by *Mark Twain, a famous American author.*	Adjective phrases in which a noun follows another noun, as in (h), (i), and (j), are called "appositives."

*If an adjective clause that contains *be* + *a single adjective* is changed, the adjective is moved to its normal position in front of the noun it modifies.

      CLAUSE: ***Fruit that is fresh*** *tastes better than old, soft, mushy fruit.*
      CORRECT PHRASE: ***Fresh fruit*** *tastes better than old, soft, mushy fruit.*
      INCORRECT PHRASE: Fruit fresh tastes better than old, soft, mushy fruit.

□ **EXERCISE 33. Adjective phrases. (Charts 13-14 and 13-15)**
Directions: Change the adjective clauses to adjective phrases.

1. Do you know the woman who is coming toward us?
   → *Do you know the woman coming toward us?*
2. The people who are waiting for the bus in the rain are getting wet.
3. I come from a city that is located in the southern part of the country.
4. The children who attend that school receive a good education.
5. The scientists who are researching the causes of cancer are making progress.
6. The fence which surrounds our house is made of wood.
7. They live in a house that was built in 1890.
8. We have an apartment which overlooks the park.

□ **EXERCISE 34. Adjective phrases. (Charts 13-14 and 13-15)**
Directions: Change the adjective clauses to adjective phrases.

1. Dr. Stanton, ~~who is~~ the president of the university, will give a speech at the commencement ceremonies.
2. Be sure to follow the instructions that are given at the top of the page.
3. The rules that allow public access to wilderness areas need to be reconsidered.
4. The photographs which were published in the newspaper were extraordinary.
5. There is almost no end to the problems that face a head of state.
6. The psychologists who study the nature of sleep have made important discoveries.
7. The experiment which was conducted at the University of Chicago was successful.
8. Kuala Lumpur, which is the capital city of Malaysia, is a major trade center in Southeast Asia.
9. Antarctica is covered by a huge ice cap that contains 70 percent of the earth's fresh water.
10. When I went to Alex's house to drop off some paperwork, I met Jerry, who is his longtime partner.
11. Our solar system is in a galaxy that is called the Milky Way.
12. Two out of three people who are struck by lightning survive.
13. Simon Bolivar, who was a great South American general, led the fight for independence early in the 19th century.
14. Many of the students who hope to enter the university will be disappointed because only one-tenth of those who apply for admission will be accepted.
15. There must exist in a modern community a sufficient number of persons who possess the technical skill that is required to maintain the numerous devices upon which our physical comforts depend.
16. Many famous people did not enjoy immediate success in their early lives. Abraham Lincoln, who was one of the truly great presidents of the United States, ran for public office 26 times and lost 23 of the elections. Walt Disney, who was the creator of Mickey Mouse and the founder of his own movie production company, once was fired by a newspaper editor because he had no good ideas. Thomas Edison, who was the inventor of the light bulb and the phonograph, was believed by his teachers to be too stupid to learn. Albert Einstein, who was one of the greatest scientists of all time, performed badly in almost all of his high school courses and failed his first college entrance exam.

□ EXERCISE 35. Adjective phrases. (Charts 13-14 and 13-15)
  Directions: Change the adjective phrases to adjective clauses.

  1. We visited Barcelona, a city in northern Spain.
     → *We visited Barcelona, which is a city in northern Spain.*
  2. Corn was one of the agricultural products introduced to the European settlers by the Indians. Some of the other products introduced by the Indians were potatoes, peanuts, and tobacco.
  3. He read *The Old Man and the Sea*, a novel written by Ernest Hemingway.
  4. Mercury, the nearest planet to the sun, is also the smallest of the nine planets orbiting the sun.
  5. The pyramids, the monumental tombs of ancient Egyptian pharaohs, were constructed more than 4,000 years ago.
  6. The sloth, a slow-moving animal found in the tropical forests of Central and South America, feeds entirely on leaves and fruit.
  7. Two-thirds of those arrested for car theft are under twenty years of age.
  8. St. Louis, Missouri, known as "The Gateway to the West," traces its history to 1763, when Pierre Laclède, a French fur trader, selected this site on the Mississippi River as a fur-trading post.
  9. Any student not wanting to go on the trip should inform the office.
  10. I just purchased a volume of poems written by David Keller, a contemporary poet known for his sensitive interpretations of human relationships.

□ EXERCISE 36. Adjective phrases. (Charts 13-14 and 13-15)
  Directions: Complete the sentences in *PART II* with adjective phrases by using the information in *PART I*. Use commas as necessary.

  PART I.
     A. It is the lowest place on the earth's surface.
   ✔ B. It is the highest mountain in the world.
     C. It is the capital of Iraq.
     D. It is the capital of Argentina.
     E. It is the largest city in the Western Hemisphere.
     F. It is the largest city in the United States.
     G. It is the most populous country in Africa.
     H. It is the northernmost country in Latin America.
     I. It is an African animal that eats ants and termites.
     J. It is a small animal that spends its entire life underground.
     K. They are sensitive instruments that measure the shaking of the ground.
     L. They are devices that produce a powerful beam of light.

  PART II.

  1. Mt. Everest ___, the highest mountain in the world, ___ is in the Himalayas.

  2. One of the largest cities in the Middle East is Baghdad _____

  3. Earthquakes are recorded on seismographs _____

4. The Dead Sea _____

   is located in the Middle East between Jordan and Israel.

5. The newspaper reported an earthquake in Buenos Aires _____

6. Industry and medicine are continually finding new uses for lasers _____

   _____

7. Mexico _____

   lies just south of the United States.

8. The nation Nigeria _____ consists

   of over 250 different cultural groups even though English is the official language.

9. Both Mexico City _____ and New York

   City _____ face challenging futures.

10. The mole _____ is almost blind. The

    aardvark _____ also lives

    underground but hunts for its food above ground.

☐ EXERCISE 37. Review: adjective clauses and phrases. (Chapter 13)
   Directions: Combine each group of short, choppy sentences into one sentence. Use the
   underlined sentence as the independent clause; build your sentence around the
   independent clause. Use adjective clauses and adjective phrases wherever possible.

   1. Chihuahua is divided into two regions. It is the largest Mexican state. One region is a
      mountainous area in the west. The other region is a desert basin in the north and east.
      → **Chihuahua,** *the largest Mexican state,* **is divided into two regions,** *a mountainous*
      area in the west and a desert basin in the north and east.

   2. Disney World covers a large area of land. It is an amusement park. It is located in
      Orlando, Florida. The land includes lakes, golf courses, campsites, hotels, and a
      wildlife preserve.

   3. Jamaica is one of the world's leading producers of bauxite. It is the third largest island
      in the Caribbean Sea. Bauxite is an ore. Aluminum is made from this ore.

   4. Robert Ballard made headlines in 1985. He is an oceanographer. In 1985 he discovered
      the remains of the *Titanic*. The *Titanic* was the "unsinkable" passenger ship. It has
      rested on the floor of the Atlantic Ocean since 1912. It struck an iceberg in 1912.

   5. William Shakespeare's father was a glove maker and a town official. William Shakespeare's
      father was John Shakespeare. He owned a shop in Stratford-upon-Avon. Stratford-upon-
      Avon is a town. It is about 75 miles (120 kilometers) northwest of London.

   6. The Republic of Yemen is an ancient land. It is located at the southwestern tip of the
      Arabian Peninsula. This land has been host to many prosperous civilizations. These
      civilizations include the Kingdom of Sheba and various Islamic empires.

□ EXERCISE 38. Error analysis: adjective clauses and phrases. (Chapter 13)
   Directions: Correct the errors.

1. One of the people which I admire most is my uncle.

2. Baseball is the only sport in which I am interested in it.

3. My favorite teacher, Mr. Chu, he was always willing to help me after class.

4. It is important to be polite to people who lives in the same building.

5. She lives in a hotel is restricted to senior citizens.

6. My sister has two childrens, who their names are Ali and Talal.

7. He comes from Venezuela that is a Spanish-speaking country.

8. There are some people in the government who is trying to improve the lives of poor people.

9. I have some good advice for anyone who he wants to learn a second language.

10. My classroom is located on the second floor of Carver Hall that is a large brick building in the center of the campus.

11. A myth is a story expresses traditional beliefs.

12. There is an old legend telling among people in my country about a man lived in the seventeenth century saved a village from destruction.

13. An old man was fishing next to me on the pier was muttering to himself.

14. When I was a child, I was always afraid of the beggars whom they went from house to house in my neighborhood.

15. At the national park, there is a path leads to a spectacular waterfall.

16. The road that we took it through the forest it was narrow and steep.

17. There are ten universities in Thailand, seven of them locate in Bangkok is the capital city.

18. I would like to write about several problem which I have faced them since I come to United State.

19. There is a small wooden screen separates the bed from the rest of the room.

20. At the airport, I was waiting for some relatives which I had never met them before.

21. It is almost impossible to find two persons who their opinions are the same.

22. On the wall, there is a colorful poster which it consists of a group of young people who dancing.

23. The sixth member of our household is Alex that is my sister's son.

24. Before I came here, I didn't have the opportunity to speak with people who English is their native tongue.

☐ EXERCISE 39. Activity: adjective clauses. (Chapter 13)
Directions: A discovery and an invention are different, but they are related. A discovery occurs when something that exists in nature is recognized for the first time. Fire is an example of a discovery. An invention is something that is made for the first time by a creator. An invention never existed before the act of creation. The telephone and the automobile are two examples of important 20th-century inventions.

Either in a group or by yourself, draw up a list of inventions made in the 20th century. After your list is finished, discuss the inventions you have named, using the following questions as guidelines:

1. What are the three most important 20th-century inventions that you have listed? Why? In other words, why do you rate these as the most influential/important inventions?
2. What were some important inventions prior to the 20th century? Why?
3. Which invention has brought the most happiness to people? Which has caused the most unhappiness?
4. Are any of the inventions you have listed luxury items? Which of the inventions you have listed have become accepted as necessities?
5. What would your world be like without a certain invention? How has your life been influenced by these inventions? Would you like to go back to 1900 when none of these things existed? Can you visualize life as it was then?
6. What would you like to see invented now? What do you think will be one of the most important inventions that will be made in the future? What are you going to invent?

☐ EXERCISE 40. Activity: adjective clauses. (Chapter 13)
Directions: Form a group of three people. Together, make up one sentence with as many adjective clauses as possible. In other words, make the most awkward sentence you can while still using grammatically correct sentence structure. Count the number of adjective clauses you use. See which group can make the worst sentence by using the largest number of adjective clauses.

Example of a stylistically terrible, but grammatically correct, sentence:

The man who was sitting at a table which was at the restaurant where I usually eat dinner, which is something I do every evening, was talking to a woman who was wearing a dress which was blue, which is my favorite color.

☐ EXERCISE 41. Writing: adjective clauses and phrases. (Chapter 13)

Directions: Write on one or more of these topics. Try to use adjective clauses and phrases.

1. Write about three historical figures from your country. Give your reader information about their lives and accomplishments.

2. Write about your favorite TV shows. What are they? What are they about? Why do you enjoy them?

3. Who are some people in your country who are popular with young people (e.g., singers, movie stars, political figures, etc.)? Tell your readers about these people. Assume your readers are completely unfamiliar with them.

4. You are a tourist agent for your hometown/country. Write a descriptive brochure that would make your readers want to visit your hometown/country.

5. What kind of people do you like? What kind of people do you avoid?

6. What kind of person do you want to marry? What kind of person do you not want to marry? If you are already married: What kind of person did you marry?

☐ EXERCISE 42. Activity: speaking and writing.

Directions: Form a group of volunteers who are interested in performing a short play. Work together outside of class to prepare a performance for the rest of the class. Choose a scene from a published play, or write your own.

If you write your own, choose a situation in which there is some kind of conflict, for example, people who are facing a problem. Perhaps the characters or situations can be based on current movies or TV programs, or possibly on historical events. Write down the dialogue so that each member of the group has the exact same script.

Then present your play to the rest of the class.

Possible follow-up activities:

1. Write a synopsis of the play your classmates presented.

2. Write a letter to a character in one of the plays, giving advice on how to handle the conflict in the play.

3. With a group, discuss the relationships and the conflict in the play.

4. With others, re-enact the play you saw, without looking at a script.

CHAPTER *14*
Gerunds and Infinitives, Part 1

CONTENTS

14-1 GERUNDS: INTRODUCTION

(a) $\overset{S}{\overline{\textit{Playing}}}$ tennis $\overset{V}{\overline{\text{is}}}$ fun.

(b) $\overset{S}{\overline{\text{We}}}$ $\overset{V}{\overline{\text{enjoy}}}$ $\overset{O}{\overline{\textit{playing}}}$ tennis.

(c) He's excited $\overset{PREP}{\overline{\text{about}}}$ $\overset{O}{\overline{\textit{playing}}}$ tennis.

A *gerund* is the *-ing* form of a verb used as a noun.* A gerund is used in the same ways as a noun, i.e., as a subject or as an object.

In (a): *playing* is a gerund. It is used as the subject of the sentence. *Playing tennis* is a *gerund phrase*.

In (b): *playing* is a gerund used as the object of the verb *enjoy*.

In (c): *playing* is a gerund used as the object of the preposition *about*.

*COMPARE the uses of the *-ing* form of verbs:
(1) *Walking* is good exercise.
    → *walking* = a gerund used as the subject of the sentence.
(2) *Bob and Ann are **playing** tennis.*
    → *playing* = a present participle used as part of the present progressive tense.
(3) *I heard some **surprising** news.*
    → *surprising* = a present participle used as an adjective.

14-2 USING GERUNDS AS THE OBJECTS OF PREPOSITIONS

(a) We talked *about going* to Canada for our vacation. (b) Sue is in charge *of organizing* the meeting. (c) I'm interested *in learning* more about your work.	A gerund is frequently used as the object of a preposition.
(d) I'm *used to sleeping* with the window open. (e) I'm *accustomed to sleeping** with the window open. (f) I *look forward to going* home next month. (g) They *object to changing* their plans at this late date.	In (d) through (g): *to* is a preposition, not part of an infinitive form, so a gerund follows.
(h) We *talked about not going* to the meeting, but finally decided we should go.	Negative form: *not* precedes a gerund.

*Possible in British English: *I'm accustomed to sleep* with the window open.*

☐ **EXERCISE 1. Preview. (Chart 14-3)**

Directions: Without referring to Chart 14-3, see how many of the preposition combinations you already know by completing these sentences with an appropriate preposition and verb form.

1. Alice isn't interested ___in___ *(look)* ___looking___ for a new job.

2. Henry is excited _____ *(leave)* _____ for India.

3. You are capable _____ *(do)* _____ better work.

4. I have no excuse _____ *(be)* _____ late.

5. I'm accustomed _____ *(have)* _____ a big breakfast.

6. The rain prevented us _____ *(complete)* _____ the work.

7. Fred is always complaining _____ *(have)* _____ a headache.

8. Instead _____ *(study)* _____, Margaret went to a ballgame with some of her friends.

9. Thank you _____ *(help)* _____ me carry my suitcases.

10. Mrs. Grant insisted _____ *(know)* _____ the whole truth.

11. I believe _____ *(be)* _____ honest at all times.

12. You should take advantage _____ *(live)* _____ here.

13. Fatima had a good reason _____ *(go, not)* _____ to class yesterday.

14. Everyone in the neighborhood participated _____ *(search)* _____ for the lost child.

15. I apologized to Yoko _____ *(make)* _____ her wait for me.

16. The weather is terrible tonight. I don't blame you _____ (want, not) _____ _____ to go to the meeting.

17. Who is responsible _____ (wash) _____ and (dry) _____ the dishes after dinner?

18. In addition _____ (go) _____ to school full time, Spiro has a part-time job.

19. I stopped the child _____ (run) _____ into the street.

20. Where should we go for dinner tonight? Would you object _____ (go) _____ to an Italian restaurant?

21. The mayor made another public statement for the purpose _____ (clarify) _____ the new tax proposal.

22. The thief was accused _____ (steal) _____ a woman's purse.

23. The jury found Mr. Adams guilty _____ (take) _____ money from the company he worked for and (keep) _____ it for himself.

24. Larry isn't used _____ (wear) _____ a suit and tie every day.

25. I'm going to visit my family during the school vacation. I'm looking forward _____ (eat) _____ my mother's cooking and (sleep) _____ in my own bed.

14-3 COMMON PREPOSITION COMBINATIONS FOLLOWED BY GERUNDS

be excited
be worried } *about doing* it

complain
dream
talk
think } *about/of doing* it

apologize
blame (someone)
forgive (someone)
have an excuse
have a reason
be responsible
thank (someone) } *for doing* it

keep (someone)
prevent (someone)
prohibit (someone)
stop (someone) } *from doing* it

believe
be interested
participate
succeed } *in doing* it

be accused
be capable
for the purpose
be guilty
instead
take advantage
take care
be tired } *of doing* it

insist *on doing* it

be accustomed
in addition
be committed
be devoted
look forward
object
be opposed
be used } *to doing* it

□ **EXERCISE 2. Using gerunds as the objects of prepositions. (Charts 14-2 and 14-3)**
Directions: Using the words in parentheses complete the sentences.

1. Kostas went to bed instead _____ *of finishing his work.* _____ *(finish)*

2. I thanked my friend _____ *(lend)*

3. I'm excited _____ *(go)*

4. I'm not accustomed _____ *(live)*

5. Omar didn't feel good. He complained _____ *(have)*

6. I don't blame you _____ *(want, not)*

7. I have a good reason _____ *(be)*

8. It's getting late. I'm worried _____ *(miss)*

9. I'm interested _____ *(find out about)*

10. I'm thinking _____ *(go)*

11. I apologized to my friend _____ *(be)*

12. I am/am not used _____ *(drive)*

13. Nothing can stop me _____ *(go)*

14. In that office, who is responsible _____ *(take care of)*

15. I look forward _____ *(go)*

16. The thief was guilty _____ *(steal)*

17. Sonya has two jobs. In addition _____ *(work)*

18. Please forgive me _____ *(write, not)*

19. Sarah is an honest person. She's not capable _____ *(tell)*

20. Ill health keeps my grandfather _____ *(travel)*

□ **EXERCISE 3. Using gerunds as the objects of prepositions. (Charts 14-2 and 14-3)**
Directions: To practice using gerunds following prepositions, answer the questions in complete sentences. If working in pairs, switch roles after Item 7.

Example:
SPEAKER A *(book open):* Your friend was late. Did she apologize?
SPEAKER B *(book closed):* Yes, she apologized OR No, she didn't apologize *for being* late.

1. You were late for class yesterday. Did you have a good excuse?

2. You are going to *(a city)* to visit your friends this weekend. Are you looking forward to that?

3. (. . .) picked up your pen when you dropped it. Did you thank him/her?

4. You're living in a cold/warm climate. Are you accustomed to that?

5. You're going to *(a place)* for a vacation. Are you excited?

6. You interrupted (. . .) while s/he was speaking. Did you apologize?

7. The students in the class did pantomimes. Did all of them participate?

8. Someone broke the window. Do you know who is responsible?

9. Americans usually have their biggest meal in the evening. Are you used to doing that?

10. The weather is hot/cold. What does that prevent you from doing?

11. (. . .) has to do a lot of homework. Does s/he complain?

12. (. . .) was sick last week, so s/he stayed home in bed. Do you blame her/him?

13. (. . .) didn't study grammar last night. What did s/he do instead?

14. You studied last night. What did you do in addition?

□ EXERCISE 4. Using gerunds as the objects of prepositions. (Chart 14-2)
Directions: Complete the following using *by* + *a gerund or gerund phrase* to express how something is done.

1. Pat turned off the tape recorder ____ by pushing the stop button. ____

2. We show people we are happy ____ by smiling. ____

3. We decided who should get the last piece of pie ____ by flipping a coin. ____

4. We satisfy our hunger _____

5. We quench our thirst _____

6. I found out what "quench" means _____

7. Tony improved his listening comprehension _____

8. Alex caught my attention _____

9. They got rid of the rats in the building _____

10. My dog shows me she is happy _____

11. He accidentally electrocuted himself _____

12. Sometimes teenagers get into trouble with their parents _____
_____

14-4 COMMON VERBS FOLLOWED BY GERUNDS

(a) I $\overbrace{enjoy}^{\text{verb}} + \overbrace{playing}^{\text{gerund}}$ tennis.	Gerunds are used as the objects of certain verbs. In (a), **enjoy** is followed by a gerund *(playing)*. **Enjoy** is not followed by an infinitive. *INCORRECT:* I enjoy *to play* tennis. Common verbs that are followed by gerunds are given in the list below.
(b) Joe *quit smoking.* (c) Joe *gave up smoking.*	(b) and (c) have the same meaning. Some phrasal verbs,* e.g., **give up**, are followed by gerunds. These phrasal verbs are given in parentheses in the list below.

VERB + GERUND			
enjoy	*quit (give up)*	*avoid*	*consider*
appreciate	*finish (get through)*	*postpone (put off)*	*discuss*
mind	*stop***	*delay*	*mention*
		keep (keep on)	*suggest*

*A *phrasal verb* consists of a verb and a particle (a small word such as a preposition) that together have a special meaning. For example, *put off* means "postpone."

***Stop* can also be followed immediately by an infinitive of purpose *(in order to)*. See Chart 15-2, p. 328.
COMPARE the following:
(1) **stop** + *gerund:* When the professor entered the room, the students **stopped talking**. The room became quiet.
(2) **stop** + *infinitive of purpose:* While I was walking down the street, I ran into an old friend. I **stopped to talk** to him.
(I stopped walking *in order to talk* to him.)

☐ EXERCISE 5. Verbs followed by gerunds. (Chart 14-4)
   Directions: Create sentences from the given words, using any tense and subject. Work in pairs, in groups, or as a class. The cuer's book is open. The responder's book is closed.

   Example: enjoy + read the newspaper
   SPEAKER A *(book open):* "enjoy" (pause) "read the newspaper"
   SPEAKER B *(book closed):* I enjoy reading the newspaper every morning while I'm having my first cup of coffee.

   1. enjoy + watch TV
   2. mind + open the window
   3. quit + eat desserts
   4. give up + eat desserts
   5. finish + eat dinner
   6. get through + eat dinner
   7. stop + rain
   8. avoid + answer my question
   9. postpone + do my work
   10. put off + do my work
   11. delay + leave on vacation
   12. keep + work
   13. keep on + work
   14. consider + get a job
   15. think about + get a job
   16. discuss + go to a movie
   17. talk about + go to a movie
   18. mention + go to a concert
   19. suggest + go on a picnic*
   20. enjoy + listen to music

---
*For other ways of expressing ideas with *suggest*, see Chart 12-8, p. 263.

☐ EXERCISE 6. Verbs followed by gerunds. (Chart 14-4)

Directions: Complete each sentence with any appropriate gerund.

1. When Beth got tired, she stopped ___working/studying___.

2. Would you mind _____ the door? Thanks.

3. The weather will get better soon. We can leave as soon as it quits
_____.

4. The police officer told him to stop, but the thief kept _____.

5. I enjoy _____ a long walk every morning.

6. I have a lot of homework tonight, but I'd still like to go with you later on. I'll call you
when I get through _____.

7. I would like to have some friends over. I'm thinking about _____ a
dinner party.

8. He told a really funny joke. We couldn't stop _____!

9. Jack almost had an automobile accident. He barely avoided _____
another car at the intersection of 4th and Elm.

10. Where are you considering _____ for vacation?

11. Sometimes I put off _____ my homework.

12. You have to decide where you want to go to school next year. You can't postpone
_____ that decision much longer.

13. I wanted to go to Mexico. Sally suggested _____ to Hawaii.

14. Tony mentioned _____ the bus to school instead of walking.

15. I appreciate _____ able to study in peace and quiet.

14-5 *GO* + GERUND

(a) Did you *go shopping*? (b) We *went fishing* yesterday.	*Go* is followed by a gerund in certain idiomatic expressions to express, for the most part, recreational activities.

GO + GERUND

go birdwatching	go fishing*	go sailing	go skinnydipping
go boating	go hiking	go shopping	go sledding
go bowling	go hunting	go sightseeing	go snorkeling
go camping	go jogging	go skating	go swimming
go canoeing/kayaking	go mountain climbing	go skateboarding	go tobogganing
go dancing	go running	go skiing	go window shopping

*Also, in British English: *go angling*

□ **EXERCISE 7. GO + gerund. (Chart 14-5)**
   Directions: Discuss the activities listed in Chart 14-5.

   1. Which ones have you done? When? Briefly describe your experiences.
   2. Which ones do you like to do?
   3. Which ones do you never want to do?
   4. Which ones have you not done but would like to do?

□ **EXERCISE 8. GO + gerund. (Chart 14-5)**
   Directions: Create sentences from the given words, using any tense and subject. Work in pairs, in groups, or as a class. The cuer's book is open. The responder's book is closed.

   Example: enjoy + go
   SPEAKER A *(book open):* "enjoy" (pause) "go"
   SPEAKER B *(book closed):* I enjoy going to the zoo. / My friend and I enjoyed going to a rock concert last weekend. / Where do you enjoy going in *(this city)* when you have some free time?

   1. finish + study
   2. go + dance
   3. keep + work
   4. go + bowl
   5. think about + wear
   6. enjoy + play
   7. go + fish
   8. talk about + go + swim
   9. stop + fight
   10. postpone + go + camp
   11. quit + rain
   12. avoid + go + shop
   13. give up + ask
   14. discuss + go + birdwatch
   15. appreciate + hear
   16. mind + wait
   17. think about + not go
   18. talk about + go + run

14-6 SPECIAL EXPRESSIONS FOLLOWED BY -ING

(a) We *had fun*
 We *had a good time* } *playing* volleyball.
	-ing forms follow certain special expressions:
	    have fun/a good time + *-ing*
	    have trouble/difficulty + *-ing*
	    have a hard time/difficult time + *-ing*

(b) I *had trouble* I *had difficulty* I *had a hard time* I *had a difficult time* } *finding* his house.	
(c) Sam *spends* most of his time *studying*. (d) I *waste a lot of time watching* TV.	*spend* + expression of time or money + *-ing* *waste* + expression of time or money + *-ing*
(e) She *sat* at her desk *writing* a letter. (f) I *stood* there *wondering* what to do next. (g) He *is lying* in bed *reading* a novel.	*sit* + expression of place + *-ing* *stand* + expression of place + *-ing* *lie* + expression of place + *-ing*
(h) When I walked into my office, I *found* George *using* my telephone. (i) When I walked into my office, I *caught* a thief *looking* through my desk drawers.	*find* + (pro)noun + *-ing* *catch* + (pro)noun + *-ing* In (h) and (i): Both *find* and *catch* mean "discover." *Catch* often expresses anger or displeasure.

☐ EXERCISE 9. Special expressions followed by -ING. (Chart 14-6)
     Directions: Complete the sentences.

1. We had a lot of fun _____playing_____ games at the picnic.

2. I have trouble _____ Mrs. Maxwell when she speaks. She talks too fast.

3. I spent five hours _____ my homework last night.

4. Olga is standing at the corner _____ for the bus.

5. Ricardo is sitting in class _____ notes.

6. It was a beautiful spring day. Dorothy was lying under a tree _____ to the birds sing.

7. We wasted our money _____ to that movie. It was very boring.

8. Omar spent all day _____ ready to leave on vacation.

9. Ted is an indecisive person. He has a hard time _____ up his mind about anything.

10. I wondered what the children were doing while I was gone. When I got home, I found them _____ TV.

11. When Mr. Chan walked into the kitchen, he caught the children _____ some candy even though he'd told them not to spoil their dinners.

12. Ms. Gray is a commuter. Every work day, she spends almost two hours _____ to and from work.

13. A: My friend is going to Germany next month, but he doesn't speak German. What do you suppose he will have difficulty _____?

    B: Well, he might have trouble _____.

14. A: Did you enjoy your trip to New York City?

    B: Very much. We had a good time _____.

15. A: This is your first semester at this school. Have you had any problems?

    B: Not really, but sometimes I have a hard time _____.

16. A: What did you do yesterday?

    B: I spent almost all day _____.

☐ EXERCISE 10. Special expressions followed by -ING. (Chart 14-6)
Directions: Create sentences from the given verb combinations. Work in pairs, in groups, or as a class. The cuer's book is open. The responder's book is closed.

Example: have a difficult time + understand
SPEAKER A *(book open):* "have a difficult time" (pause) "understand"
SPEAKER B *(book closed):* I have a difficult time understanding the teacher's explanations in calculus.

Example: spend *(time)* + polish
SPEAKER A *(book open):* "spend an hour" (pause) "polish"
SPEAKER B *(book closed):* The soldier spent an hour polishing his boots.

1. have trouble + remember

2. stand *(place)* + wait

3. have a hard time + learn

4. sit *(place)* + think

5. have a good time + play

6. lie *(place)* + dream

7. have difficulty + pronounce

8. have fun + sing and dance

9. find *(someone)* + study

10. spend *(time)* + chat

11. waste *(money)* + try

12. catch *(someone)* + take

14-7 COMMON VERBS FOLLOWED BY INFINITIVES

VERB + INFINITIVE (a) I *hope to see* you again soon. (b) He *promised to be* here by ten. (c) He *promised not to be* late.	An *infinitive* = **to** + *the simple form of a verb (to see, to be, to go, etc.).* Some verbs are followed immediately by an infinitive, as in (a) and (b). See Group A below. Negative form: **not** precedes the infinitive, as in (c).
VERB + (PRO)NOUN + INFINITIVE (d) Mr. Lee *told me to be* here at ten o'clock. (e) The police *ordered the driver to stop.*	Some verbs are followed by a (pro)noun and then an infinitive, as in (d) and (e). See Group B below.
(f) I *was told to be* here at ten o'clock. (g) The driver *was ordered to stop.*	These verbs are followed immediately by an infinitive when they are used in the passive, as in (f) and (g).

(h) I *expect to pass* the test.
(i) I *expect Mary to pass* the test.
	Ask, expect, would like, want, and *need* may or may not be followed by a (pro)noun object.
	COMPARE
	   In (h): I think I will pass the test.
	   In (i): I think Mary will pass the test.

GROUP A: VERB + INFINITIVE

hope *to (do something)*	**promise** *to*	**seem** *to*	**expect** *to*
plan *to*	**agree** *to*	**appear** *to*	**would like** *to*
intend *to**	**offer** *to*	**pretend** *to*	**want** *to*
decide *to*	**refuse** *to*	**ask** *to*	**need** *to*

GROUP B: VERB + (PRO)NOUN + INFINITIVE

tell *someone to*	**permit** *someone to*	**force** *someone to*	**need** *someone to*
advise *someone to***	**allow** *someone to*	**ask** *someone to*	
encourage *someone to*	**warn** *someone to*	**expect** *someone to*	
remind *someone to*	**require** *someone to*	**would like** *someone to*	
invite *someone to*	**order** *someone to*	**want** *someone to*	

***Intend** is usually followed by an infinitive (*I intend to go* to the meeting), but sometimes may be followed by a gerund (*I intend going* to the meeting) with no change in meaning.

A gerund is used after **advise (active) if there is no (pro)noun object.
COMPARE:
   (1) He **advised buying** a Fiat.
   (2) He **advised me to buy** a Fiat. I **was advised to buy** a Fiat.

☐ EXERCISE 11. Verb + gerund or infinitive. (Charts 14-4 and 14-7)
Directions: Use a gerund or an infinitive to complete each sentence.

1. We're going out for dinner. Would you like _____to join_____ us?

2. Jack avoided _____looking at_____ me.

3. Fred didn't have any money, so he decided _____ a job.

4. The teacher reminded the students _____ their assignments.

5. Do you enjoy _____ soccer?

6. I was broke, so Jenny offered _____ me a little money.

7. Mrs. Allen promised _____ tomorrow.

8. My boss expects me _____ this work ASAP.*

9. Would you mind _____ the door for me?

10. Even though I asked the people in front of me at the movie _____ quiet, they kept _____.

11. Joan and David were considering _____ married in June, but they finally decided _____ until August.

12. Our teacher encourages us _____ a dictionary whenever we are uncertain of the spelling of a word.

13. Before I went away to college, my mother reminded me _____ her a letter at least once a week.

14. Mrs. Jackson had warned her young son

_____

the hot stove.

15. I don't mind _____ alone.

16. The teacher seems _____ in a good mood today, don't you think?

17. Lucy pretended _____ the answer to my question.

18. Paulo intends _____ his friend a letter.

19. Residents are not allowed _____ pets in my apartment building.

20. All applicants are required _____ an entrance examination.

21. Someone asked me _____ this package.

22. I was asked _____ this package.

23. Jack advised me _____ a new apartment.

24. I was advised _____ a new apartment.

25. Jack advised _____ a new apartment.

26. Jack suggested _____ a new apartment.

27. Ann advised her sister _____ the plane instead of driving to Oregon.

28. Ann advised _____ the plane instead of driving to Oregon.

_____

*ASAP = *as soon as possible*

□ EXERCISE 12. Verbs followed by infinitives. (Chart 14-7)

Directions: Use an infinitive phrase to create active and passive sentences using the given ideas and the verbs in parentheses. (Omit the *by*-phrase in passive sentences.)

1. The teacher said to me, "You may leave early."
   (permit) The teacher permitted me to leave early. (active)
   I was permitted to leave early. (passive)

2. The secretary said to me, "Please give this note to Sue."
   (ask)

3. My advisor said to me, "You should take Biology 109."
   (advise)

4. When I went to traffic court, the judge said to me, "You must pay a fine."
   (order)

5. During the test, the teacher said to Greg, "Keep your eyes on your own paper."
   (warn)

6. During the test, the teacher said to Greg, "Don't look at your neighbor's paper."
   (warn)

7. At the meeting, the head of the department said to the faculty, "Don't forget to turn in your grade reports by the 15th."
   (remind)

8. Mr. Lee said to the children, "Be quiet."
   (tell)

9. The hijacker said to the pilot, "You must land the plane."
   (force)

10. When I was growing up, my parents said to me, "You may stay up late on Saturday night."
    (allow)

11. The teacher said to the students, "Speak slowly and clearly."
    (encourage)

12. The teacher always says to the students, "You are supposed to come to class on time."
    (expect)

☐ EXERCISE 13. Using infinitives to report speech. (Chart 14-7)
Directions: Report what someone said by using one of the verbs in the list to introduce an infinitive phrase.

advise	*expect*	*remind*
allow	*force*	*require*
ask	*order*	*tell*
encourage	*permit*	*warn*

1. The professor said to Alan, "You may leave early."
   → *The professor allowed Alan to leave early.* OR
   → *Alan was allowed to leave early.*
2. The general said to the soldiers, "Surround the enemy!"
3. Nancy said to me, "Would you please open the window?"
4. Bob said to me, "Don't forget to take your book back to the library."
5. Paul thinks I have a good voice, so he said to me, "You should take singing lessons."
6. Mrs. Anderson was very stern and a little angry. She shook her finger at the children and said to them, "Don't play with matches!"
7. I am very relieved because the Dean of Admissions said to me, "You may register for school late."
8. The law says, "Every driver must have a valid driver's license."
9. My friend said to me, "You should get some automobile insurance."
10. The robber had a gun. He said to me, "Give me all of your money."
11. Before the examination began, the teacher said to the students, "Work quickly."
12. My boss said to me, "Come to the meeting ten minutes early."

☐ EXERCISE 14. Common verbs followed by infinitives. (Chart 14-7)
Directions: Work in groups of three. The cuer's book is open. The responders' books are closed.

Speaker A: Your book is open. Give the cue.
Speaker B: Your book is closed. Make an active sentence from the verb combination.
Speaker C: Your book is closed. Change the sentence to the passive; omit the *by*-phrase as appropriate.

Example: allow me + leave

SPEAKER A *(book open):*   "allow me" (pause) "leave"

SPEAKER B *(book closed):* The teacher allowed me to leave class early last Friday because I had an appointment with my doctor.

SPEAKER C *(book closed):* (. . .) was allowed to leave class early last Friday because he/she had an appointment with his/her doctor.

	Switch roles.	*Switch roles.*
1. remind me + finish	4. expect me + be	7. tell me + open
2. ask me + go	5. warn me + not go	8. encourage me + visit
3. permit me + have	6. advise me + take	9. require us + take

14-8 COMMON VERBS FOLLOWED BY EITHER INFINITIVES OR GERUNDS

Some verbs can be followed by either an infinitive or a gerund, sometimes with no difference in meaning, as in Group A below, and sometimes with a difference in meaning, as in Group B below.

GROUP A: VERB + INFINITIVE OR GERUND, WITH NO DIFFERENCE IN MEANING			The verbs in Group A may be followed by either an infinitive or a gerund with little or no difference in meaning.
begin	*like*	*hate*	
start	*love*	*can't stand*	
continue	*prefer**	*can't bear*	

(a) It *began to rain.* / It *began raining.* (b) I *started to work.* / I *started working.*	In (a): There is no difference between ***began to rain*** and ***began raining.***
(c) It *was beginning to rain.*	If the main verb is progressive, an infinitive (not a gerund) is usually used, as in (c).

GROUP B: VERB + INFINITIVE OR GERUND, WITH A DIFFERENCE IN MEANING		The verbs in Group B may be followed by either an infinitive or a gerund, but the meaning is different.
remember	*regret*	
forget	*try*	

(d) Judy always *remembers to lock* the door.	***Remember*** + *infinitive* = remember to perform responsibility, duty, or task, as in (d).
(e) Sam often *forgets to lock* the door.	***Forget*** + *infinitive* = forget to perform a responsibility, duty, or task, as in (e).
(f) I *remember seeing* the Alps for the first time. The sight was impressive.	***Remember*** + *gerund* = remember (recall) something that happened in the past, as in (f).
(g) I'll *never forget seeing* the Alps for the first time.	***Forget*** + *gerund* = forget something that happened in the past, as in (g).**

(h) I *regret to tell* you that you failed the test.	***Regret*** + *infinitive* = regret to say, to tell someone, to inform someone of some bad news, as in (h).
(i) I *regret lending* him some money. He never paid me back.	***Regret*** + *gerund* = regret something that happened in the past, as in (i).

(j) I'm *trying to learn* English.	***Try*** + *infinitive* = make an effort, as in (j).
(k) The room was hot. I *tried opening* the window, but that didn't help. So I *tried turning* on the fan, but I was still hot. Finally, I turned on the air conditioner.	***Try*** + *gerund* = experiment with a new or different approach to see if it works, as in (k).

*Notice the patterns with ***prefer****:
    prefer + *gerund:* I ***prefer staying*** home ***to going*** to the concert.
    prefer + *infinitive:* I'd ***prefer to stay*** home (rather) ***than (to) go*** to the concert.

****Forget*** followed by a gerund usually occurs in a negative sentence or in a question: e.g., *I'll never forget, I can't forget, Have you ever forgotten,* and *Can you ever forget* are often followed by a gerund phrase.

□ EXERCISE 15. Gerund vs. infinitive. (Chart 14-8)

Directions: Complete the sentences with the correct form(s) of the verbs in parentheses.

1. I like *(go)* _____to go / going_____ to the zoo.

2. The play wasn't very good. The audience started *(leave)* _____ before it was over.

3. After a brief interruption, the professor continued *(lecture)* _____ _____.

4. The children love *(swim)* _____ in the ocean.

5. I hate *(see)* _____ any living being suffer. I can't bear it.

6. I'm afraid of flying. When a plane begins *(move)* _____ down the runway, my heart starts *(race)* _____. Oh-oh! The plane is beginning *(move)* _____, and my heart is starting *(race)* _____.

7. When I travel, I prefer *(drive)* _____ to *(take)* _____ a plane.

8. I prefer *(drive)* _____ rather than *(take)* _____ _____ a plane.

9. I always remember *(turn)* _____ off all the lights before I leave my house.

10. I can remember *(be)* _____ very proud and happy when I graduated.

11. Did you remember *(give)* _____ Jake my message?

12. I remember *(play)* _____ with dolls when I was a child.

13. What do you remember *(do)* _____ when you were a child?

14. What do you remember *(do)* _____ before you leave for class every day?

15. What did you forget *(do)* _____ before you left for class this morning?

16. I'll never forget *(carry)* _____ my wife over the threshold when we moved into our first home.

17. I can't ever forget *(watch)* _____ our team score the winning goal in the last seconds of the championship game.

18. Don't forget *(do)* _____ your homework tonight!

19. I regret *(inform)* _____ you that your loan application has not been approved.

20. I regret *(listen, not)* _____ to my father's advice. He was right.

21. When a student asks a question, the teacher always tries *(explain)* _____ _____ the problem as clearly as possible.

22. I tried everything, but the baby still wouldn't stop crying. I tried *(hold)* _____ _____ him, but that didn't help. I tried *(feed)* _____ _____ him, but he refused the food and continued to cry. I tried *(burp)* _____ him. I tried *(change)* _____ his diapers. Nothing worked. The baby wouldn't stop crying.

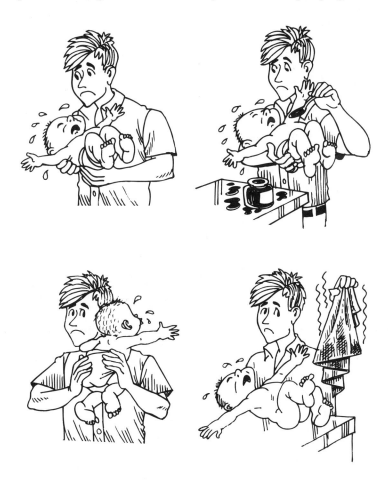

☐ EXERCISE 16. Gerund vs. infinitive. (Charts 14-4 → 14-8)

Directions: Supply an appropriate form, gerund or infinitive, of the verbs in parentheses.

1. Mary reminded me *(be, not)* _____ not to be _____ late for the meeting.

2. We went for a walk after we finished *(clean)* _____ up the kitchen.

3. I forgot *(take)* _____ a book back to the library, so I had to pay a fine.

4. When do you expect *(leave)* _____ on your trip?

5. The baby started *(talk)* _____ when she was about eighteen months old.

6. I don't mind *(wait)* _____ for you. Go ahead and finish *(do)*
   _____ your work.

7. I've decided *(stay)* _____ here over vacation and *(paint)*
   _____ my room.

8. We discussed *(quit)* _____ our jobs and *(open)* _____
   our own business.

9. I'm getting tired. I need *(take)* _____ a break.

10. Sometimes students avoid *(look)* _____ at the teacher if they don't
    want *(answer)* _____ a question.

11. The club members discussed *(postpone)* _____ the next meeting until
    March.

12. Most children prefer *(watch)* _____ television to *(listen)*
    _____ to the radio.

13. My grandfather prefers *(read)* _____ .

14. Did Carol agree *(go)* _____ *(camp)* _____ with you?

15. As the storm approached, the birds quit *(sing)* _____ .

16. The taxi driver refused *(take)* _____ a check. He wanted the passenger
    (pay) _____ cash.

17. The soldiers were ordered *(stand)* _____ at attention.

18. The travel agent advised us *(wait, not)* _____ until August.

□ EXERCISE 17. Gerund vs. infinitive. (Charts 14-4 → 14-8)

Directions: Use the correct form of the verbs in parentheses and complete the sentences. Include a (pro)noun object between the two verbs if necessary. Work in pairs, in groups, or as a class.

Examples: The fire marshal *(tell + unlock)*
   → *The fire marshall told us to unlock the back doors of the school to provide a fast exit in the event of an emergency.*

   (. . .) *(be asked + lead)*
   → *Maria was asked to lead a group discussion in class yesterday.*

1. (. . .) *(remind + finish)*
2. We *(have fun + swim)*
3. Students *(be required + have)*
4. The counselor *(advise + take)*
5. I *(try + learn)*
6. (. . .) *(warn + not open)*
7. I *(like + go + camp)*
8. (. . .) *(invite + go)*
9. (. . .) *(promise + not tell)*
10. We *(not be permitted + take)*
11. My friend *(ask + tell)*
12. When the wind *(begin + blow)*
13. I *(remember + call)*
14. (. . .) *(tell + not worry about + be)*
15. (. . .) *(be told + be)*
16. I *(spend + write)*

□ EXERCISE 18. Gerund vs. infinitive. (Charts 14-4 → 14-8)

Directions: Work in pairs or small groups.
Speaker A: Your book is open. Give the cues.
Speaker B: Your book is closed. Make sentences from the verb combinations. Use "I" or the name of another person in the room. Use any verb tense or modal.

Examples:

SPEAKER A *(book open):* like + go

SPEAKER B *(book closed):* I like to go (OR: going) to the park.

SPEAKER A *(book open):* ask + open

SPEAKER B *(book closed):* Kostas asked me to open the window.

1. enjoy + listen
2. offer + lend
3. start + laugh
4. remind + take

Switch roles.

5. postpone + go
6. look forward to + see
7. forget + bring
8. remember + go

Switch roles.

9. prefer + live
10. finish + do
11. encourage + go
12. can't stand + have to wait

Switch roles.

13. continue + walk
14. stop + walk
15. be interested in + learn
16. be used to + speak

Switch roles.
17. suggest + go
18. advise + go
19. be allowed + have
20. like + go + swim

Switch roles.
21. regret + take
22. consider + not go
23. keep + put off + do
24. decide + ask + come

☐ EXERCISE 19. Gerund vs. infinitive. (Charts 14-4 → 14-8)
   Directions: Supply an appropriate form, gerund or infinitive, of the verbs in parentheses.

1. Keep *(talk)* _____. I'm listening to you.

2. The children promised *(play)* _____ more quietly. They promised *(make, not)* _____ so much noise.

3. Linda offered *(look after)* _____ my cat while I was out of town.

4. You shouldn't put off *(pay)* _____ your bills.

5. Alex's dog loves *(chase)* _____ sticks.

6. Mark mentioned *(go)* _____ to the market later today. I wonder if he's still planning *(go)* _____.

7. Igor suggested *(go)* _____ *(ski)* _____ in the mountains this weekend. How does that sound to you?

8. The doctor ordered Mr. Gray *(smoke, not)* _____.

9. Don't tell me his secret. I prefer *(know, not)* _____.

10. Could you please stop *(whistle)* _____? I'm trying *(concentrate)* _____ on my work.

11. Recently, Jo has been spending most of her time *(do)* _____ research for a book on pioneer women.

12. Nadia finally decided *(quit)* _____ her present job and *(look for)* _____ another one.

13. Did you remember *(turn off)* _____ the stove?

14. Toshi was allowed *(renew)* _____ his student visa.

15. Pat told us *(wait, not)* _____ for her.

16. Mr. Buck warned his daughter *(play, not)* _____ with matches.

17. Would you please remind me *(call)* _____ Gina tomorrow?

18. The little boy had a lot of trouble *(convince)* _____ anyone he had
    seen a mermaid.

19. Liz encouraged me *(throw away)* _____ my old running shoes
    with holes in the toes and *(buy)* _____ a new pair.

20. I'm considering *(drop out of)* _____ school, *(hitchhike)*
    _____ to New York, and *(try)* _____ *(find)*
    _____ a job.

21. Don't forget *(tell)* _____ Jane *(call)* _____ me
    about *(go)* _____ *(swim)* _____ tomorrow.

22. Sally reminded me *(ask)* _____ you *(tell)* _____
    Bob *(remember)* _____ *(bring)* _____ his
    soccer ball to the picnic.

Verbs with a bullet (•) can also be followed by infinitives. See Chart 14-10.

1.	*admit*	He *admitted stealing* the money.
2.	*advise*•	She *advised waiting* until tomorrow.
3.	*anticipate*	I *anticipate having* a good time on vacation.
4.	*appreciate*	I *appreciated hearing* from them.
5.	*avoid*	He *avoided answering* my question.
6.	*can't bear*•	I *can't bear waiting* in long lines.
7.	*begin*•	It *began raining*.
8.	*complete*	I finally *completed writing* my term paper.
9.	*consider*	I *will consider going* with you.
10.	*continue*•	He *continued speaking*.
11.	*delay*	He *delayed leaving* for school.
12.	*deny*	She *denied committing* the crime.
13.	*discuss*	They *discussed opening* a new business.
14.	*dislike*	I *dislike driving* long distances.
15.	*enjoy*	We *enjoyed visiting* them.
16.	*finish*	She *finished studying* about ten.
17.	*forget*•	I'*ll never forget visiting* Napoleon's tomb.
18.	*hate*•	I *hate making* silly mistakes.
19.	*can't help*	I *can't help worrying* about it.
20.	*keep*	I *keep hoping* he will come.
21.	*like*•	I *like going* to movies.
22.	*love*•	I *love going* to operas.
23.	*mention*	She *mentioned going* to a movie.
24.	*mind*	*Would* you *mind helping* me with this?
25.	*miss*	I *miss being* with my family.
26.	*postpone*	Let's *postpone leaving* until tomorrow.
27.	*practice*	The athlete *practiced throwing* the ball.
28.	*prefer*•	Ann *prefers walking* to driving to work.
29.	*quit*	He *quit trying* to solve the problem.
30.	*recall*	I *don't recall meeting* him before.
31.	*recollect*	I *don't recollect meeting* him before.
32.	*recommend*	She *recommended seeing* the show.
33.	*regret*•	I *regret telling* him my secret.
34.	*remember*•	I can *remember meeting* him when I was a child.
35.	*resent*	I *resent her interfering* in my business.
36.	*resist*	I *couldn't resist eating* the dessert.
37.	*risk*	She *risks losing* all of her money.
38.	*can't stand*•	I *can't stand waiting* in long lines.
39.	*start*•	It *started raining*.
40.	*stop*	She *stopped going* to classes when she got sick.
41.	*suggest*	She *suggested going* to a movie.
42.	*tolerate*	She *won't tolerate cheating* during an examination.
43.	*try*•	I *tried changing* the light bulb, but the lamp still didn't work.
44.	*understand*	I *don't understand his leaving* school.

14-10 REFERENCE LIST OF VERBS FOLLOWED BY INFINITIVES

Verbs with a bullet (•) can also be followed by gerunds. See Chart 14-9.

A. VERBS FOLLOWED IMMEDIATELY BY AN INFINITIVE

1. *afford*	I *can't afford to buy* it.	24. *love•*	I *love to go* to operas.
2. *agree*	They *agreed to help* us.	25. *manage*	She *managed to finish* her work early.
3. *appear*	She *appears to be* tired.	26. *mean*	I *didn't mean to hurt* your feelings.
4. *arrange*	I'll *arrange to meet* you at the airport.	27. *need*	I *need to have* your opinion.
5. *ask*	He *asked to come* with us.	28. *offer*	They *offered to help* us.
6. *can't bear•*	I *can't bear to wait* in long lines.	29. *plan*	I *am planning to have* a party.
7. *beg*	He *begged to come* with us.	30. *prefer•*	Ann *prefers to walk* to work.
8. *begin•*	It *began to rain*.	31. *prepare*	We *prepared to welcome* them.
9. *care*	I *don't care to see* that show.	32. *pretend*	He *pretends not to understand*.
10. *claim*	She *claims to know* a famous movie star.	33. *promise*	I *promise not to be* late.
11. *consent*	She finally *consented to marry* him.	34. *refuse*	I *refuse to believe* his story.
12. *continue•*	He *continued to speak*.	35. *regret•*	I *regret to tell* you that you failed.
13. *decide*	I *have decided to leave* on Monday.	36. *remember•*	I *remembered to lock* the door.
14. *demand*	I *demand to know* who is responsible.	37. *seem*	That cat *seems to be* friendly.
15. *deserve*	She *deserves to win* the prize.	38. *can't stand•*	I *can't stand to wait* in long lines.
16. *expect*	I *expect to enter* graduate school in the fall.	39. *start•*	It *started to rain*.
17. *fail*	She *failed to return* the book to the library on time.	40. *struggle*	I *struggled to stay* awake.
18. *forget•*	I *forgot to mail* the letter.	41. *swear*	She *swore to tell* the truth.
19. *hate•*	I *hate to make* silly mistakes.	42. *threaten*	She *threatened to tell* my parents.
20. *hesitate*	*Don't hesitate to ask* for my help.	43. *try•*	I'm *trying to learn* English.
21. *hope*	Jack *hopes to arrive* next week.	44. *volunteer*	He *volunteered to help* us.
22. *learn*	He *learned to play* the piano.	45. *wait*	I *will wait to hear* from you.
23. *like•*	I *like to go* to the movies.	46. *want*	I *want to tell* you something.
		47. *wish*	She *wishes to come* with us.

B. VERBS FOLLOWED BY A (PRO)NOUN + AN INFINITIVE

48. *advise•*	She *advised me to wait* until tomorrow.	61. *instruct*	He *instructed them to be* careful.
49. *allow*	She *allowed me to use* her car.	62. *invite*	Harry *invited the Johnsons to come* to his party.
50. *ask*	I *asked John to help* us.	63. *need*	We *needed Chris to help* us figure out the solution.
51. *beg*	They *begged us to come*.	64. *order*	The judge *ordered me to pay* a fine.
52. *cause*	Her laziness *caused her to fail*.	65. *permit*	He *permitted the children to stay* up late.
53. *challenge*	She *challenged me to race* her to the corner.	66. *persuade*	I *persuaded him to come* for a visit.
54. *convince*	I couldn't *convince him to accept* our help.	67. *remind*	She *reminded me to lock* the door.
55. *dare*	He *dared me to do* better than he had done.	68. *require*	Our teacher *requires us to be* on time.
56. *encourage*	He *encouraged me to try* again.	69. *teach*	My brother *taught me to swim*.
57. *expect*	I *expect you to be* on time.	70. *tell*	The doctor *told me to take* these pills.
58. *forbid*	I *forbid you to tell* him.	71. *urge*	I *urged her to apply* for the job.
59. *force*	They *forced him to tell* the truth.	72. *want*	I *want you to be* happy.
60. *hire*	She *hired a boy to mow* the lawn.	73. *warn*	I *warned you not to drive* too fast.

☐ EXERCISE 20. Gerund vs. infinitive. (Charts 14-9 and 14-10)

Directions: Work in pairs.

Speaker A: Your book is open. Give the cue. Don't lower your intonation at the end of the cue.

Speaker B: Your book is closed. Complete the sentence with ***doing it*** or ***to do it***.

Speaker A: If you are unsure about the correctness of B's completion, refer to Charts 14-9 and 14-10.

Example:

SPEAKER A *(book open):*   I promise . . . .
SPEAKER B *(book closed):*   . . . to do it.

1. I enjoyed . . . .
2. I can't afford . . . .
3. She didn't allow me . . . .
4. We plan . . . .
5. Please remind me . . . .
6. I am considering . . . .
7. Our director postponed . . . .
8. He persuaded me . . . .
9. I don't mind . . . .
10. Everyone avoided . . . .

Switch roles.

11. I refused . . . .
12. I hope . . . .
13. She convinced me . . . .
14. He mentioned . . . .
15. I expect . . . .
16. I encouraged him . . . .
17. I warned him not . . . .
18. We prepared . . . .
19. I don't recall . . . .
20. We decided . . . .

Switch roles.

21. Did someone offer . . . .
22. When will you finish . . . .
23. Did you practice . . . .
24. She agreed . . . .
25. Keep . . . .

26. Stop . . . .
27. I didn't force him . . . .
28. I couldn't resist . . . .
29. Somehow, the cat managed . . . .
30. Did the little boy admit . . . .

Switch roles.

31. He denied . . . .
32. I didn't mean . . . .
33. She swore . . . .
34. I volunteered . . . .
35. He suggested . . . .
36. He advised me . . . .
37. He struggled . . . .
38. I don't want to risk . . . .
39. Do you recommend . . . .
40. I miss . . . .

Switch roles.

41. I can't imagine . . . .
42. She threatened . . . .
43. He seems to dislike . . . .
44. The children begged . . . .
45. She challenged me . . . .
46. Did he deny . . . .
47. Don't hesitate . . . .
48. Do you anticipate . . . .
49. Why did she fail . . . .
50. I'll arrange . . . .

□ EXERCISE 21. Gerund vs. infinitive. (Charts 14-9 and 14-10)
Directions: Complete the sentences with the correct form, gerund or infinitive, of the words in parentheses.

1. Hassan volunteered *(bring)* _____ some food to the reception.

2. The students practiced *(pronounce)* _____ the "th" sound in the phrase "these thirty-three dirty trees."

3. In the fairy tale, the wolf threatened *(eat)* _____ a girl named Little Red Riding Hood.

4. Susie! How many times do I have to remind you *(hang up)* _____ your coat when you get home from school?

5. The horses struggled *(pull)* _____ the wagon out of the mud.

6. Anita demanded *(know)* _____ why she had been fired.

7. My skin can't tolerate *(be)* _____ in the sun all day. I get sunburned easily.

8. I avoided *(tell)* _____ Mary the truth because I knew she would be angry.

9. Fred Washington claims *(be)* _____ a descendant of George Washington.

10. Mr. Kwan broke the antique vase. I'm sure he didn't mean *(do)* _____ it.

11. I urged Omar *(return)* _____ to school and *(finish)* _____ his education.

12. Mrs. Freeman can't help *(worry)* _____ about her children.

13. Children, I forbid you *(play)* _____ in the street. There's too much traffic.

14. My little cousin is a blabbermouth! He can't resist *(tell)* _____ everyone my secrets!

15. I appreciate your *(take)* _____ the time to help me.

16. I can't afford *(buy)* _____ a new car.

17. Kim managed *(change)* _____ my mind.

18. I think Sam deserves *(have)* _____ another chance.

19. Olga finally admitted *(be)* _____ responsible for the problem.

20. I don't recall ever *(hear)* _____ you mention his name before.

21. Nadia keeps *(promise)* _____ *(visit)* _____ us, but she never does.

22. Margaret challenged me *(race)* _____ her across the pool.

23. Oscar keeps *(hope)* _____ and *(pray)* _____ that things will get better.

24. I finally managed *(persuade)* _____ Yoko *(stay)* _____ in school and *(finish)* _____ her degree.

☐ **EXERCISE 22. Activity: gerund vs. infinitive. (Charts 14-9 and 14-10)**
Directions: Return to Exercise 20, but this time use your own words instead of *to do it* or ***doing it***. Work with a partner.

Example:
SPEAKER A *(book open):* I promise . . . .
SPEAKER B *(book closed):* . . . to be on time for our meeting tomorrow.

☐ **EXERCISE 23. Activity: gerund vs. infinitive. (Charts 14-9 and 14-10)**
Directions: Divide into two teams. Your teacher will begin a sentence by using any of the verbs in Charts 14-9 and 14-10 or by using the verbs in Exercise 20. Complete the sentence with a gerund or infinitive phrase. Each correct completion scores one point.

14-11 *IT* + INFINITIVE; GERUNDS AND INFINITIVES AS SUBJECTS

(a) *It* is difficult *to learn a second language.*	Often an infinitive phrase is used with *it* as the subject of a sentence. The word *it* refers to and has the same meaning as the infinitive phrase at the end of the sentence. In (a): *It = to learn a second language.*
(b) *Learning a second language* is difficult.	A gerund phrase is frequently used as the subject of a sentence, as in (b).
(c) *To learn a second language* is difficult.	An infinitive can also be used as the subject of a sentence, as in (c), but far more commonly an infinitive phrase is used with *it*, as in (a).
(d) It is easy *for young children to learn a second language.* *Learning a second language* is easy *for young children.* *To learn a second language* is easy *for young children.*	The phrase *for (someone)* may be used to specify exactly who the speaker is talking about, as in (d).

☐ **EXERCISE 24. IT + infinitive. (Chart 14-11)**

Directions: Create sentences beginning with *it*. Use a form of the given expression in your sentence, followed by an infinitive phrase.

1. be dangerous → *It's dangerous to ride a motorcycle without wearing a helmet.*
2. be important
3. not be easy
4. be foolish
5. must be interesting
6. be always a pleasure
7. be clever of you
8. not cost much money
9. be necessary
10. take time

☐ **EXERCISE 25. IT + infinitive. (Chart 14-11)**

Directions: Add *for (someone)* and any other words to give a more specific and accurate meaning to the sentences.

1. It isn't possible to be on time.
   → *It isn't possible for me to be on time for class if the bus drivers are on strike and I have to walk to class in a rainstorm.*
2. It's easy to speak Spanish.
3. It's important to learn English.
4. It is essential to get a visa.
5. It's important to take advanced math courses.
6. It's difficult to communicate.
7. It was impossible to come to class.
8. It is a good idea to study gerunds and infinitives.

□ **EXERCISE 26. Gerunds as subjects. (Chart 14-11)**
Directions: Complete the sentences. Use gerund phrases as subjects.

1. . . . isn't easy. → *Climbing to the top of a mountain isn't easy.*
2. . . . is hard.
3. . . . can be interesting.
4. . . . was a good experience.
5. Does . . . sound like fun to you?
6. . . . demands patience and a sense of humor.
7. . . . is a complicated process.
8. . . . is considered impolite in my country.

□ **EXERCISE 27. IT + infinitive; gerunds as subjects. (Chart 14-11)**
Directions: Work in pairs.
Speaker A: Your book is open. Give the cue.
Speaker B: Your book is closed. Complete the sentence with an infinitive phrase.
Speaker A: Create a sentence with the same meaning by using a gerund phrase as the subject.

Example:
SPEAKER A *(book open):*   It's fun . . . .
SPEAKER B *(book closed):*   . . . to ride a horse.
SPEAKER A: Riding a horse is fun.

Switch roles.

1. It's dangerous . . . .
2. It's easy . . . .
3. It's impolite . . . .
4. It is important . . . .
5. It is wrong . . . .
6. It takes a lot of time . . . .
7. It's a good idea . . . .
8. Is it difficult . . . ?

□ **EXERCISE 28. Activity: gerunds and infinitives. (Chapter 14)**
Directions: Form a group of three to five members. Choose one of the story beginnings or make up your own. Each group member continues the story by adding a sentence or two. At least one of the sentences should contain words from the given list, plus a gerund or infinitive phrase (but it is okay simply to continue the story without using a gerund or infinitive if it works out that way). As a group, use as many of the words in the list which follows as you can.

Example: (Yoko) had a bad night last night. First, when she got home, she discovered that . . . .
SPEAKER A: . . . her door was unlocked. She didn't ***recall leaving*** her door unlocked. She always ***remembers to lock*** her door and in fact specifically ***remembered locking*** it that morning. So she became afraid that someone had broken into her apartment.
SPEAKER B: She ***thought about going*** inside, but then decided ***it*** would be better ***not to go*** into her apartment alone. What if there was a burglar inside?
SPEAKER C: ***Instead of going*** into her apartment alone, Yoko walked to her next-door neighbor's door and knocked.
SPEAKER D: Her neighbor answered the door. He could see that something was the matter. "Are you all right?" he asked her.
SPEAKER A: Etc.

Story beginnings:

1. (. . .) is having trouble with (her/his) roommate, whose name is (. . .). (Her/His) roommate keeps many pets even though the lease they signed forbids residents to keep animals in their apartments. Yesterday, one of these pets, a/an . . . .

2. Not long ago, (. . .) and (. . .) were walking home together after dark. They heard a strange whooshing sound. When they looked up in the night sky, they saw a huge hovering aircraft. It glowed! It was round and green! (. . .) was frightened and curious at the same time. (She/He) wanted to . . . , but . . . .

3. Once upon a time, (. . .) lived in a faraway village in a remote mountainous region. All of the villagers were terrified because of the dragon that lived nearby. At least once a week, the dragon would descend on the village and . . . .

4. It was a dark and stormy night. (. . .) was all alone at home. Suddenly . . . .

5. (. . .) had a bad day yesterday. First of all, when (she/he) got up in the morning, (she/he) discovered that . . . .

List of words and phrases to work into the story:

PREPOSITIONAL EXPRESSIONS FOLLOWED BY GERUNDS	VERBS FOLLOWED BY GERUNDS OR INFINITIVES		IT + INFINITIVE OR A GERUND SUBJECT
be accused of	admit	mind	be a bad experience
be accustomed to	advise	need	be a bad idea
in addition to	afford	offer	be better
be afraid	agree	permit	be clever
apologize (to someone) for	ask	persuade	be dangerous
believe in	avoid	plan	be difficult
blame (someone) for	beg	postpone	be easy
be capable of	begin	prefer	be essential
be committed to	consider	prepare	be foolish
complain about	continue	pretend	be a good experience
dream of	convince	promise	be a good idea
forgive (someone) for	decide	quit	be fun
be excited about	demand	recall	be hard
be guilty of	deny	refuse	be important
instead of	discuss	regret	be impossible
be interested in	dislike	remember	be interesting
look forward to	encourage	remind	be necessary
be opposed to	enjoy	risk	be a pleasure
prevent (someone) from	expect	seem	be possible
be scared of	fail	start	be relaxing
stop (someone) from	force	stop	take effort
succeed in	forget	struggle	take energy
take advantage of	forget	suggest	take money
be terrified of	hesitate	threaten	take patience
thank (someone) for	hope	wait	take time
think of	invite	want	
be tired of	learn	warn	
be worried about	like		
	manage		

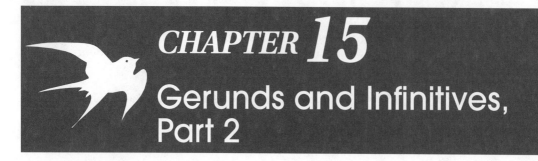

CHAPTER 15
Gerunds and Infinitives, Part 2

CONTENTS

15-1   INFINITIVE OF PURPOSE: *IN ORDER TO*

(a) He came here *in order to study* English. (b) He came here *to study* English.	*In order to* is used to express *purpose*. It answers the question "Why?" *In order* is often omitted, as in (b).
(c) *INCORRECT:* He came here *for studying* English. (d) *INCORRECT:* He came here *for to study* English. (e) *INCORRECT:* He came here *for study* English.	To express purpose, use *(in order) to*, not *for*, with a verb.*
(f) I went to the store *for some bread*. (g) I went to the store *to buy some bread*.	*For* can be used to express purpose, but it is a preposition and is followed by a noun object, as in (f).

*Exception: The phrase *be used for* expresses the typical or general purpose of a thing. In this case, the preposition *for* is followed by a gerund: *A saw is used for cutting wood.* Also possible: *A saw is used to cut wood.*

However, to talk about a particular thing and a particular situation, *be used* + *an infinitive* is used: *A chain saw was used to cut* (NOT *for cutting*) *down the old oak tree.*

☐ EXERCISE 1. Error analysis: IN ORDER TO. (Chart 15-1)

Directions: Correct the errors.

1. I went to the library ~~for~~ study last night.
   to

2. Helen borrowed my dictionary for to look up the spelling of "occurred."

3. The teacher opened the window for letting some fresh air in the room.

4. I came to this school for learn English.

5. I traveled to Osaka for to visit my sister.

326

☐ EXERCISE 2. IN ORDER TO vs. FOR. (Chart 15-1)
   Directions: Make up completions. Express the *purpose* of the action.

   1. I went to Chicago to _____ visit my relatives. _____

   2. Tom went to Chicago for _____ a business conference. _____

   3. I went to the market for _____

   4. Mary went to the market for _____

   5. I went to the doctor to _____

   6. My son went to the doctor for _____

   7. I swim every day to _____

   8. My friend swims every day for _____

   9. I drove into the service station to _____

   10. They stopped at the service station for _____

☐ EXERCISE 3. IN ORDER TO. (Chart 15-1)
   Directions: Add ***in order*** wherever possible. If nothing should be added, write **Ø**.

   1. I went to the garden center _____ in order _____ to get some fertilizer for my flowers.

   2. When the teacher asked him a question, Jack pretended _____ Ø _____ to understand what she was saying.

   3. My roommate asked me _____ to clean up the dishes after dinner.

   4. I bought a new screwdriver _____ to repair my bicycle.

   5. My mother always said I should eat lots of green vegetables _____ to make my body strong.

   6. Mustafa climbed onto a chair _____ to change a light bulb in the ceiling.

   7. I really want _____ to learn Italian before I visit Venice next year.

   8. I jog three times a week _____ to stay healthy.

   9. It is a good idea _____ to know where your children are at all times.

   10. I need to find her _____ to talk to her.

   11. Rita has to work at two jobs _____ to support herself and her three children.

12. Jim finally went to the dentist _____ to get some relief from his toothache.

13. It's easier for me _____ to understand written English than it is to understand spoken English.

14. I practice speaking English into a tape recorder _____ to improve my pronunciation.

15. It isn't important _____ to speak English without an accent as long as people understand what you're saying.

15-2 ADJECTIVES FOLLOWED BY INFINITIVES

(a) We *were sorry to hear* the bad news. (b) I *was surprised to see* Tim at the meeting.	Certain adjectives can be immediately followed by infinitives, as in (a) and (b). In general, these adjectives describe a person (or persons), not a thing. Many of these adjectives describe a person's feelings or attitudes.

SOME COMMON ADJECTIVES FOLLOWED BY INFINITIVES

glad to (do it)	*sorry to**	*ready to*	*careful to*	*surprised to**
happy to	*sad to**	*prepared to*	*hesitant to*	*amazed to**
pleased to	*upset to**	*anxious to*	*reluctant to*	*astonished to**
delighted to	*disappointed to**	*eager to*	*afraid to*	*shocked to**
content to		*willing to*		*stunned to**
relieved to	*proud to*	*motivated to*	*likely to*	
lucky to	*ashamed to*	*determined to*	*certain to*	
fortunate to				

*The expressions with asterisks are usually followed by infinitive phrases with verbs such as *see, learn, discover, find out, hear.*

☐ EXERCISE 4. Adjectives followed by infinitives. (Chart 15-2)
Directions: Complete the sentences, using the expressions listed in Chart 15-2 and your own words. Use infinitive phrases in your completions.

1. Maria always speeds on the expressway. She's . . . .
   → *She's certain to get stopped by the police.*
   → *She's likely to get a ticket.*
2. There have been a lot of burglaries in my neighborhood recently, so I have started taking precautions. Now I am always very . . . .
3. I've worked hard all day long. Enough's enough! I'm . . . .
4. Next month, I'm going to a family reunion—the first one in 25 years. I'm very much looking forward to it. I'm . . . .
5. Some children grow up in unhappy homes. My family, however, has always been loving and supportive. I'm . . . .
6. Ivan's run out of money again, but he doesn't want anyone to know his situation. He needs money desperately, but he's . . . .

7. Rosalyn wants to become an astronaut. That has been her dream since she was a little girl. She has been working hard toward her goal and is . . . .

8. Mr. Wah was offered an excellent job in another country, but his wife and children don't want to move. He's not sure what to do. Although he would like the job, he's . . . .

9. Our neighbors had extra tickets to the ballet, so they invited us to go with them. Since both of us love the ballet, we were . . . .

10. Sally recently told me what my wayward brother is up to these days. I couldn't believe my ears! I was . . . .

☐ EXERCISE 5. Adjectives followed by infinitives. (Chart 15-2)
Directions: Work in pairs.
Speaker A: Your book is open. Give the cues.
Speaker B: Your book is closed. Answer "yes" to the question. Use an infinitive phrase in your response.

Example:
SPEAKER A *(book open):* You saw your friend at the airport. Were you happy?
SPEAKER B *(book closed):* Yes. I was happy to see my friend at the airport.

1. (. . .) has a lot of good friends. Is he/she fortunate?
2. You're leaving on vacation soon. Are you eager?
3. You met (. . .)'s wife/husband. Were you delighted?
4. You went to *(name of a faraway place in the world)* last summer. You saw (. . .) there. Were you surprised?

Switch roles.
5. You're going to take a test tomorrow. Are you prepared?
6. You're thinking about asking (. . .) a personal question. Are you hesitant?
7. Your friend was ill. Finally you found out that she was okay. Were you relieved?
8. You heard about (. . .)'s accident. Were you sorry?

☐ EXERCISE 6. Adjectives followed by infinitives. (Chart 15-2)
Directions: Work in pairs, in groups, or as a class.
Speaker A: Your book is open. Ask the questions.
Speaker B: Your book is closed. Answer in complete sentences.

1. What are you careful to do before you cross a busy street?
2. What are children sometimes afraid to do?
3. When you're tired in the evening, what are you content to do?
4. If one of your friends has a problem, what are you willing to do?
5. Sometimes when people don't know English very well, what are they reluctant to do?
6. If the teacher announces there is a test tomorrow, what will you be motivated to do?
7. What are you determined to do before you are 70 years old?
8. What are some things people should be ashamed to do?
9. Is there anything you are eager to do today or tomorrow?
10. In what ways are you a fortunate person?
11. Can you tell me something you were shocked to find out?/astonished to learn?
12. Can you tell me something you were disappointed to discover?/sad to hear?

15-3 USING INFINITIVES WITH *TOO* AND *ENOUGH*

COMPARE (a) That box is *too heavy* for Bob to lift. (b) That box is *very heavy,* but Bob can lift it.	In the speaker's mind, the use of *too* implies a negative result. In (a): *too heavy* = It is *impossible* for Bob to lift that box. In (b): *very heavy* = It is *possible but difficult* for Bob to lift that box.
(c) I am *strong enough to lift* that box. I can lift it. (d) I have *enough strength to lift* that box. (e) I have *strength enough to lift* that box.	*Enough* follows an adjective, as in (c). Usually *enough* precedes a noun, as in (d). In formal English, it may follow a noun, as in (e).

☐ EXERCISE 7. Using infinitives with TOO and ENOUGH. (Chart 15-3)
Directions: Think of a negative result, and then complete the sentence with an infinitive phrase.

1. That ring is too expensive. → Negative result: *I can't buy it. That ring is too expensive for me to buy.*

2. I'm too tired. → Negative result: *I can't/don't want to go to the meeting. I'm too tired to go to the meeting.*

3. It's too late. → Negative result: . . . .

4. It's too cold.

5. Nuclear physics is too difficult.

6. I'm too busy.

7. My son is too young.

8. The mountain cliff is too steep.

Now think of a positive result, and complete the sentence with an infinitive phrase.

9. That ring is very expensive, but it isn't too expensive → Positive result: *I can buy it. That ring isn't too expensive for me to buy.*

10. I'm very tired, but I'm not too tired → Positive result: . . . .

11. My suitcase is very heavy, but it's not too heavy.

12. I'm very busy, but I'm not too busy.

☐ EXERCISE 8. Activity: using infinitives with TOO and ENOUGH. (Chart 15-3)
Directions: Discuss the questions.

1. (. . .)'s daughter is 18 months old. Is she too young or very young?
2. What is a child too young to do but an adult old enough to do?
3. Who had a good dinner last night? Was it too good or very good?
4. Is it very difficult or too difficult to learn English?
5. After you wash your clothes, are they too clean or very clean?
6. Who stayed up late last night? Did you stay up too late or very late?
7. What is your pocket big enough to hold? What is it too small to hold?

8. Compare a mouse with an elephant. Is a mouse too small or very small?

9. What is the highest mountain in *(this country/the world)*? Is it too high or very high?

10. What did you have enough time to do before class today?

11. What's the difference between the following situations?
    a. We don't have enough big envelopes.
    b. We don't have big enough envelopes.

12. If you apologize for something, do you say you're very sorry or too sorry?

13. What is the sun too bright for you to do?

14. What can't you do if a room is too dark?

15. In what circumstances would you say your cup of tea or coffee is too full?

15-4 PASSIVE AND PAST FORMS OF INFINITIVES AND GERUNDS

FORMS

	SIMPLE	PAST
ACTIVE	*to see* *seeing*	*to have seen* *having seen*
PASSIVE	*to be seen* *being seen*	*to have been seen* *having been seen*

PAST INFINITIVE: ***to have*** + *past participle* (a) The rain seems *to have stopped*.	The event expressed by a past infinitive or past gerund happened before the time of the main verb. In (a): *The rain seems now to have stopped a few minutes ago.*★
PAST GERUND: ***having*** + *past participle* (b) I appreciate *having had* the opportunity to meet the king.	In (b): I met the king yesterday. *I appreciate now having had the opportunity to meet the king yesterday.*★
PAST INFINITIVE: ***to be*** + *past participle* (c) I didn't expect *to be invited* to his party.	In (c): ***to be invited*** is passive. The understood *by*-phrase is "by him": *I didn't expect to be invited by him.*
PAST GERUND: ***being*** + *past participle* (d) I appreciated *being invited* to your home.	In (d): ***being invited*** is passive. The understood *by*-phrase is "by you": *I appreciated being invited by you.*
PAST-PASSIVE INFINITIVE: ***to have been*** + *past participle* (e) Nadia is fortunate *to have been given* a scholarship.	In (e): Nadia was given a scholarship last month by her government. She is fortunate. *Nadia is fortunate now to have been given a scholarship last month by her government.*
PAST-PASSIVE GERUND: ***having been*** + *past participle* (f) I appreciate *having been told* the news.	In (f): I was told the news yesterday by someone. I appreciate that. *I appreciate now having been told the news yesterday by someone.*

★If the main verb is past, the action of the past infinitive or gerund happened before a time in the past:
The rain **seemed to have stopped**. = The rain seemed at six P.M. to have stopped before six P.M.
I **appreciated having had** *the opportunity to meet the king.* = I met the king in 1995. In 1997 I appreciated having had the opportunity to meet the king in 1995.

☐ **EXERCISE 9. Passive and past forms of infinitives and gerunds. (Chart 15-4)**
   Directions: Supply an appropriate form for each verb in parentheses.

1. I don't enjoy *(laugh)* ___being laughed___ at by other people.

2. I'm angry at him for *(tell, not)* ___not telling / not having told*___ me the truth.

3. It is easy *(fool)* ___to be fooled___ by his lies.

4. I expected *(invite)* _____ to the party, but I wasn't.

5. Sometimes adolescents complain about not *(understand)* _____
   _____ by their parents.

6. Your compositions are supposed *(write)* _____ in ink.

7. Jin Won had a narrow escape. He was almost hit by a car. He barely avoided *(hit)*
   _____ by a speeding automobile.

8. Ms. Thompson is always willing to help if there is a problem in the office, but she
   doesn't want *(call)* _____ at home unless there is an emergency.

9. Jack Welles has a good chance of *(elect)* _____. I know I'm
   going to vote for him.

10. Carlos appears *(lose)* _____ some weight. Has he been ill?

11. You must tell me the truth. I insist on *(tell)* _____ the truth.

12. Don't all of us want *(love)* _____ and *(need)* _____
    by other people?

13. Dear Hiroki,
        I feel guilty about *(write, not)* _____ to you sooner, but
    I've been swamped with work lately.

14. A: You know Jim Frankenstein, don't you?
    B: Jim Frankenstein? I don't think so. I don't recall ever *(meet)* _____
       _____ him.

15. Mr. Gow mentioned *(injure)* _____ in an accident as a child,
    but he never told us the details.

16. Tim was in the army during the war. He was caught by the enemy, but he managed to
    escape. He is lucky *(escape)* _____ with his life.

_____

*The past gerund is used to emphasize that the action of the gerund took place before that of the main verb.
However, often there is little difference in meaning between a simple gerund and a past gerund.

17. A: Is Abdul a transfer student?

    B: Yes.

    A: Where did he go to school before he came here?

    B: I'm not sure, but I think he mentioned something about *(go)* _____ _____ to UCLA or USC.

18. We would like *(invite)* _____ to the president's reception at the Pearl Hotel last week, but we weren't.*

15-5 USING GERUNDS OR PASSIVE INFINITIVES FOLLOWING *NEED*

(a) I *need to borrow* some money. (b) John *needs to be told* the truth.	Usually an infinitive follows *need*, as in (a) and (b).
(c) The house *needs painting*. (d) The house *needs to be painted*.	In certain circumstances, a gerund may follow *need*. In this case, the gerund carries a passive meaning. Usually the situations involve fixing or improving something. (c) and (d) have the same meaning.

☐ EXERCISE 10. Using gerunds or passive infinitives following NEED. (Chart 15-5)
  Directions: Supply an appropriate form of the verbs in parentheses.

1. The chair is broken. I need *(fix)* _____to fix_____ it. The chair needs *(fix)* ___fixing / to be fixed___.

2. The baby's diaper is wet. It needs *(change)* _____.

3. What a mess! This room needs *(clean)* _____ up. We need *(clean)* _____ it up before the company arrives.

4. My shirt is wrinkled. It needs *(iron)* _____.

5. There is a hole in our roof. The roof needs *(repair)* _____.

6. I have books and papers all over my desk. I need *(take)* _____ some time to straighten up my desk. It needs *(straighten)* _____ up.

7. The apples on the tree are ripe. They need *(pick)* _____.

8. The dog's been digging in the mud. He needs *(wash)* _____.

---

*Sometimes native speakers use both a past modal and a past infinitive even though only one past form is necessary: *We would have liked to have been invited* .... Also possible, with the same meaning: *We would have liked to be invited* ....

□ **EXERCISE 11. Gerunds vs. infinitives following NEED. (Chart 15-5)**
   Directions: Look at the picture.
   What needs doing/to be done?

15-6 USING A POSSESSIVE TO MODIFY A GERUND

We came to class late. Mr. Lee complained about that fact. (a) FORMAL: Mr. Lee complained about *our coming* to class late.★ (b) INFORMAL: Mr. Lee complained about *us coming* to class late.	In formal English, a possessive adjective (e.g., *our*) is used to modify a gerund, as in (a). In informal English, the object form of a pronoun (e.g., *us*) is frequently used, as in (b).
(c) FORMAL: Mr. Lee complained about *Mary's coming* to class late. (d) INFORMAL: Mr. Lee complained about *Mary coming* to class late.	In very formal English, a possessive noun (e.g., *Mary's*) is used to modify a gerund. The possessive form is often not used in informal English, as in (d).

★*Coming to class late* occurred before *Mr. Lee complained*, so a past gerund is also possible: *Mr. Lee complained about our having come to class late.*

□ **EXERCISE 12. Using a possessive to modify a gerund. (Chart 15-6)**
   Directions: Combine the pairs of sentences. Change *that fact* to a gerund phrase. Use formal English. Discuss informal usage.

1. Mary won a scholarship. We are excited about *that fact*.
   → *We are excited about Mary's (Mary) winning a scholarship.*

2. He didn't want to go. I couldn't understand *that fact*.
   → *I couldn't understand his (him) not wanting to go.*

3. You took the time to help us. We greatly appreciate *that fact*.

4. We talked about him behind his back. The boy resented *that fact*.

5. They ran away to get married. *That fact* shocked everyone.

6. You are late to work every morning. I will no longer tolerate *that fact*.

7. Ann borrowed Sally's clothes without asking her first. Sally complained about *that fact*.

8. Helen is here to answer our questions about the company's new insurance plan. We should take advantage of *that fact*.

☐ EXERCISE 13. Review: verb forms. (Charts 14-1 → 15-6)
   Directions: Supply an appropriate form for each verb in parentheses.

1. Alice didn't expect *(ask)* _____ to Bill's party.

2. I'm not accustomed to *(drink)* _____ coffee with my meals.

3. I'll help you with your homework as soon as I finish *(wash)* _____ the dishes.

4. She took a deep breath *(relax)* _____ herself before she got up to give her speech.

5. I'm prepared *(answer)* _____ any question that might be asked during my job interview tomorrow.

6. Matthew left without *(tell)* _____ anyone.

7. It's useless. Give up. Enough's enough. Don't keep *(beat)* _____ your head against a brick wall.

8. His *(be, not)* _____ able to come is disappointing.

9. I hope *(award)* _____ a scholarship for the coming semester.

10. We are very pleased *(accept)* _____ your invitation.

11. I have considered *(get)* _____ a part-time job *(help)* _____ pay for my school expenses.

12. It is exciting *(travel)* _____ to faraway places and *(leave)* _____ one's daily routine behind.

13. *(Help)* _____ the disadvantaged children learn how to read was a rewarding experience.

14. He wants *(like)* _____ and *(trust)* _____ by everyone.

15. I can't help *(wonder)* _____ why Larry did such a foolish thing.

16. Mr. Carson is very lucky *(choose)* _____ by the committee as their representative to the meeting in Paris.

17. *(Live)* _____ in a city has certain advantages.

18. Keep on *(do)* _____ whatever you were doing. I didn't mean *(interrupt)* _____ you.

19. It is very kind of you *(take)* _____ care of that problem for me.

20. She opened the window *(let)* _____ in some fresh air.

21. They agreed *(cooperate)* _____ with us to the fullest extent.

22. Jack wastes a lot of time *(hang)* _____ out with his friends on street corners.

23. Did you remember *(turn)* _____ in your assignment?

24. I don't remember ever *(hear)* _____ that story before.

25. Does your son regret *(leave)* _____ home and *(go)* _____
to a foreign country *(study)* _____ ?

26. I appreciate your *(ask)* _____ my opinion on the matter.

27. You should stop *(drive)* _____ if you get sleepy. It's dangerous *(drive)*
_____ when you're not alert.

28. I have trouble *(fall)* _____ asleep at night.

29. After driving for three hours, we stopped *(get)* _____ something to eat.

30. Please forgive me for *(be, not)* _____ here to help you yesterday.

☐ **EXERCISE 14. Review: gerunds and infinitives. (Charts 14-1 → 15-6)**
Directions: Complete the sentences with your own words. Each sentence should contain a
GERUND or an INFINITIVE.

Example: You are required . . . .
→ *You are required to stop at the border when entering Canada by car.*

1. Your not wanting . . . .
2. It's important for . . . .
3. I'll never forget . . . .
4. Jack advised not . . . .
5. I'm not willing . . . .
6. My apartment needs . . . .
7. . . . enough energy . . . .
8. . . . in order to save . . . .
9. . . . to be told about . . . .
10. . . . had just begun . . . when . . . .
11. Do you think it is easy . . . ?
12. . . . my having been . . . .
13. Have you ever considered . . . ?
14. . . . is likely . . . .
15. Most people object . . . .
16. . . . try to avoid . . . .

15-7 USING VERBS OF PERCEPTION

(a) I *saw* my friend *run* down the street. (b) I *saw* my friend *running* down the street. (c) I *heard* the rain *fall* on the roof. (d) I *heard* the rain *falling* on the roof.	Certain verbs of perception are followed by either *the simple form** or *the -ing form*** of a verb. There is often little difference in meaning between the two forms, except that the *-ing* form usually gives the idea of "while." In (b): I saw my friend while she was running down the street.
(e) When I walked into the apartment, I *heard* my roommate *singing* in the shower. (f) I *heard* a famous opera star *sing* at the concert last night.	Sometimes (not always) there is a clear difference between using the simple form or the *-ing* form. The use of the *-ing* form gives the idea that an activity is already in progress when it is perceived, as in (e): The singing was in progress when I first heard it. In (f): I heard the singing from beginning to end. It was not in progress when I first heard it.

VERBS OF PERCEPTION FOLLOWED BY THE SIMPLE FORM OR THE *-ING* FORM

see	*look at*	*hear*	*feel*	*smell*
notice	*observe*	*listen to*		
watch				

**The simple form of a verb* = the infinitive form without "to." INCORRECT: I saw my friend *to run* down the street.

**The -ing form refers to the present participle.

☐ EXERCISE 15. Using verbs of perception. (Chart 15-7)

PART I. Complete the sentences with any appropriate verbs. Both the simple form and the **-ing** form are possible with little, if any, difference in meaning.

1. Polly was working in her garden, so she didn't hear the phone ___ring / ringing___ .

2. I like to listen to the birds _____ when I get up early in the morning.

3. The guard observed a suspicious-looking person _____ into the bank.

4. There was an earthquake in my hometown last year. It was just a small one, but I could feel the ground _____ .

5. I was almost asleep last night when I suddenly heard someone _____ on the door.

6. While I was waiting for my plane, I watched other planes _____ and _____ .

PART II. Both the simple form and the **-ing** form are grammatically correct, so you can't make a grammar mistake. But a speaker might choose one over the other. Read the situation, then decide which form seems better to you in the sentence that contains a verb of perception. Remember that the **-ing** form gives the idea that an activity is in progress when it is perceived.

1. SITUATION: *I was downtown yesterday. I saw the police. They were chasing a thief.*

   When I was downtown yesterday, I saw the police ___chasing___ a thief.

2. SITUATION: *The front door slammed. I got up to see if someone had come in.*

   When I heard the front door _____, I got up to see if someone had come in.

3. SITUATION: *Uncle Jake is in the bedroom. He is snoring.*

   I know Uncle Jake is in the bedroom because I can hear him _____ .

4. SITUATION: *When I walked past the park, some children were playing softball.*

   When I walked past the park, I saw some children _____ softball.

5. SITUATION: *It was graduation day in the auditorium. When the school principal called my name, I walked to the front of the room.*

   When I heard the school principal _____ my name, I walked to the front of the auditorium to receive my diploma.

6. SITUATION: *I glanced out the window. Jack was walking toward the house. I was surprised.*

   I was surprised when I glanced out the window and saw Jack _____
   toward the house.

7. SITUATION: *Someone is calling for help in the distance. I suddenly hear that.*

   Listen! Do you hear someone _____ for help? I do.

8. SITUATION: *My daughter's team plays soccer every weekend. I always watch the team when they play a game.*

   I enjoy watching my daughter _____ soccer every weekend.

9. SITUATION: *I went to bed around eleven. At that time, the people in the next apartment were singing and laughing.*

   When I went to bed last night around eleven, I could hear the people in the next

   apartment _____ and _____. I had trouble getting to
   sleep because they were making so much noise.

10. SITUATION: *A fly landed on the table. I swatted it with a rolled up newspaper.*

    As soon as I saw the fly _____ on the table, I swatted it with a rolled up
    newspaper.

11. SITUATION: *I smell smoke. Something must be burning.*

    Do you smell something _____? I do.

12. SITUATION: *I was sitting in class. Suddenly someone touched my shoulder.*

    I was startled in class yesterday when I felt someone _____ my shoulder.
    I didn't mind. It just surprised me. It was Olga. She wanted to borrow my dictionary.

☐ EXERCISE 16. Activity: using verbs of perception. (Chart 15-7)
Directions: Describe what you see and hear.

1. What do you see happening around you right now?
2. Ask (. . .) to stand up and sit back down. What did you just see (. . .) do?
3. Close your eyes. What do you hear happening right now?
4. Ask (. . .) to say something. What did you just hear (. . .) say?
5. Ask (. . .) to do something. As he/she continues to do this, describe what you see and hear him/her doing.

15-8 USING THE SIMPLE FORM AFTER *LET* AND *HELP*

(a) My father *lets* me *drive* his car. (b) I *let* my friend *borrow* my bicycle. (c) *Let's go* to a movie.	*Let* is followed by the simple form of a verb, not an infinitive. *INCORRECT:* My father lets me *to drive* his car.
(d) My brother *helped* me *wash* my car. (e) My brother *helped* me *to wash* my car.	*Help* is often followed by the simple form of a verb, as in (d). An infinitive is also possible, as in (e). Both (d) and (e) are correct.

☐ **EXERCISE 17. Using the simple form after LET and HELP. (Chart 15-8)**
Directions: Complete the sentences with verb phrases.

1. Don't let me __forget to take my keys to the house with me.__

2. The teacher usually lets us _____

3. Why did you let your roommate _____

4. You shouldn't let other people _____

5. A stranger helped the lost child _____

6. It was very kind of my friend to help me _____

7. Keep working. Don't let me _____

8. Could you help me _____

15-9 USING CAUSATIVE VERBS: *MAKE, HAVE, GET*

(a) I *made* my brother *carry* my suitcase. (b) I *had* my brother *carry* my suitcase. (c) I *got* my brother *to carry* my suitcase.	*Make*, *have*, and *get* can be used to express the idea that "X" causes "Y" to do something. When they are used as causative verbs, their meanings are similar but not identical. In (a): My brother had no choice. I insisted that he carry my suitcase. In (b): My brother carried my suitcase because I asked him to. In (c): I managed to persuade my brother to carry my suitcase.
FORMS X *makes* Y *do* something. (simple form) X *has* Y *do* something. (simple form) X *gets* Y *to do* something. (infinitive)	
CAUSATIVE *MAKE* (d) Mrs. Lee *made* her son *clean* his room. (e) Sad movies *make* me *cry*.	Causative *make* is followed by the simple form of a verb, not an infinitive. (*INCORRECT*: She made him *to clean* his room.) *Make* gives the idea that "X" **forces** "Y" to do something. In (d): Mrs. Lee's son had no choice.
CAUSATIVE *HAVE* (f) I *had* the plumber *repair* the leak. (g) Jane *had* the waiter *bring* her some tea.	Causative *have* is followed by the simple form of a verb, not an infinitive. (*INCORRECT*: I had him *to repair* the leak.) *Have* gives the idea that "X" **requests** "Y" to do something. In (f): The plumber repaired the leak because I asked him to.
CAUSATIVE *GET* (h) The students *got* the teacher *to dismiss* class early. (i) Jack *got* his friends *to play* soccer with him after school.	Causative *get* is followed by an infinitive. *Get* gives the idea that "X" **persuades** "Y" to do something. In (h): The students managed to persuade the teacher to let them leave early.
PASSIVE CAUSATIVES (j) I *had* my watch *repaired* (by someone). (k) I *got* my watch *repaired* (by someone).	The past participle is used after *have* and *get* to give a passive meaning. In this case, there is usually little or no difference in meaning between *have* and *get*. In (j) and (k): I caused my watch to be repaired by someone.

☐ EXERCISE 18. Causative verbs. (Chart 15-9)

Directions: Complete the sentences with the words in parentheses.

1. The doctor made the patient *(stay)* _____stay_____ in bed.

2. Mrs. Crane had her house *(paint)* _____painted_____.

3. The teacher had the class *(write)* _____ a 2000-word research paper.

4. I made my son *(wash)* _____ the windows before he could go outside to play.

5. Kostas got some kids in the neighborhood *(clean)* _____ out his garage.

6. I went to the bank to have a check *(cash)* _____.

7. Tom had a bad headache yesterday, so he got his twin brother, Tim, *(go)* _____ to class for him. The teacher didn't know the difference.

8. When Scott went shopping, he found a jacket that he really liked. After he had the sleeves *(shorten)* _____, it fit him perfectly.

9. My boss made me *(redo)* _____ my report because he wasn't satisfied with it.

10. Alice stopped at the service station to have the tank *(fill)* _____.

11. I got Rosa *(lend)* _____ me some money so I could go to a movie last night.

12. Mr. Fields went to a doctor to have a wart on his nose *(remove)* _____.

13. I spilled some tomato sauce on my suit coat. Now I need to get my suit *(clean)* _____.

14. Peeling onions always makes me *(cry)*

    _____.

15. Tom Sawyer was supposed to paint the fence, but he didn't want to do it. He was a very clever boy. Somehow he got his friends *(do)*

    _____ it for him.

16. We had a professional photographer *(take)*

    _____ pictures of everyone who participated in our wedding.

☐ **EXERCISE 19. Causative verbs. (Chart 15-9)**
Directions: Complete the sentences with verb phrases.

1. I got my friend ___*to translate a letter for me.*___

2. Sometimes parents make their children ___

3. When I was at the restaurant, I had the waiter ___

4. Many people take their cars to service stations to get the oil ___

5. Teachers sometimes have their students ___

6. I'm more than willing to help you ___

7. Before I left on my trip, I had the travel agent ___

8. My cousin's jokes always make me ___

9. When I was a child, my parents wouldn't let me ___

10. We finally got our landlady ___

☐ **EXERCISE 20. Activity: causative verbs. (Chart 15-9)**
Directions: Answer the questions in complete sentences.

1. Who has had something fixed recently? What was it? Who fixed it? Where did you go to get it repaired?
2. What did your parents make you do when you were a child? What did they let you do? What did they help you do?
3. In one of the jobs you've held in the past, what did your boss have you do?
4. Have you persuaded someone to do something recently? What did you get him/her to do?
5. Where do you usually go to get . . .
   a. a check cashed?
   b. your clothes drycleaned?
   c. your laundry done?
   d. your blood pressure checked?
   e. your hair cut?

☐ **EXERCISE 21. Error analysis: gerunds, infinitives, causatives. (Chapters 14 and 15)**
Directions: Correct the errors.

1. Stop tell me what to do! Let me to make up my own mind.

2. My English is pretty good, but sometimes I have trouble to understand lectures at school.

3. When I entered the room, I found my wife to cry over the broken vase that had belonged to her great-grandmother.

4. Sara is going to spend next year for studying Chinese at a university in Taiwan.

5. I went to the pharmacy for having my prescription to be filled.

6. You shouldn't let children playing with matches.

7. When I got home, Irene was lying in bed think about what a wonderful time she'd had.

8. When Shelley needed a passport photo, she had her picture taking by a professional photographer.

9. I've finally assembled enough information for beginning writing my thesis.

10. Omar is at the park right now. He is sit on a park bench watch the ducks swiming in the pond. The sad expression on his face makes me to feel sorry for him.

☐ EXERCISE 22. Review: verb forms. (Chapters 14 and 15)
    Directions: Supply an appropriate form for each verb in parentheses.

1. As he contemplated the meaning of life, Edward stood on the beach *(look)*
   _____*looking*_____ out over the ocean.

2. It was a hot day, and the work was hard. I could feel sweat *(trickle)* _____ down my back.

3. It is foolish *(ignore)* _____ physical ailments.

4. You can lead a horse to water, but you can't make him
   (drink) _____ .

5. My cousins helped me *(move)* _____ into my new apartment.

6. I was tired, so I just watched them *(play)*
   _____ volleyball instead of
   (join) _____ them.

7. Many people think Mr. Peel will win the
   election. He has a good chance of *(elect)*
   _____ .

8. If you hear any news, I want *(tell)*
   _____ immediately.

9. Let's *(have)* _____ Ron and Maureen *(join)* _____ us
   for dinner tonight, okay?

10. I was getting sleepy, so I had my friend *(drive)* _____ the car.

11. We sat in his kitchen *(sip)* _____ very hot, strong tea and *(eat)* _____ chunks of hard cheese.

12. Emily stopped her car *(let)* _____ a black cat *(run)* _____ across the street.

13. He's a terrific soccer player! Did you see him *(make)* _____ that goal?

14. We spent the entire class period *(talk)* _____ about the revolution.

15. I don't like *(force)* _____
(leave) _____ the room *(study)*
_____ whenever my roommate feels
like *(have)* _____ a party.

16. Yuko got along very well in France despite not *(be)*
_____ able to speak French. She used
English a lot.

17. He's at an awkward age. He's old enough *(have)*
_____ adult problems but too young
(know) _____ how *(handle)* _____
_____ them.

18. *(Look)* _____ at the car after the accident made him *(realize)*
_____ that he was indeed lucky *(be)* _____ alive.

19. I'm tired. I wouldn't mind just *(stay)* _____ home tonight and *(get)*
_____ to bed early.

20. I don't anticipate *(have)* _____ any difficulties *(adjust)*
_____ to a different culture when I go abroad.

☐ **EXERCISE 23. Review: verb forms. (Chapters 14 and 15)**
Directions: Complete the sentence with an appropriate form of the verb in parentheses.

1. My children enjoy *(allow)* _____ to stay up late when there's something special on TV.

2. *(Observe)* _____ the sun *(climb)* _____ above the horizon at dawn makes one *(realize)* _____ the earth is indeed turning.

3. John admitted *(surprise)* _____ by the unexpected birthday party last night. We had a lot of fun *(plan)* _____ it.

4. I don't understand how you got the wrong results. When I look over your notes, your chemistry experiment seems (perform) _____ correctly. But something is wrong somewhere.

5. The witness to the murder asked not (identify) _____ in the newspaper. She wanted her name kept secret.

6. It is generally considered impolite (pick) _____ your teeth at the dinner table.

7. I don't recall (meet) _____ Mr. Tanaka before. I'm sure I haven't. I'd like (introduce) _____ to him. Would you do the honors?

8. Ed's boss recommended him for the job. Ed was pleased (consider) _____ _____ for the job even though he didn't get it.

9. I wasn't tired enough (sleep) _____ last night. For a long time, I just lay in bed (think) _____ about my career and my future.

10. It is the ancient task of the best artists among us (force) _____ us (use) _____ our ability (feel) _____ and (share) _____ _____ emotions.

11. Jeff applied to medical school many months ago. Now he's so concerned about (accept) _____ into medical school that he's having a difficult time (concentrate) _____ on the courses he's taking this term.

12. It may be impossible (persuade) _____ my mother (give) _____ _____ up her job even though she's having health problems. We can't even get her (cut) _____ down on her working hours. She enjoys (work) _____ so much that she refuses (retire) _____ and (take) _____ it easy. I admire her for (dedicate) _____ _____ to her work, but I also want her to take care of her health.

13. Traffic has become too heavy for the Steinbergs (commute) _____ easily to their jobs in the city. They're considering (move) _____ to an apartment close to their places of work. They don't want (give) _____ up their present home, but they need (live) _____ in the city (be) _____ closer to their work so they can spend more time (do) _____ the things they really enjoy (do) _____ in their free time.

14. Last week I was sick with the flu. It made me *(feel)* _____ awful. I didn't have enough energy *(get)* _____ out of bed. I just lay there *(feel)* _____ sorry for myself. When my father heard me *(sneeze)* _____ and *(cough)* _____, he opened my bedroom door *(ask)* _____ me if I needed anything. I was really happy *(see)* _____ his kind and caring face, but there wasn't anything he could do to make the flu *(go)* _____ away.

15. Fish don't use their teeth for *(chew)* _____. They use them for *(grab)* _____, *(hold)* _____, or *(tear)* _____. Most fish *(swallow)* _____ their prey whole.

16. I can't seem *(get)* _____ rid of the cockroaches in my apartment. Every night I see them *(run)* _____ all over my kitchen counters. It drives me crazy. I'm considering *(have)* _____ the whole apartment *(spray)* _____ by a professional pest control expert.

17. The employees were unhappy when the new management took over. They weren't accustomed to *(treat)* _____ disrespectfully by the managers of the production departments. By *(threaten)* _____ *(stop)* _____ *(work)* _____, they got the company *(listen)* _____ to their grievances. In the end, a strike was averted.

18. According to some estimates, well over half of the world's population is functionally illiterate. Imagine *(be)* _____ a parent with a sick child and *(be)* _____ unable to read the directions on a medicine bottle. We all know that it is important for medical directions *(understand)* _____ clearly. Many medical professionals are working today *(bridge)* _____ the literacy gap by *(teach)* _____ health care through pictures.

☐ EXERCISE 24. Error analysis: gerunds, infinitives, causatives. (Chapters 14 and 15)
Directions: Correct the errors.

1. My parents made me to promise to write them once a week.

2. I don't mind to have a roommate.

3. Most students want return home as soon as possible.

4. When I went to shopping last Saturday, I saw a man to drive his car onto the sidewalk.

5. I asked my roommate to let me to use his shoe polish.

6. To learn about another country it is very interesting.

7. I don't enjoy to play card games.

8. I heard a car door to open and closing.

9. I had my friend to lend me his car.

10. I tried very hard to don't make any mistakes.

11. You should visit my country. It is too beautiful.

12. The music director tapped his baton for beginning the rehearsal.

13. Some people prefer to save their money to spend it.

14. The task of find a person who could help us wasn't difficult.

15. All of us needed to went to the cashier's window.

16. I am looking forward to go to swim in the ocean.

17. When your planting a garden, it's important to be known about soils.

18. My mother always make me to be slow down if she think I am driving to fast.

19. One of our fights ended up with me having to sent to the hospital for getting stitches.

20. Please promise not telling anybody my secret.

21. I would appreciate having heard from you soon.

22. Maria has never complained about have a handicap.

23. Lillian deserves to be tell the truth about what happened last night.

24. Barbara always makes me laughing. She has a great sense of humor.

25. Ali no speak Spanish, and Juan not know Arabic. But they communicate well by speak English when they be together.

26. I enjoyed to talk to her on the phone. I look forward to see her next week.

27. During a fire drill, everyone is required leaving the building.

28. Ski in the Alps was a big thrill for me.

29. Don't keep to be asking me the same questions over and over.

30. When I entered the room, I found my young son stand on the kitchen table.

☐ EXERCISE 25. Writing. (Chapters 14 and 15)

Directions: Choose one to write about.

1. Write about your first day or week here (in this city/at this school/etc.). Did you have any unusual, funny, or difficult experiences? What were your first impressions and reactions? Whom did you meet?

2. Write about your childhood. What are some of the pleasant memories you have of your childhood? Do you have any unpleasant memories?

3. Whom do you like to spend some of your free time with? What do you enjoy doing together? Include an interesting experience the two of you have had.

☐ EXERCISE 26. Writing. (Chapters 14 and 15)

Directions: Write a composition for me, your reader, in which you explain exactly how to do something. Choose any topic that you know well. Assume that I know almost nothing about your topic. I have not had the experiences you have had. I don't know what you know. You must teach me. In your composition, use the words "I" and "you." Explain why/how you know about this topic. Address your information directly to your reader.

Possible topics:

How to: buy a used car   prepare a meal
        travel to a particular place   write a story
        open a bank account   paint a room
        get a job   repair a car
        design a bridge   study a language
        plant a garden   organize a meeting
        rent an apartment   decorate a home
        register at a hotel   teach a class
        breed dairy cows   maintain a farm
        interpret an X-ray   start a business
        change a flat tire   live abroad
        play a guitar   play a game
        catch a fish   take care of someone who has the flu

Example of an introductory paragraph:

Have you ever thought about buying a used car? When I was in my late teens, I decided I had to have a car. I worked hard and saved my money. When the time came, I convinced my best friend to accompany me to a used car lot. I didn't really know what I was doing, so I knew I needed him to help me. When we got to the lot, the salesman had us look at lots of cars. Suddenly we came upon the car of my dreams: a small, black sports convertible. It was classy, comfortable, shiny, and it had leather seats, not to mention a powerful engine and lots of speed. My friend urged me to think it over, but I was so excited I handed the salesman my check for the first of many payments. Of course, I had no idea that the car was simply a beautiful pile of junk. I learned that later when everything started to go wrong with it. I'm older and wiser now, and even though I'm not an expert on automobiles, I'd like to share my experiences with you and discuss what you should consider before you buy a used car.

CHAPTER 16
Coordinating Conjunctions

CONTENTS

16-1 PARALLEL STRUCTURE

One use of a conjunction is to connect words or phrases that have the same grammatical function in a sentence. This use of conjunctions is called "parallel structure." The conjunctions used in this pattern are *and*, *but*, *or*, *nor*. These words are called "coordinating conjunctions."

(a) *Steve **and** his friend* are coming to dinner.	In (a): *noun + **and** + noun*
(b) Susan *raised* her hand **and** *snapped* her fingers.	In (b): *verb + **and** + verb*
(c) He *is waving* his arms **and** *(is) shouting* at us.	In (c): *verb + **and** + verb* (The second auxiliary may be omitted if it is the same as the first auxiliary.)
(d) These shoes are *old **but** comfortable*.	In (d): *adjective + **but** + adjective*
(e) He wants *to watch* TV **or** *(to) listen* to some music.	In (e): *infinitive + **or** + infinitive* (The second *to* is usually omitted.)
(f) *Steve, Joe, **and** Alice* are coming to dinner.	A parallel structure may contain more than two parts. In a series, commas are used to separate each unit.
(g) Susan *raised* her hand, *snapped* her fingers, **and** *asked* a question.	The final comma that precedes the conjunction is optional; also correct: *Steve, Joe and Alice* are coming to dinner.
(h) The colors in that fabric are *red, gold, black, **and** green*.	
(i) *INCORRECT: Steve, and Joe* are coming to dinner.	Note: No commas are used if there are only two parts to a parallel structure.

☐ EXERCISE 1. Parallel structure. (Chart 16-1)
> *Directions:* Underline the parallel structure in each sentence and give the pattern that is used, as shown in the examples.

> 1. The old man is extremely <u>kind</u> and <u>generous</u>.   *adjective* + and + *adjective*

> 2. He received a pocket <u>calculator</u> and a wool <u>sweater</u> for his birthday.   *noun* + and + *noun*

3. She spoke angrily and bitterly about the war.   _____   + and +

4. I looked for my book but couldn't find it.   _____   + but +

5. I hope to go to that university and study under Dr. Liu.   _____   + and +

6. In my spare time, I enjoy reading novels or watching television.   _____   + or +

7. He will leave at eight and arrive at nine.   _____   + and +

8. He should have broken his engagement to Beth and married Sue instead.   _____   + and +

☐ **EXERCISE 2. Parallel structure. (Chart 16-1)**

Directions: Parallel structure makes repeating the same words unnecessary.* Combine the given sentences into one concise sentence that contains parallel structure. Punctuate carefully.

1. Mary opened the door. Mary greeted her guests.
   → *Mary opened the door and greeted her guests.*
2. Mary is opening the door. Mary is greeting her guests.
3. Mary will open the door. Mary will greet her guests.
4. Alice is kind. Alice is generous. Alice is trustworthy.
5. Please try to speak more loudly. Please try to speak more clearly.
6. He gave her flowers on Sunday. He gave her candy on Monday. He gave her a ring on Tuesday.
7. While we were in New York, we attended an opera. While we were in New York, we ate at marvelous restaurants. While we were in New York, we visited some old friends.
8. He decided to quit school. He decided to go to California. He decided to find a job.
9. I am looking forward to going to Italy. I am looking forward to eating wonderful pasta every day.
10. I should have finished my homework. I should have cleaned up my room.
11. The boy was old enough to work. The boy was old enough to earn some money.
12. He preferred to play baseball. Or he preferred to spend his time in the streets with other boys.
13. I like coffee. I do not like tea.
    → *I like coffee but not tea.***
14. I have met his mother. I have not met his father.
15. Jake would like to live in Puerto Rico. He would not like to live in Iceland.

---

*This form of parallel structure, in which unnecessary words are omitted but are understood, is called "ellipsis."

Sometimes a comma precedes **but not: *I like coffee, but not tea.*

☐ EXERCISE 3. Parallel structure. (Chart 16-1)
   Directions: In each group, complete the unfinished sentence. Then combine the sentences into one concise sentence that contains parallel structure. Punctuate carefully.

1. The country lane was narrow.
   The country lane was steep.
   The country lane was _____ muddy. _____
   _____ The country lane was narrow, steep, and muddy. _____

2. I like to become acquainted with the people of other countries.
   I like to become acquainted with the customs of other countries.

   I like to become acquainted with _____ of other countries.

   _____

3. I dislike living in a city because of the air pollution.
   I dislike living in a city because of the crime.

   I dislike living in a city because of _____

   _____

4. We discussed some of the social problems of the United States.
   We discussed some of the political problems of the United States.

   We discussed some of the _____ problems of the United States.

   _____

   _____

5. Hawaii has _____
   Hawaii has many interesting tropical trees.
   Hawaii has many interesting tropical flowers.
   Hawaii has beautiful beaches.

   _____

   _____

6. Mary Hart would make a good president because she _____
   Mary Hart would make a good president because she works effectively with others.
   Mary Hart would make a good president because she has a reputation for integrity.
   Mary Hart would make a good president because she has a reputation for independent thinking.

   _____

   _____

   _____

☐ EXERCISE 4. Parallel structure. (Chart 16-1)
Directions: With your own words, complete each sentence, using parallel structure.

1. Judge Holmes served the people of this country with impartiality, ability, and
   ____integrity____.

2. Ms. Polanski has proven herself to be a sincere, hardworking, and
   _____ supervisor.

3. The professor walked through the door and _____.

4. I was listening to music and _____ when I heard a
   knock at the door.

5. I get up at seven every morning, eat a light breakfast, and _____.

6. _____ and attending concerts in the park are two
   of the things my wife and I like to do on summer weekends.

7. Our whole family enjoys camping. We especially enjoy fishing in mountain streams
   and _____.

8. Resolve to be tender with the young, compassionate with the aged, understanding of
   those who are wrong, and _____.
   Sometime in your life, you will have been all of these.

☐ EXERCISE 5. Error analysis: parallel structure. (Chart 16-1)
Directions: Correct the errors.

1. By obeying the speed limit, we can save energy, lives, and it costs us less.

2. My home offers me a feeling of security, warm, and love.

3. The pioneers labored to clear away the forest and planting crops.

4. When I refused to help her, she became very angry and shout at me.

5. In my spare time, I enjoy taking care of my aquarium and to work on my stamp
   collection.

6. With their keen sight, fine hearing, and they have a refined sense of smell, wolves hunt
   elk, deer, moose, and caribou.

7. All plants need light, to have a suitable climate, and an ample supply of water and
   minerals from the soil.

8. Slowly and being cautious, the firefighter ascended the burned staircase.

9. The Indian cobra snake and the king cobra use poison from their fangs in two ways: by injecting it directly into their prey or they spit it into the eyes of the victim.

10. On my vacation I lost a suitcase, broke my glasses, and I missed my flight home.

11. When Anna moved, she had to rent an apartment, make new friends, and to find a job.

☐ **EXERCISE 6. Error anlysis: parallel structure. (Chart 16-1)**
Directions: Correct the errors.

What do people in your country think of bats? Are they mean and scary creatures, or are they symbols of happiness and lucky?

In Western countries, many people have an unreasoned fear of bats. According to scientist Dr. Sharon Horowitz, bats are beneficial mammals and harmless. "When I was a child, I believed that a bat would attack me and tangled itself in my hair. Now I know better," said Dr. Horowitz.

Contrary to popular Western myths, bats do not attack humans and not blind. Although a few bats may be infected, they are not major carriers of rabies or carry other dread diseases. Bats help natural plant life by pollinating plants, spreading seeds, and they eat insects. If you get rid of bats that eat overripe fruit, then fruit flies can flourish and destroying the fruit industry.

According to Dr. Horowitz, bats make loving pets, and they are trainable, and are gentle pets. Not many people, however, are known to have bats as pets, and bats themselves prefer to avoid people.

16-2 PAIRED CONJUNCTIONS: *BOTH . . . AND; NOT ONLY . . . BUT ALSO; EITHER . . . OR; NEITHER . . . NOR*

(a) **Both** *my mother* **and** *my sister* **are** here.	Two subjects connected by **both . . . and** take a plural verb, as in (a).
(b) **Not only** *my mother* **but also** *my sister* **is** here. (c) **Not only** *my sister* **but also** *my parents* **are** here. (d) **Neither** *my mother* **nor** *my sister* **is** here. (e) **Neither** *my sister* **nor** *my parents* **are** here.	When two subjects are connected by **not only . . . but also**, **either . . . or**, or **neither . . . nor**, the subject that is closer to the verb determines whether the verb is singular or plural.
(f) The research project will take **both** *time* **and** *money*. (g) Yesterday it **not only** *rained* **but (also)** *snowed*. (h) I'll take **either** *chemistry* **or** *physics* next quarter. (i) That book is **neither** *interesting* **nor** *accurate*.	Notice the parallel structure in the examples. The same grammatical form should follow each part of the paired conjunctions.* In (f): **both** + *noun* + **and** + *noun* In (g): **not only** + *verb* + **but also** + *verb* In (h): **either** + *noun* + **or** + *noun* In (i): **neither** + *adjective* + **nor** + *adjective*

*Paired conjunctions are also called "correlative conjunctions."

☐ EXERCISE 7. Paired conjunctions. (Chart 16-2)
Directions: Add *is* or *are* to each sentence.

1. Both the teacher and the student ___are___ here.

2. Neither the teacher nor the student _____ here.

3. Not only the teacher but also the student _____ here.

4. Not only the teacher but also the students _____ here.

5. Either the students or the teacher _____ planning to come.

6. Either the teacher or the students _____ planning to come.

7. Both the students and the teachers _____ planning to come.

8. Both the students and the teacher _____ planning to come.

☐ EXERCISE 8. Error anlysis: paired conjunctions. (Chart 16-2)
Directions: What is wrong with these sentences?

1. Either John will call Mary or Bob.

2. Not only Sue saw the mouse but also the cat.

3. Both my mother talked to the teacher and my father.

4. Either Mr. Anderson or Ms. Wiggins are going to teach our class today.

5. I enjoy not only reading novels but also magazines.

6. Oxygen is plentiful. Both air contains oxygen and water.

□ EXERCISE 9. Paired conjunctions. (Chart 16-2)
Directions: Answer the questions, using paired conjunctions. Work in pairs, in groups, or as a class.

PART I. Use ***both . . . and***.

1. You have met his father. Have you met his mother?
   → *Yes, I have met both his father and his mother.*

2. The driver was injured in the accident. Was the passenger injured in the accident?

3. Wheat is grown in Kansas. Is corn grown in Kansas?

4. He buys used cars. Does he sell used cars?

5. You had lunch with your friends. Did you have dinner with them?

6. The city suffers from air pollution. Does it suffer from water pollution?

PART II. Use ***not only . . . but also***.

7. I know you are studying math. Are you studying chemistry too?
   → *Yes, I'm studying not only math but also chemistry.*

8. I know his cousin is living with him. Is his mother-in-law living with him too?

9. I know your country has good universities. Does the United States have good universities too?

10. I know you lost your wallet. Did you lose your keys too?

11. I know she goes to school. Does she have a full-time job too?

12. I know he bought a coat. Did he buy a new pair of shoes too?

PART III. Use ***either . . . or***.

13. Omar has your book, or Rosa has your book. Is that right?
    → *Yes, either Omar or Rosa has my book.*

14. You're going to give your friend a book for her birthday, or you're going to give her a pen. Is that right?

15. Your sister will meet you at the airport, or your brother will meet you there. Right?

16. They can go swimming, or they can play tennis. Is that right?

17. You're going to vote for Mr. Smith, or you're going to vote for Mr. Jones. Right?

18. You'll go to New Orleans for your vacation, or you'll go to Miami. Right?

PART IV. Use ***neither . . . nor***.

19. He doesn't like coffee. Does he like tea?
    → *No, he likes neither coffee nor tea.*

20. Her husband doesn't speak English. Do her children speak English?

21. The students aren't wide awake today. Is the teacher wide awake today?

22. They don't have a refrigerator for their new apartment. Do they have a stove?

23. She doesn't enjoy hunting. Does she enjoy fishing?

24. The result wasn't good. Was the result bad?

Directions: Combine the following into sentences that contain parallel structure. Use ***both . . . and; not only . . . but also; either . . . or; neither . . . nor.***

1. He does not have a pen. He does not have paper.
   → *He has neither a pen nor paper.*
2. Ron enjoys horseback riding. Bob enjoys horseback riding.
3. You can have tea, or you can have coffee.
4. Arthur is not in class today. Ricardo is not in class today.
5. Arthur is absent. Ricardo is absent.
6. We can fix dinner for them here, or we can take them to a restaurant.
7. She wants to buy a Chevrolet, or she wants to buy a Toyota.
8. The leopard faces extinction. The tiger faces extinction.
9. The library doesn't have the book I need. The bookstore doesn't have the book I need.
10. We could fly, or we could take the train.
11. The president's assistant will not confirm the story. The president's assistant will not deny the story.
12. Coal is an irreplaceable natural resource. Oil is an irreplaceable natural resource.
13. Smallpox is a dangerous disease. Malaria is a dangerous disease.
14. Her roommates don't know where she is. Her brother doesn't know where she is.
15. According to the news report, it will snow tonight, or it will rain tonight.

16-3 COMBINING INDEPENDENT CLAUSES WITH COORDINATING CONJUNCTIONS

(a) It was raining hard. There was a strong wind. (b) INCORRECT PUNCTUATION: It was raining hard**,** there was a strong wind.	Example (a) contains two *independent clauses* (i.e., two complete sentences). Notice the punctuation. A period,* NOT A COMMA, is used to separate two independent clauses. The punctuation in (b) is not correct; the error in (b) is called "a run-on sentence."
(c) It was raining hard, *and* there was a strong wind. (d) It was raining hard *and* there was a strong wind. (e) It was raining hard. *And* there was a strong wind.	A *conjunction* may be used to connect two independent clauses. PUNCTUATION: Usually a comma immediately precedes the conjunction, as in (c). In short sentences, the comma is sometimes omitted, as in (d). In informal writing, a conjunction sometimes begins a sentence, as in (e).
(f) He was tired, *so* he went to bed. (g) The child hid behind his mother's skirt, *for* he was afraid of the dog. (h) She did not study, *yet* she passed the exam.	In addition to ***and, but, or,*** and ***nor,*** other conjunctions are used to connect two independent clauses: ***so*** (meaning "therefore, as a result") ***for*** (meaning "because") ***yet*** (meaning "but, nevertheless") A comma almost always precedes ***so, for,*** and ***yet*** when they are used as coordinating conjunctions.**

* In British English, a period is called "a full stop."

** ***So, for,*** and ***yet*** have other meanings in other structures: e.g., *He is not **so** tall as his brother.* (***so*** = as) *We waited **for** the bus.* (***for*** = a preposition) *She hasn't arrived **yet**.* (***yet*** = an adverb meaning "up to this time")

☐ **EXERCISE 11. Combining independent clauses with coordinating conjunctions. (Chart 16-3)**

Directions: Punctuate the sentences by adding commas or periods. Do not add any words. Capitalize where necessary.

1. The boys walked the girls ran. → *The boys walked. The girls ran.*

2. The teacher lectured the students took notes.

3. The teacher lectured and the students took notes.

4. Elena came to the meeting but Pedro stayed home.

5. Elena came to the meeting her brother stayed home.

6. Her academic record was outstanding yet she was not accepted by the university.

7. I have not finished writing my term paper yet I will not be finished until sometime next week.

8. We had to go to the grocery store for some milk and bread.

9. We had to go to the grocery store for there was nothing in the house to fix for dinner.

10. Kostas didn't have enough money to buy an airplane ticket so he couldn't fly home for the holiday.

☐ **EXERCISE 12. Combining independent clauses with coordinating conjunctions. (Chart 16-3)**

Directions: Punctuate the sentences by adding commas or periods. Do not add any words. Capitalize where necessary.

1. A thermometer is used to measure temperature a barometer measures air pressure.

2. Daniel made many promises but he had no intention of keeping them.

3. I always enjoyed mathematics in high school so I decided to major in it in college.

4. Anna is in serious legal trouble for she had no car insurance at the time of the accident.

5. Last night Martha had to study for a test so she went to the library.

6. The ancient Egyptians had good dentists archaeologists have found mummies that had gold fillings in their teeth.

7. Both John and I had many errands to do yesterday John had to go to the post office and the bookstore I had to go to the post office the travel agency and the bank.

8. I did not like the leading actor yet the movie was quite good on the whole.

9. The team of researchers has not finished compiling the statistics yet their work will not be made public until later.

10. We have nothing to fear for our country is strong and united.

11. He slapped his desk in disgust he had failed another examination and had ruined his chances for a passing grade in the course.

12. I struggled to keep my head above water I tried to yell for help but no sound came from my mouth.

13. The earthquake was devastating tall buildings crumbled and fell to the earth.

14. It was a wonderful picnic the children waded in the stream collected rocks and insects and flew kites the teenagers played an enthusiastic game of baseball the adults busied themselves preparing the food supervising the children and playing a game or two of volleyball.

15. Some people collect butterflies for a hobby these collectors capture them with a net and put them in a jar that has poison in it the dead butterflies are then mounted on a board.

16. Caterpillars eat plants and cause damage to some crops but adult butterflies feed principally on nectar from flowers and do not cause any harm.

17. The butterfly is a marvel it begins as an ugly caterpillar and turns into a work of art.

18. The sight of a butterfly floating from flower to flower on a warm sunny day brightens anyone's heart a butterfly is a charming and gentle creature.

19. When cold weather comes some butterflies travel great distances to reach tropical climates.★

20. Butterflies are admired throughout the world because they are beautiful they can be found on every continent except Antarctica.★

★See Chart 5-1, p. 70, for ways to punctuate sentences that contain adverb clauses.

□ EXERCISE 13. Writing. (Chapter 16)

Directions: Write two descriptive paragraphs on one of the topics below. The first paragraph should be a draft, and the second should be a "tightened" revision of the first. Look for places where two or three sentences can be combined into one by using parallel structure. Pay special attention to punctuation, and be sure all of your commas and periods are used correctly.

Topics:

1. Give a physical description of your place of residence (apartment, dorm room, etc.)
2. Describe the characteristics and activities of a successful student.
3. Give your reader directions for making a particular food dish.

Example:

FIRST DRAFT

To make spaghetti sauce, you will need several ingredients. First, you will need some ground beef. Probably about one pound of ground beef will be sufficient. You should also have an onion. If the onions are small, you should use two. Also, find a green pepper and put it in the sauce. Of course, you will also need some tomato sauce or tomatoes.

REVISION

To make spaghetti sauce you will need one pound of ground beef, one large or two small onions, a green pepper, and some tomato sauce or tomatoes.

CHAPTER 17
Adverb Clauses

CONTENTS

17-1 INTRODUCTION

(a) *When we were in New York,* we saw several plays. (b) We saw several plays *when we were in New York.*	*When we were in New York* is an adverb clause. PUNCTUATION: When an adverb clause precedes an independent clause, as in (a), a comma is used to separate the clauses. When the adverb clause follows, as in (b), usually no comma is used.
(c) *Because he was sleepy,* he went to bed. (d) He went to bed *because he was sleepy.*	Like *when*, *because* introduces an adverb clause. *Because he was sleepy* is an adverb clause.
(e) INCORRECT: *When we were in New York. We saw several plays.* (f) INCORRECT: *He went to bed. Because he was sleepy.*	Adverb clauses are dependent clauses. They cannot stand alone as a sentence in written English. They must be connected to an independent clause.★

SUMMARY LIST OF WORDS USED TO INTRODUCE ADVERB CLAUSES★★

TIME		CAUSE AND EFFECT	CONTRAST	CONDITION
after	*by the time (that)*	*because*	*even though*	*if*
before	*once*	*now that*	*although*	*unless*
when	*as/so long as*	*since*	*though*	*only if*
while	*whenever*			*whether or not*
as	*every time (that)*		DIRECT CONTRAST	*even if*
as soon as	*the first time (that)*		*while*	*in case*
since	*the last time (that)*		*whereas*	*in the event that*
until	*the next time (that)*			

★See Chart 13-1, p. 267, for the definition of dependent and independent clauses.

★★Words that introduce adverb clauses are called "subordinating conjunctions."

☐ EXERCISE 1. Adverb clauses. (Chart 17-1)

   Directions: Add periods, commas, and capitalization. Do not change, add, or omit any words. <u>Underline</u> each adverb clause. (NOTE: Item 12 contains an adjective clause. Item 13 contains an adjective clause and a noun clause. Can you find these other dependent clauses?)

1. Sue was in the other room when the phone rang as soon as she heard it she ran to the front room to answer it.

     → *Sue was in the other room <u>when the phone rang</u>.* ***A**s soon as she heard it* , *she ran to the front room to answer it.*

2. When it began to rain he closed the windows.

3. He closed the windows when it began to rain.

4. As soon as the rain began the children wanted to go outdoors they love to play outside in the warm summer rain I used to do the same thing when I was a child.

5. Jack got to the airport early after he checked in at the airline counter he went to the waiting area near his gate he sat and read until his flight was announced.

6. Jack walked onto the plane found his seat and stowed his bag in an overhead compartment.

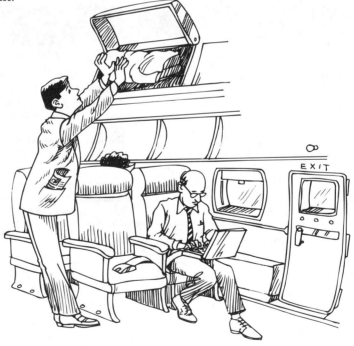

7. Before the plane took off he fastened his seat belt and put his seat in an upright position.

8. Jack's wife doesn't like to fly because she gets nervous on airplanes.

9. When Jack and his wife go on vacation they have to drive or take the train because his wife is afraid of flying.

10. I had a cup of tea before I left for work this morning but I didn't have anything to eat I rarely eat breakfast.

11. After Ellen gets home from work she likes to read the newspaper she follows the same routine every day after work as soon as she gets home she changes her clothes gets a snack and a drink and sits down in her favorite chair to read the newspaper in peace and quiet she usually has about half an hour to read the paper before her husband arrives home from his job.

12. When you speak to someone who is hard of hearing you do not have to shout it is important to face the person directly and speak clearly my elderly father is hard of hearing but he can understand me if I face him speak slowly and say each word clearly.

13. Greg Adams has been blind since he was two years old today he is a key scientist in a computer company he is able to design complex electronic equipment because he has a special computer that reads writes and speaks out loud his blindness neither helps nor hinders him it is irrelevant to how well he does his job.

☐ EXERCISE 2. Review of adverb clauses of time. (Chapter 5 and Chart 17-1)
Directions: Complete the sentences. Punctuate carefully. Pay special attention to verb tense usage.

1. Since I came to . . . .
2. Just as I was falling asleep last night . . . .
3. I'll help you with your homework as soon as I . . . .
4. I was late. By the time I got to the airport . . . .
5. One of my friends gets nervous every time . . . .
6. I will be here until I . . . .
7. . . . as long as I live.
8. I heard . . . while I . . . .
9. Once summer/winter comes . . . .
10. Shortly before I . . . .
11. I have been in . . . for . . . . By the time I leave, I . . . .
12. The last time I . . . .
13. The next time you . . . .
14. I . . . just as soon as . . . .
15. Not long after I . . . .
16. I had already . . . when . . . .
17. Whenever . . . .
18. Ever since . . . .

17-2 USING ADVERB CLAUSES TO SHOW CAUSE AND EFFECT

because	(a) **Because** *he was sleepy*, he went to bed. (b) He went to bed **because** *he was sleepy*.	An adverb clause may precede or follow the independent clause. Notice the punctuation in (a) and (b).
now that	(c) **Now that** *the semester is over*, I'm going to rest a few days and then take a trip. (d) Jack lost his job. **Now that** *he's unemployed*, he can't pay his bills.	**Now that** means "because now." In (c): *Now that the semester is over* means "because the semester is now over." **Now that** is used for present causes of present or future situations.
since	(e) **Since** *Monday is a holiday*, we don't have to go to work. (f) **Since** *you're a good cook and I'm not,* you should cook the dinner.	When **since** is used to mean "because," it expresses a known cause; it means "because it is a fact that" or "given that it is true that." Cause and effect sentences with **since** say: "Given the fact that X is true, Y is the result." In (e): "Given the fact that Monday is a holiday, we don't have to go to work." Note: **Since** has two meanings. One is "because." It is also used in time clauses: e.g., *Since I came here, I have met many people.* See Chart 5-2, p. 72.

□ **EXERCISE 3. Using adverb clauses to show cause and effect. (Chart 17-2)**
Directions: Combine the sentences, using the word or phrase in parentheses. Add commas where necessary.

1. We can go swimming every day. The weather is warm. *(now that)*
   → *We can go swimming every day now that the weather is warm.*

2. All of the students had done poorly on the test. The teacher decided to give it again. *(since)*
   → *Since all of the students had done poorly on the test, the teacher decided to give it again.*

3. Cold air hovers near the earth. It is heavier than hot air. *(because)*

4. You paid for the theater tickets. Please let me pay for our dinner. *(since)*

5. Larry is finally caught up on his work. He can start his vacation tomorrow. *(now that)*

6. Our TV set was broken. We listened to the news on the radio. *(because)*

7. My brother got married last month. He's a married man now, so he has more responsibilities. *(now that)*

8. Oil is an irreplaceable natural resource. We must do whatever we can in order to conserve it. *(since)*

9. Do you want to go for a walk? The rain has stopped. *(now that)*

10. Many young people move to the cities in search of employment. There are few jobs available in the rural areas. *(since)*

11. The civil war has ended. A new government is being formed. *(now that)*

12. Ninety-two thousand people already have reservations with an airline company for a trip to the moon. I doubt that I'll get the chance to go on one of the first tourist flights. *(since)*

☐ EXERCISE 4. Using adverb clauses to show cause and effect. (Chart 17-2)
Directions: Complete the sentences. Punctuate carefully.

1. Now that I've finally finished . . . .
2. The teacher didn't . . . because . . . .
3. Since it's too expensive to . . . .
4. Jack can't stay out all night with his friends now that . . . .
5. Since we don't have class tomorrow . . . .

17-3 EXPRESSING CONTRAST (UNEXPECTED RESULT): USING *EVEN THOUGH*

(a) *Because* the weather was cold, I *didn't go* swimming. (b) *Even though* the weather was cold, I *went* swimming. (c) *Because* I wasn't tired, I *didn't go* to bed. (d) *Even though* I wasn't tired, I *went* to bed.	*Because* is used to express expected results. *Even though* is used to express unexpected results. Note: Like *because*, *even though* introduces an adverb clause.

☐ EXERCISE 5. Using EVEN THOUGH. (Chart 17-3)

    Directions: Complete the sentences by using either *even though* or *because*.

1. Tim's in good shape physically _____*even though*_____ he doesn't get much exercise.

2. Larry's in good shape physically _____*because*_____ he gets a lot of exercise.

3. I put on my sunglasses _____ it was a dark, cloudy day.

4. I put on my sunglasses _____ the sun was bright.

5. _____ Maria has a job, she doesn't make enough money to support her four children.

6. _____ Anna has a job, she is able to pay her rent and provide food for her family.

7. Susan didn't learn Spanish _____ she lived in Mexico for a year.

8. Joe speaks Spanish well _____ he lived in Mexico for a year.

9. Jing-Won jumped into the river to rescue the little girl who was drowning _____ he wasn't a good swimmer.

10. A newborn kangaroo can find its mother's pouch _____ its eyes are not yet open.

11. Some people protest certain commercial fishing operations _____ dolphins, considered to be highly intelligent mammals, are killed unnecessarily.

12. _____ the earthquake damaged the bridge across Skunk River, the Smiths were able to cross the river _____ they had a boat.

☐ EXERCISE 6. Using EVEN THOUGH. (Chart 17-3)

    Directions: Work in pairs, in groups, or as a class.
    Speaker A: Your book is open. Give Student B the cues in the text.
    Speaker B: Your book is closed. Answer each question by using a sentence with *even though*. Begin your response with either *yes* or *no*.

Examples:

SPEAKER A *(book open):* It was raining. Did you go to the zoo anyway?
SPEAKER B *(book closed):* Yes, even though it was raining, I went to the zoo.

SPEAKER A *(book open):* You studied hard. Did you pass the test?
SPEAKER B *(book closed):* No, even though I studied hard, I didn't pass the test.

1. You weren't tired. Did you go to bed anyway?
2. The telephone rang many times, but did . . . wake up?
3. The food was terrible. Did you eat it anyway?
4. You didn't study. Did you pass the test anyway?

5. The weather is terrible today. Did you stay home?

6. You fell down the stairs. Did you get hurt?

7. You took a nap. Do you still feel tired?

(Switch roles if working in pairs.)

8. You told the truth, but did anyone believe you?

9. You turned on the air conditioner. Is it still hot in here?

10. You mailed the letter three days ago. Has it arrived yet?

11. You have a lot of money. Can you afford to buy an airplane?

12. Your grandmother is ninety years old. Is she still young at heart?

13. (. . .) told a joke. You didn't understand it. Did you laugh anyway?

14. Your house burned down. You lost your job. Your wife/husband left you. Are you still cheerful?

☐ EXERCISE 7. Using EVEN THOUGH and BECAUSE. (Charts 17-2 and 17-3)
Directions: Write sentences that include the verbs in parentheses. Use any verb tense or modal.

1. Because the bus drivers went on strike, I *(walk)* ___had to walk___ all the way home.

2. Even though I was dead tired, I *(walk)* ___walked___ all the way home.

3. Because _____, I *(go)* _____ fishing.

4. Even though _____, I *(go)* _____ fishing.

5. Even though there *(be)* _____ very few customers in the store,

_____

6. Because there *(be)* _____ very few customers in the store,

_____

7. I *(wear)* _____ heavy gloves because _____

8. Even though my feet *(be)* _____ killing me and my head *(be)* _____

pounding, I _____

9. Even though _____, I *(get, not)* _____ a

traffic ticket.

10. Even though I *(be)* _____ tired, I _____

because _____

11. Even though _____ when _____,

I _____ because _____

12. Because _____ while _____, I

_____ even though _____

17-4 SHOWING DIRECT CONTRAST: *WHILE* AND *WHEREAS*

(a) Mary is rich, *while John is poor.* (b) John is poor, *while Mary is rich.* (c) Mary is rich, *whereas John is poor.* (d) *Whereas Mary is rich,* John is poor.	*While* and *whereas* are used to show direct contrast: "this" is exactly the opposite of "that." *While* and *whereas* may be used with the idea of either clause with no difference in meaning. *Whereas* mostly occurs in formal written English. Note: A comma is usually used even if the adverb clause comes second.
COMPARE (e) *While I was studying,* the phone rang.	*While* is also used in time clauses and means "during the time that," as in (e). See Chart 5-2, p. 72.

□ EXERCISE 8. Using WHILE and WHEREAS. (Chart 17-4)
   Directions: Choose the best completion.

1. Some people are tall, whereas others are ___C___ .
   A. intelligent   C. short
   B. thin   D. large

2. A box is square, whereas _____ .
   A. a rectangle has four sides   C. we use envelopes for letters
   B. my village has a town square   D. a circle is round
      in the center

3. While some parts of the world get an abundance of rain, others _____ .
   A. are warm and humid   C. get little or none
   B. are cold and wet   D. get a lot

4. In some nations the favorite beverage is coffee, while _____ .
   A. I like tea   C. in others it is tea
   B. it has caffeine   D. tea has caffeine too

5. Some people like cream and sugar in their coffee, while _____ .
   A. others drink hot coffee   C. milk is good in coffee, too
   B. others like it black   D. sugar can cause cavities

6. Jack is an interesting storyteller and conversationalist. His brother, on the other
   hand, _____ .
   A. is a newspaper reporter   C. has four children
   B. bores other people by talking D. knows a lot of stories, too
      about himself all the time

□ EXERCISE 9. Using WHILE and WHEREAS. (Chart 17-4)
   Directions: Complete the sentences. Discuss other ways of expressing the same idea by
   moving the position of *while* or *whereas*.

1. Some people are fat, whereas . . .
   → *Some people are fat, whereas others are thin.*
   → *Whereas some people are fat, others are thin.*
   → *Some people are thin, whereas others are fat.*

2. Some people are tall, whereas . . . .

3. Some people prefer to live in the country, while . . . .

4. While some people know only their native language . . . .

5. A mouse is small, whereas . . . .

6. The climate at sea level at the equator is always hot, whereas the climate at the North and South poles . . . .

7. Some people . . . , while . . . .

8. Some countries . . . , whereas . . . .

17-5 EXPRESSING CONDITIONS IN ADVERB CLAUSES: *IF*-CLAUSES

(a) *If it rains*, the streets get wet.	*If*-clauses (also called "adverb clauses of condition") present possible conditions. The main clause expresses results. In (a): POSSIBLE CONDITION = *it rains* RESULT = *the streets get wet*
(b) *If it rains tomorrow*, I will take my umbrella.	A present tense, not a future tense, is used in an *if*-clause even though the verb in the *if*-clause may refer to a future event or situation, as in (b).*

WORDS THAT INTRODUCE ADVERB CLAUSES OF CONDITION (*IF*-CLAUSES)		
if *whether or not* *even if*	*in case* *in the event that*	*unless* *only if*

*See Chapter 20 for uses of other verb forms in sentences with *if*-clauses.

☐ EXERCISE 10. IF-clauses. (Chart 17-5)
Directions: Make sentences from the given possibilities. Use *if*.

1. It may be cold tomorrow.
   → *If it's cold tomorrow, I'm going to stay home.*
   → *If it's cold tomorrow, let's go skating.*
   → *If it's cold tomorrow, you should wear your wool sweater.*
   → *We can't go on a picnic if it's cold tomorrow.*

2. Maybe it will be hot tomorrow.

3. Maybe you will have some free time tomorrow.

4. Maybe you will lock yourself out of your apartment.

5. Maybe the sun will be shining when you get up tomorrow morning.

6. You will probably be too tired to finish your work today.

7. You might not have enough money to take your trip next month.

8. We might continue to destroy our environment.

17-6 ADVERB CLAUSES OF CONDITION: USING *WHETHER OR NOT* AND *EVEN IF*

WHETHER OR NOT	
(a) I'm going to go swimming tomorrow *whether or not it is cold*. (OR: *whether it is cold or not*.)	*Whether or not* expresses the idea that neither this condition nor that condition matters; the result will be the same. In (a): "If it is cold, I'm going swimming. If it is not cold, I'm going swimming. I don't care about the temperature. It doesn't matter."
EVEN IF	
(b) I have decided to go swimming tomorrow. *Even if the weather is cold*, I'm going to go swimming.	Sentences with *even if* are close in meaning to those with *whether or not*. *Even if* gives the idea that a particular condition does not matter. The result will not change.

☐ EXERCISE 11. Using WHETHER OR NOT and EVEN IF. (Chart 17-6)
   Directions: Use the given information to complete the sentences.

1. *Usually people need to graduate from school to get a good job. But it's different for Ed. Maybe Ed will graduate from school, and maybe he won't. It doesn't matter because he has a good job waiting for him in his father's business.*

   a. Ed will get a good job whether or not . . . *he graduates.*
   b. Ed will get a good job even if . . . *he doesn't graduate.*

2. *Sam's uncle tells a lot of jokes. Sometimes they're funny, and sometimes they're not. It doesn't matter.*

   a. Sam laughs at the jokes whether . . . or not.
   b. Sam laughs at the jokes even if . . . .

3. *Maybe you are finished with the exam, and maybe you're not. It doesn't matter. The time is up.*

   a. You have to hand in your examination paper whether . . . or not.
   b. You have to hand in your examination paper even if . . . .

4. *It might snow, or it might not. We don't want to go camping in the snow, but it doesn't matter.*

   a. We're going to go camping in the mountains whether . . . or not.
   b. We're going to go camping in the mountains even if . . . .

5. *Max's family doesn't have enough money to send him to college. He would like to get a scholarship, but it doesn't matter because he's saved some money to go to school and has a part-time job.*

   a. Max can go to school whether or not . . . .
   b. Max can go to school even if . . . .

6. *Sometimes the weather is hot, and sometimes the weather is cold. It doesn't matter. My grandfather always wears his gray sweater.*

   a. My grandfather wears his gray sweater whether or not . . . .
   b. My grandfather always wears his gray sweater even if . . . .

7. *Your approval doesn't matter to me.*

   a. I'm going to marry Harry whether . . . or not.
   b. I'm going to marry Harry even if . . . .

□ EXERCISE 12. Using WHETHER OR NOT and EVEN IF. (Chart 17-6)
   Directions: Complete the sentences with your own words.

   Examples: Even if . . . , I'm not going to go.
   → *Even if I get an invitation to the reception, I'm not going to go.*

   . . . whether I feel better or not.
   → *I have to go to work tomorrow whether I feel better or not.*

   1. . . . even if the weather improves.
   2. Even if . . . , Maria may lose her job.
   3. Getting that job depends on whether or not . . . .
   4. . . . whether you want me to or not.
   5. I won't tell you even if . . . .
   6. I'm really angry! Maybe he'll apologize, and maybe he won't. It doesn't matter. Even if . . . , I won't forgive him!
   7. I'm exhausted. Please don't wake me up even if . . . .
   8. I'm not going to . . . even if . . . .
   9. Even if . . . , I'm going to . . . .
   10. I'm going to . . . whether or not . . . .

17-7 ADVERB CLAUSES OF CONDITION: USING *IN CASE* AND *IN THE EVENT THAT*

(a) I'll be at my uncle's house *in case* you (should) need to reach me.	*In case* and *in the event that* express the idea that something probably won't happen, but it might. *In case/in the event that* means "if by chance this should happen."
(b) *In the event that* you (should) need to reach me, I'll be at my uncle's house.	Notes: *In the event that* is more formal than *in case*. The use of *should* in the adverb clause emphasizes the speaker's uncertainty that something will happen.

□ EXERCISE 13. Using IN CASE and IN THE EVENT THAT. (Chart 17-7)
   Directions: Show the relationship between the ideas in the two sentences by using *in case* and/or *in the event that*.

   1. You probably won't need to get in touch with me, but maybe you will. If so, I'll give you my phone number.
      → *I'll give you my phone number in case you (should) need to get in touch with me/in the event that you (should) need to get in touch with me.*
   2. You probably won't need to see me, but maybe you will. If so, I'll be in my office tomorrow morning around ten.
   3. I don't think you need any more information, but maybe you do. If so, you can call me.
   4. You probably don't have any more questions, but maybe you do. If so, ask Dr. Smith.
   5. Jack probably won't call, but maybe he will. If so, please tell him that I'm at the library.

6. You will probably be satisfied with your purchase, but maybe not. If not, you can return it to the store.

Complete the following.

7. I've told you all I know. In the event that you need more information, ...
8. It's a good idea for you to keep a written record of your credit card numbers in case . . . .
9. I think I'd better clean up the apartment in case . . . .
10. I have my umbrella with me just in case . . . .
11. In the event that the two countries agree to a peace treaty, ...
12. I'll try to be there on time, but in case I'm not, ...
13. According to the manufacturer's guarantee, I should return my new camera to the factory in the event that . . . .

17-8 ADVERB CLAUSES OF CONDITION: USING *UNLESS*

(a) I'll go swimming tomorrow *unless* it's cold.	*unless = if . . . not*
(b) I'll go swimming tomorrow *if* it isn't cold.	In (a): *unless it's cold* means "if it isn't cold."
	(a) and (b) have the same meaning.

☐ EXERCISE 14. Using UNLESS. (Chart 17-8)
Directions: Make sentences with the same meaning by using *unless*.

1. I will go to the zoo if it isn't cold.
   → *I will go to the zoo unless it's cold.*
2. You can't travel abroad if you don't have a passport.
3. You can't get a driver's license if you're not at least sixteen years old.
4. If I don't get some film, I won't be able to take pictures when Ann and Rob get here.
5. You'll get hungry during class if you don't eat breakfast.

☐ EXERCISE 15. Using UNLESS. (Chart 17-8)
> *Directions:* Complete the sentences.

1. Your letter won't be delivered unless . . . .
   → *Your letter won't be delivered unless it has the correct postage.*
2. I'm sorry, but you can't see the doctor unless . . . .
3. I can't graduate from school unless . . . .
4. . . . unless you put it in the refrigerator.
5. Unless it rains, ...
6. Certain species of animals will soon become extinct unless . . . .
7. . . . unless I get a raise in salary.
8. Tomorrow I'm going to . . . unless . . . .
9. The political situation in . . . will continue to deteriorate unless . . . .
10. Ivan never volunteers in class. He doesn't say anything unless . . . .
11. Unless you . . . .

17-9 ADVERB CLAUSES OF CONDITION: USING *ONLY IF*

(a) The picnic will be canceled *only if it rains.* If it's windy, we'll go on the picnic. If it's cold, we'll go on the picnic. If it's damp and foggy, we'll go on the picnic. If it's unbearably hot, we'll go on the picnic.	*Only if* expresses the idea that there is only one condition that will cause a particular result.
(b) *Only if* it rains *will the picnic be canceled.*	When *only if* begins a sentence, the subject and verb of the main clause are inverted, as in (b).*

*Other subordinating conjunctions and prepositional phrases fronted by *only* at the beginning of a sentence require subject-verb inversion in the main clause:
> *Only when* the teacher dismisses us *can we stand* and *leave* the room.
> *Only after* the phone rang *did I realize* that I had fallen asleep in my chair.
> *Only in* my hometown *do I feel* at ease.

☐ EXERCISE 16. Using ONLY IF. (Chart 17-9)
> *Directions:* Use the given information to complete the sentences.

1. John must get a scholarship in order to go to school. That is the only condition under which he can go to school. If he doesn't get one, he can't go to school.
   He can go to school only if . . . he gets a scholarship.

2. You have to have an invitation in order to go to the party. That is the only condition under which you will be admitted. If you don't have an invitation, you can't go.
   You can go to the party only if . . . .

3. You have to have a student visa in order to study here. Unless you have a student visa, you can't go to school here.
   You can attend this school only if . . . .

4. Jimmy's mother doesn't want him to chew gum, but sometimes he chews it anyway.
   Jimmy . . . only if he's sure his mother won't find out.

5. If you want to go to the movie, we'll go. If you don't want to go, we won't go.
We . . . only if you want to.

6. The temperature has to reach 32°F / 0°C before water will freeze.
Water will freeze only if . . . .

7. You must study hard. Then you will pass the exam.
Only if you study hard . . . .

8. You have to have a ticket. Then you can get into the soccer stadium.
Only if you have a ticket . . . .

9. My parents make Jake finish his homework before he can watch TV in the evening.
Only if Jake's homework is finished . . . .

10. I have to get a job. Then I will have enough money to go to school.
Only if I get a job . . . .

Complete the following.

11. Yes, John, I will marry you—but only if . . . .

12. I . . . . only if . . . .

13. Only if . . . .

☐ EXERCISE 17. Using UNLESS and ONLY IF. (Charts 17-8 and 17-9)
Directions: Create sentences with the same meaning as the given ones. Use *only if* and *unless*.

1. If you don't study hard, you won't pass the test.
    → *You will pass the test only if you study hard.*
    → *You won't pass the test unless you study hard.*
2. If I don't get a job, I can't pay my bills.
3. Your clothes won't get clean if you don't use soap.
4. I can't take any pictures if I don't buy some film.
5. I don't wake up if the alarm clock doesn't ring.
6. If eggs aren't kept at the proper temperature, they won't hatch.
7. Don't borrow money from friends if you don't absolutely have to.
8. Anita doesn't talk in class if the teacher doesn't ask her specific questions.

☐ EXERCISE 18. Adverb clauses of condition. (Charts 17-6 → 17-9)
Directions: Using the given words, combine the following two ideas.

It may or may not rain. The party will be held inside/outside.

1. if → *If it rains, the party will be held inside.*
    → *If it doesn't rain, the party will be held outside.*

2. whether or not   5. in the event that
3. even if   6. unless
4. in case   7. only if

□ EXERCISE 19. Activity: adverb clauses. (Chapter 17)
  Directions: Work in pairs.
  Speaker A: Your book is open. Say the given words, then add your own words to
                complete the adverb clause (but do not complete the whole sentence).
  Speaker B: Your book is closed. Complete Speaker A's sentence.

  Example: Although I . . . .
  SPEAKER A *(book open):*   Although I wanted to go to the park and fly a kite . . . .
  SPEAKER B *(book closed):* Although I wanted to go to the park and fly a kite, I went to my
                            English class because I really need to improve my English.

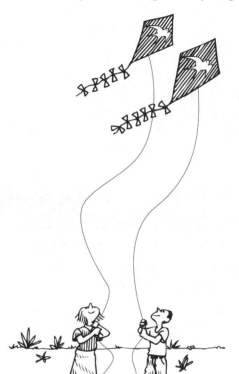

   1. Even if I . . . .
   2. Because I . . . .
   3. By the time I . . . .
   4. Even though I . . . .
   5. The next time I . . . .
   6. Until I . . . .
   7. Every time I . . . .

  Switch roles
   8. In the event that you . . . .
   9. Unless I . . . .
  10. Since I . . . .
  11. Only if I . . . .
  12. Now that I . . . .
  13. While some people are . . . .
  14. While I was walking . . . .

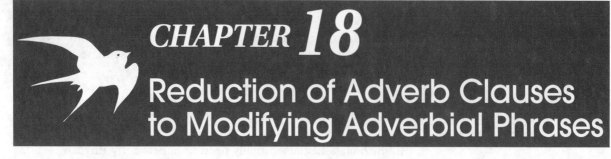

CHAPTER *18*
Reduction of Adverb Clauses to Modifying Adverbial Phrases

CONTENTS

18-1 INTRODUCTION

(a) ADVERB CLAUSE:	*While **I was walking** to class,* I ran into an old friend.	In Chapter 13, we discussed changing adjective clauses to modifying phrases (see Chart 13-13, p. 286). Some adverb clauses may also be changed to modifying phrases, and the ways in which the changes are made are the same:
(b) MODIFYING PHRASE:	*While **walking** to class,* I ran into an old friend.	
(c) ADVERB CLAUSE:	*Before **I left** for work,* I ate breakfast.	1. Omit the subject of the dependent clause and the ***be*** form of the verb, as in (b). OR
(d) MODIFYING PHRASE:	*Before **leaving** for work,* I ate breakfast.	2. If there is no ***be*** form of a verb, omit the subject and change the verb to ***-ing***, as in (d).
(e) CHANGE POSSIBLE:	*While **I** was sitting in class, **I** fell asleep.* *While sitting in class, **I** fell asleep.*	An adverb clause can be changed to a modifying phrase **only when the subject of the adverb clause and the subject of the main clause are the same.** A *modifying adverbial phrase* that is the reduction of an adverb clause *modifies the subject* of the main clause.
(f) CHANGE POSSIBLE:	*While **Ann** was sitting in class, **she** fell asleep. (clause)* *While sitting in class, **Ann** fell asleep.*	
(g) NO CHANGE POSSIBLE:	*While **the teacher** was lecturing to the class, **I** fell asleep.★*	No reduction (i.e., change) is possible if the subjects of the adverb clause and the main clause are different, as in (g) and (h).
(h) NO CHANGE POSSIBLE:	*While **we** were walking home, **a frog** hopped across the road in front of us.*	
(i) INCORRECT:	*While walking home, a frog hopped across the road in front of us.*	In (i): *While walking home* is called a "dangling modifier" or a "dangling participle," i.e., a modifier that is incorrectly "hanging alone" without an appropriate noun or pronoun subject to modify.
(j) INCORRECT:	*While watching TV last night, the phone rang.*	

★*While lecturing to the class, **I** fell asleep* means "While **I** was lecturing to the class, **I** fell asleep."

18-2 CHANGING TIME CLAUSES TO MODIFYING ADVERBIAL PHRASES

(a) CLAUSE: *Since Maria came to this country,* she has made many friends. (b) PHRASE: *Since coming to this country,* Maria has made many friends.	Adverb clauses beginning with **after**, **before**, **while**, and **since** can be changed to modifying adverbial phrases.
(c) CLAUSE: *After he (had) finished his homework,* Peter went to bed. (d) PHRASE: *After finishing his homework,* Peter went to bed. (e) PHRASE: *After having finished his homework,* Peter went to bed.	In (c): There is no difference in meaning between *After he finished* and *After he had finished.* (See Chart 3-3, p. 45.) In (d) and (e): There is no difference in meaning between *After finishing* and *After having finished.*
(f) PHRASE: Peter went to bed *after finishing his homework.*	A modifying adverbial phrase may follow the main clause, as in (f).

☐ EXERCISE 1. Changing time clauses to modifying adverbial phrases.
(Charts 18-1 and 18-2)

Directions: Underline the subject of the adverb clause and the subject of the main clause. Change the adverb clauses to modifying adverbial phrases if possible.

1. While Joe was driving to school yesterday, he had an accident.
   → *While driving to school yesterday, Joe had an accident.*

2. While Joe was watching TV last night, the telephone rang. *(no change)*

3. Before I came to class, I had a cup of coffee.

4. Before the student came to class, the teacher had already given a quiz.

5. Since I came here, I have learned a lot of English.

6. Since Bob opened his new business, he has been working 16 hours a day.

7. After Omar (had) finished breakfast, he left the house and went to his office.

8. Alex hurt his back while he was chopping wood.

9. You should always read a contract before you sign your name.

10. Before the waiter came to our table, I had already made up my mind to order shrimp.

11. Before you ask the librarian for help, you should make every effort to find the materials yourself.

12. While Jack was trying to sleep last night, a mosquito kept buzzing in his ear.

13. While Susan was climbing the mountain, she lost her footing and fell onto a ledge several feet below.

14. The Wilsons have experienced many changes in their lifestyle since they adopted twins.

15. After I heard Mary describe how cold it gets in Minnesota in the winter, I decided not to go there for my vacation in January.

18-3 EXPRESSING THE IDEA OF "DURING THE SAME TIME" IN MODIFYING ADVERBIAL PHRASES

(a) *While I was walking* down the street, *I* ran into an old friend. (b) *While walking* down the street, *I* ran into an old friend. (c) *Walking* down the street, *I* ran into an old friend. (d) *Hiking* through the woods yesterday, *we* saw a bear. (e) *Pointing* to the sentence on the board, *the teacher* explained the meaning of modifying phrases.	Sometimes *while* is omitted but the *-ing* phrase at the beginning of the sentence gives the same meaning (i.e., "during the same time"). (a), (b), and (c) have the same meaning.

18-4 EXPRESSING CAUSE AND EFFECT IN MODIFYING ADVERBIAL PHRASES

(f) *Because she needed* some money to buy a book, *Sue* cashed a check. (g) *Needing* some money to buy a book, *Sue* cashed a check. (h) *Because he lacked* the necessary qualifications, *he* was not considered for the job. (i) *Lacking* the necessary qualifications, *he* was not considered for the job.	Often an *-ing* phrase at the beginning of a sentence gives the meaning of "because." (f) and (g) have the same meaning. *Because* is not included in a modifying phrase. It is omitted, but the resulting phrase expresses a cause and effect relationship, as in (g) and (i).
(j) *Having seen* that movie before, *I don't want* to go again. (k) *Having seen* that movie before, *I didn't want* to go again.	*Having* + *past participle* gives the meaning not only of "because" but also of "before."
(l) *Because she was unable* to afford a car, *she* bought a bicycle. (m) *Being unable* to afford a car, *she* bought a bicycle. (n) *Unable* to afford a car, *she* bought a bicycle.	A form of *be* in the adverb clause may be changed to *being*. The use of *being* makes the cause and effect relationship clear. (l), (m), and (n) have the same meaning.

☐ EXERCISE 2. Modifying adverbial phrases. (Charts 18-3 and 18-4)
   Directions: Discuss the meaning of these sentences. Which ones give the meaning of *because?* Which ones give the meaning of *while?* Do some of the sentences give the idea of both *because* and *while?*

   1. Sitting on the airplane and watching the clouds pass beneath me, I let my thoughts wander to the new experiences that were in store for me during the next two years of living abroad.
   2. Being a self-supporting widow with three children, she has no choice but to work.
   3. Lying on her bed in peace and quiet, she soon forgot her troubles.
   4. Having already spent all of his last paycheck, he does not have any money to live on for the rest of the month.
   5. Watching the children's energetic play, I felt like an old man even though I am only forty.

6. Having brought up ten children of their own, the Smiths may be considered experts on child behavior.
7. Being totally surprised by his proposal of marriage, Carol could not find the words to reply.
8. Driving to my grandparents' house last night, we saw a young woman who was selling flowers. We stopped so that we could buy some for my grandmother.
9. Struggling against fatigue, I forced myself to put one foot in front of the other.
10. Having guessed at the correct answers for a good part of the test, I did not expect to get a high score.
11. Realizing that I had made a dreadful mistake when I introduced him as George Johnson, I walked over to him and apologized. I know his name is John George.
12. Tapping his fingers loudly on the desk top, he made his impatience and dissatisfaction known.

☐ EXERCISE 3. Modifying adverbial phrases. (Chart 18-4)
Directions: Change the adverb clauses to modifying adverbial phrases.

1. Because Sam didn't want to hurt her feelings, he didn't tell her the bad news.
   → *Not wanting to hurt her feelings, Sam didn't tell her the bad news.*
2. Because the little boy believed that no one loved him, he ran away from home.
3. Because she was not paying attention to where she was going, Rosa stepped into a hole and sprained her ankle.
4. Because I had forgotten to bring a pencil to the examination, I had to borrow one.
5. Because Chelsea is a vegetarian, she does not eat meat.
6. Because he has already flunked out of school once, Mike is determined to succeed this time.

☐ EXERCISE 4. Modifying adverbial phrases. (Charts 18-2 → 18-4)
Directions: Change the adverb clauses to modifying adverbial phrases.

1. Before I talked to you, I had never understood that formula.
2. Because he did not want to spend any more money this month, Larry decided against going to a restaurant for dinner. He made himself a sandwich instead.
3. After I read the chapter four times, I finally understood the author's theory.
4. Because I remembered that everyone makes mistakes, I softened my view of his seemingly inexcusable error.
5. Since he completed his Bachelor's degree, he has had three jobs, each one better than the last.
6. While I was traveling across the United States, I could not help being impressed by the great differences in terrain.
7. Before he gained national fame, the union leader had been an electrician in a small town.
8. Because we were enjoying the cool evening breeze and listening to the sounds of nature, we lost track of time.
9. Because she had never flown in an airplane before, the little girl was surprised and a little frightened when her ears popped.
10. Before he became vice-president of marketing and sales, Peter McKay worked as a sales representative.

☐ EXERCISE 5. Modifying adverbial phrases. (Charts 18-3 and 18-4)
   Directions: Combine the two sentences, making a modifying phrase out of the first sentence if possible.

   1. The children had nothing to do. They were bored.
      → *Having nothing to do, the children were bored.*
   2. I heard that Nadia was in the hospital. I called her family to find out what was wrong.
   3. We slowly approached the door to the hospital. The nurse stepped out to greet us.
   4. I live a long distance from my work. I have to commute daily by train.
   5. Heidi lives a long distance from her work. She has to commute daily by train.
   6. Abdul lives a long distance from his work. His car is essential.
   7. I did not want to inconvenience my friend by asking her to drive me to the airport. I decided to take a taxi.
   8. I was sitting on a large rock at the edge of a mountain stream. I felt at peace with the world.
   9. I am a married man. I have many responsibilities.
   10. The little boy was trying his best not to cry. He swallowed hard and began to speak.
   11. Anna kept one hand on the steering wheel. She opened a can of soda pop with her free hand.
   12. Anna kept one hand on the steering wheel. Bob handed her a can of pop to hold in the other hand.
   13. I recognized his face, but I had forgotten his name. I just smiled and said, "Hi."
   14. Martha was picking strawberries in the garden. A bumblebee stung her.
   15. Ann was convinced that she could never learn to play the piano. She stopped taking lessons.

☐ EXERCISE 6. Modifying adverbial phrases. (Charts 18-3 and 18-4)
   Directions: Make sentences by combining the ideas in Column A and Column B. Use the idea in Column A as a modifying adverbial phrase. Show logical relationships.

   Examples:

Column A	Column B
1. She was looking in the want ads in the Sunday newspaper.	A. Mary has a lot of responsibilities.
2. She had grown up overseas.	B. Ann found a good used car at a price she could afford to pay.
3. She is the vice-president of a large company.	C. Alice enjoys trying foods from other countries.

   → 1. *Looking in the want ads in the Sunday newspaper, Ann found a good used car at a price she could afford to pay.*

   → 2. *Having grown up overseas, Alice enjoys trying foods from other countries.*

   → 3. *Being the vice-president of a large company, Mary has a lot of responsibilities.*

Column A	Column B
1. They have sticky pads on their feet.	A. Sally didn't know what to expect when she went to the Thai restaurant for dinner.
2. He has worked with computers for many years.	B. Mice can hide in almost any part of a house.
3. She was born two months prematurely.	C. Rhinos are protected by law from poachers who kill them solely for their horns.
4. He had done everything he could for the patient.	D. The doctor left to attend other people.
5. She had never eaten Thai food before.	E. Nancy expects to be hired by a top company after graduation.
6. He had no one to turn to for help.	F. Diamonds are used extensively in industry to cut other hard minerals.
7. They are endangered species.	G. Flies can easily walk on the ceiling.
8. They are able to crawl into very small places.	H. Sam was forced to work out the problem by himself.
9. She has done very well in her studies and is finally nearly finished.	I. Mary needed special care for the first few days of her life.
10. They are extremely hard and nearly indestructible.	J. Ed has an excellent understanding of their limitations as well as their potential.

□ EXERCISE 7. Modifying adverbial phrases. (Charts 18-1 → 18-4)
Directions: Some (but not all) of the sentences contain DANGLING MODIFIERS (i.e., incorrectly used modifying adverbial phrases). Correct these errors.

1. After leaving the theater, we stopped at a coffee shop for a late night snack. *(no change)*

2. After leaving the theater, Tom's car wouldn't start, so we had to take a taxi home.
   → *After we left the theater, Tom's car wouldn't start, so we had to take a taxi home.*
   → *After leaving the theater, we discovered that Tom's car wouldn't start, so we took a taxi home.*

3. Not wanting to interrupt the conversation, I stood quietly and listened until I could have a chance to talk.

4. Being too young to understand death, my mother gave me a simple explanation of where my grandfather had gone.

5. When asked to explain his mistake, the new employee cleared his throat nervously.

6. While working in my office late last night, someone suddenly knocked loudly at my door and nearly scared me to death!

7. After hurrying to get everything ready for the picnic, it began to rain just as we were leaving.

8. While walking across the street at a busy intersection, a truck nearly ran over my foot.

18-5 USING *UPON* + *-ING* IN MODIFYING ADVERBIAL PHRASES

(a) ***Upon reaching*** the age of 21, I received my inheritance. (b) ***When I reached*** the age of 21, I received my inheritance.	Modifying adverbial phrases beginning with ***upon*** + ***-ing*** usually have the same meaning as adverb clauses introduced by ***when***. (a) and (b) have the same meaning.
(c) ***On reaching*** the age of 21, I received my inheritance.	***Upon*** can be shortened to ***on***. (a), (b), and (c) all have the same meaning.

☐ EXERCISE 8. Using UPON + -ING. (Chart 18-5)

Directions: Using the given information, make sentences with ***upon*** + ***-ing***.

1. When Tom saw his wife and child get off the airplane, he broke into a big smile.
   → *Upon seeing his wife and child get off the airplane, Tom broke into a big smile.*

2. When Tina crossed the marathon finish line, she fell in exhaustion.

3. When I looked in my wallet, I discovered I didn't have enough money to pay my restaurant bill.

4. I bowed my head when I met the king.

5. When Sam re-read the figures, he found that he had made a mistake.

6. The small child reached toward the lighted candle. When he discovered it was hot, he jerked his hand back, held it in front of himself, and stared at it curiously. Then he began to scream.

7. Mrs. Alexander nearly fainted when she learned that she had won the lottery.

8. When you finish the examination, bring your paper to the front of the room.

9. There must have been 300 students in the room on the first day of class. The professor slowly read through the list of names. When I heard my name, I raised my hand to identify myself.

10. Captain Cook had been sailing for many weeks with no land in sight. Finally, one of the sailors shouted, "Land ho!" When he heard this, Cook grabbed his telescope and searched the horizon.

☐ EXERCISE 9. Review: modifying adverbial phrases. (Chapter 18)

Directions: Change the adverb clause in each sentence to a modifying adverbial phrase if possible. Make any necessary changes in punctuation, capitalization, or word order.

1. After it spends some time in a cocoon, a caterpillar will emerge as a butterfly.

   → *After spending some time in a cocoon, a caterpillar will emerge as a butterfly.*

2. When the movie started, it suddenly got very quiet inside the theater. *(no change)*

3. When we entered the theater, we handed the usher our tickets.

   → *Upon entering the theater, we handed the usher our tickets.*

4. Because I was unprepared for the test, I didn't do well.

   → *Being unprepared for the test, I didn't do well.* OR: *Unprepared for the test, I didn't do well.*

5. Before I left on my trip, I checked to see what shots I would need.

6. Since Indians in the high Andes Mountains live in thin air, their hearts grow to be a larger than average size.

7. Because I hadn't understood the directions, I got lost.

8. My father reluctantly agreed to let me attend the game after he had talked it over with my mother.

9. When I discovered I had lost my key to the apartment, I called the building superintendent.

10. Jane's family hasn't received any news from her since she arrived in Australia two weeks ago.

11. Garcia Lopez de Cardenas accidentally discovered the Grand Canyon while he was looking for the legendary Lost City of Gold.

12. Because the forest area is so dry this summer, it is prohibited to light camp fires.

13. After we had to wait for more than half an hour, we were finally seated at the restaurant.

14. Before Maria got accepted on her country's Olympic running team, she had spent most of the two previous years in training.

15. Because George wasn't paying attention to his driving, he didn't see the large truck until it was almost too late.

☐ EXERCISE 10. Review: modifying adverbial phrases. (Chapter 18)

Directions: <u>Underline</u> the adverb clauses in the following. Change the adverb clauses to adverb phrases if possible. Make any necessary changes in punctuation, capitalization, or word order.

1. Alexander Graham Bell, a teacher of the deaf in Boston, invented the first telephone. One day in 1875, <u>while he was running a test on his latest attempt to create a machine</u> that could carry voices, he accidentally spilled acid on his coat. Naturally, he called for his assistant, Thomas A. Watson, who was in another room. Bell said, "Mr. Watson, come here. I want you." When Watson heard words coming from the machine, he immediately realized that their experiments had at last been successful. He rushed excitedly into the other room to tell Bell that he had heard his words over the machine.

    After Bell had successfully tested the new apparatus again and again, he confidently announced his invention to the world. For the most part, scientists appreciated his accomplishment, but the general public did not understand the revolutionary nature of Bell's invention. Because they believed the telephone was a toy with little practical application, most people paid little attention to Bell's announcement.

2. Wolves are much misunderstood animals. Because many people believe that wolves eagerly kill human beings, they fear them. However, the truth is that wolves avoid any contact with human beings. Wildlife biologists in the United States say there is no documented case of wolves attacking humans in the lower 48 states. More people are hurt and killed by buffaloes in Yellowstone Park than have ever been hurt by wolves in North America.

    Because they are strictly carnivorous, wolves hunt large animals such as elk and deer, as well as their mainstay, small animals such as mice and rabbits. And they are particularly fond of sheep. Killing ranchers' livestock has helped lead to wolves' bad reputation among people.

    Because it was relentlessly poisoned, trapped, and shot by ranchers and hunters, the timber wolf, a subspecies of the gray wolf, was eradicated in the lower 48 states by the 1940s. Not one wolf remained. In the 1970s, after they realized a mistake had been made, U.S. lawmakers passed laws to protect wolves.

Long ago, wolves could be found in almost all areas of the Northern Hemisphere throughout Asia, Europe, and North America. Today, after they have been unremittingly destroyed for centuries, they are found in few places, principally in sparsely populated areas of Alaska, Minnesota, Canada, and the northernmost regions of Russia and China.

□ EXERCISE 11. Review: modifying adverbial phrases. (Chapter 18)
Directions: Complete the sentences. Punctuate carefully.

1. After having finished my . . . .
2. Before going to . . . .
3. Since coming to . . . .
4. Sitting in the park the other day . . . .
5. Having heard a strange noise in the other room . . . .
6. Being new on the job . . . .
7. Being the largest city in the United States . . . .
8. Upon reaching our destination . . . .
9. Receiving no answer when he knocked on the door . . . .
10. Exhausted by the long hours of work . . . .

☐ EXERCISE 12. Error analysis: general review. (Chapters 16, 17, and 18)
   Directions: Correct the errors.

1. I was very tired, go to bed.

   → *I was very tired, so I went to bed.* OR: *I was very tired and went to bed.*

2. Because our leader could not attend the meeting, so it was canceled.

3. I and my wife likes to travel.

4. I always fasten my seat belt before to start the engine.

5. I don't like our classroom. Because it is hot and crowded. I hope we can change to a different room.

6. The day was very warm and humid, for that I turned on the air conditioner.

7. Upon I learned that my car couldn't be repaired for three days, I am very distressed.

8. Having missed the final examination because, the teacher gave me a failing grade.

9. Both my sister and my brother is going to be at the family reunion.

10. I hope my son will remain in school until he will finish his degree.

11. My brother has succeeded in business because of he works hard.

12. Luis stood up, turned toward me, and speaking so softly that I couldn't hear what he said.

13. I was lost. I could not find my parents neither my brother.

14. Having studied Greek for several years, Sarah's pronunciation was easy to understand.

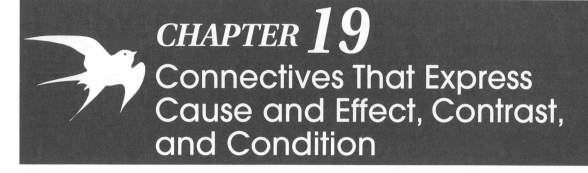

CHAPTER *19*
Connectives That Express Cause and Effect, Contrast, and Condition

---

CONTENTS

☐ EXERCISE 1. Preview. (Charts 19-1 → 19-3)
Directions: Correct the errors.

1. Because of Rosa's computer skills were poor she was not considered for the job.

2. Rosa's computer skills were poor therefore she was not considered for the job.

3. Because Rosa's computer skills were poor, therefore she was not considered for the job.

4. Because Rosa's computer skills were poor, so she was not considered for the job.

5. Due to her poor computer skills, Rosa was not considered for the job therefore.

6. Consequently Rosa's computer skills were poor, she was not considered for the job.

19-1 USING *BECAUSE OF* AND *DUE TO*

(a) **Because** *the weather was cold*, we stayed home.	**Because** introduces an adverb clause; it is followed by a subject and verb, as in (a).
(b) **Because of** *the cold weather*, we stayed home. (c) **Due to** *the cold weather*, we stayed home.	**Because of** and **due to** are phrasal prepositions; they are followed by a noun object, as in (b) and (c).
(d) **Due to the fact that** *the weather was cold*, we stayed home.	Sometimes, usually in more formal writing, **due to** is followed by a noun clause introduced by **the fact that**.
(e) We stayed home *because of the cold weather*. We stayed home *due to the cold weather*. We stayed home *due to the fact that the weather was cold*.	Like adverb clauses, these phrases can also follow the main clause, as in (e).

☐ **EXERCISE 2. Using BECAUSE and BECAUSE OF. (Charts 17-2 and 19-1)**
   Directions: Complete the sentences with either *because* or *because of*.

   1. We postponed our trip _____because of_____ the bad driving conditions.

   2. Sue's eyes were red _____because_____ she had been swimming in a chlorinated pool.

   3. We can't visit the museum tomorrow _____ it isn't open.

   4. Jim had to give up jogging _____ his sprained ankle.

   5. _____ heavy fog at the airport, we had to stay in London an extra day.

   6. _____ the elevator was broken, we had to walk up six flights of stairs.

   7. Thousands of Irish people emigrated to the United States _____ the potato famine in Ireland in the mid-19th century.

   8. The young couple decided not to buy the house _____ its dilapidated condition.

☐ **EXERCISE 3. Using BECAUSE OF and DUE TO. (Chart 19-1)**
   Directions: Using the ideas given in parentheses, complete the sentences.

   1. *(Our parents are generous.)* Because of _____our parents' generosity_____, all of the children in our family have received the best of everything.

   2. *(The traffic was heavy.)* We were late to the meeting due to _____

   _____ .

3. *(Bill's wife is ill.)* Bill has to do all of the cooking and cleaning because of

   _____ .

4. *(Dr. Robinson has done excellent research on wolves.)* Due to _____

   _____ , we know much more

   today about that endangered species than we did even five years ago.

5. *(It was noisy in the next apartment.)* I couldn't get to sleep last night because of

   _____ .

6. *(Circumstances are beyond my control.)* Due to _____

   _____ , I regret to say that I cannot be present at your daughter's

   wedding.

19-2 USING TRANSITIONS TO SHOW CAUSE AND EFFECT: *THEREFORE* AND *CONSEQUENTLY*

(a) Al failed the test because he didn't study. (b) Al didn't study. ***Therefore,*** he failed the test. (c) Al didn't study. ***Consequently,*** he failed the test.	(a), (b), and (c) have the same meaning. ***Therefore*** and ***consequently*** mean "as a result." In grammar, they are called *transitions* (or *conjunctive adverbs)*. Transitions connect the ideas between two sentences.

(d) Al didn't study. ***Therefore,*** he failed the test.
(e) Al didn't study. He, ***therefore,*** failed the test.
(f) Al didn't study. He failed the test, ***therefore.***
 	
POSITIONS OF A TRANSITION
    transition + s + v (+ rest of sentence)
    s + ***transition*** + v (+ rest of sentence)
    s + v (+ rest of sentence) + ***transition***
	A transition occurs in the second of two related sentences. Notice the patterns and punctuation in the examples. A period (NOT a comma) is used at the end of the first sentence.* The transition has several positions in the second sentence. The transition is separated from the rest of the sentence by commas.

(g) Al didn't study, *so* he failed the test.	COMPARE: A *transition* (e.g., ***therefore***) has several possible positions within the second sentence of the pair, as in (d), (e), and (f). A *conjunction* (e.g., ***so***) has only one possible position: between the two sentences. (See Chart 16-3, p. 355.) ***So*** cannot move around in the second sentence as ***therefore*** can.

*A semicolon is also possible in this situation. See the footnote to Chart 19-3, p. 389.

☐ **EXERCISE 4. Using THEREFORE and CONSEQUENTLY. (Chart 19-2)**
   Directions: Restate the sentences, using the given transitions. Use three alternative positions for the transitions, as shown in Chart 19-2. Punctuate carefully.

   1. The children stayed home because a storm was approaching. *(therefore)*

   _____

   _____

   _____

2. I didn't have my umbrella, so I got wet. *(consequently)*

_____

_____

_____

☐ EXERCISE 5. Showing cause and effect. (Charts 16-3, 17-2, 19-1, and 19-2)
Directions: Punctuate the sentences. Add capital letters if necessary.

1. *adverb clause:*   Because it was cold she wore a coat.

2. *adverb clause:*   She wore a coat because it was cold.

3. *prepositional phrase:*   Because of the cold weather she wore a coat.

4. *prepositional phrase:*   She wore a coat because of the cold weather.

5. *transition:*   The weather was cold therefore she wore a coat.

6. *transition:*   The weather was cold she therefore wore a coat.

7. *transition:*   The weather was cold she wore a coat therefore.

8. *conjunction:*   The weather was cold so she wore a coat.

☐ EXERCISE 6. Showing cause and effect. (Charts 17-2, 19-1, and 19-2)
Directions: Punctuate the sentences. Add capital letters if necessary.

1. Pat always enjoyed studying sciences in high school therefore she decided to major in biology in college.

2. Due to recent improvements in the economy fewer people are unemployed.

3. Last night's storm damaged the power lines consequently the town was without electricity for several hours.

4. Because of the snowstorm only five students came to class the teacher therefore canceled the class.

5. Anna always makes numerous spelling mistakes in her compositions because she does not use a dictionary when she writes.

19-3 SUMMARY OF PATTERNS AND PUNCTUATION

ADVERB CLAUSE	(a) **Because** *it was hot,* we went swimming. (b) We went swimming **because** *it was hot.*	An *adverb clause* may precede or follow an independent clause. PUNCTUATION: A comma is used if the adverb clause comes first.
PREPOSITION	(c) **Because of** *the hot weather,* we went swimming. (d) We went swimming **because of** *the hot weather.*	A *preposition* is followed by a noun object, not by a subject and verb. PUNCTUATION: A comma is usually used if the prepositional phrase precedes the subject and verb of the independent clause.
TRANSITION	(e) It was hot. **Therefore,** *we went swimming.* (f) It was hot. *We,* **therefore,** *went swimming.* (g) It was hot. *We went swimming,* **therefore.**	A *transition* is used with the second sentence of a pair. It shows the relationship of the second idea to the first idea. A transition is movable within the second sentence. PUNCTUATION: A period is used between the two independent clauses.* A comma may NOT be used to separate the clauses. Commas are usually used to set the transition off from the rest of the sentence.
CONJUNCTION	(h) It was hot, **so** *we went swimming.*	A conjunction comes between two independent clauses. PUNCTUATION: Usually a comma is used immediately in front of a conjunction.

*A semicolon (;) may be used instead of a period between the two independent clauses.
   It was hot; therefore, we went swimming.
   It was hot; we, therefore, went swimming.
   It was hot; we went swimming, therefore.
In general, a semicolon can be used instead of a period between any two sentences that are closely related in meaning.
Example: *Peanuts are not nuts; they are beans.* Notice that a small letter, not a capital letter, immediately follows a semicolon.

☐ EXERCISE 7. Showing cause and effect. (Chart 19-3)
   Directions: Using the given words, combine the two ideas.

   PART I. We postponed our trip. The weather was bad.
   1. because → *We postponed our trip because the weather was bad.*
                → *Because the weather was bad, we postponed our trip.*

   2. therefore   5. because of
   3. since   6. consequently
   4. so   7. due to (the fact that)

   PART II. She missed class. She was ill.
   1. because of   4. so
   2. because   5. due to (the fact that)
   3. consequently   6. therefore

□ EXERCISE 8. Showing cause and effect. (Charts 19-2 and 19-3)
  Directions: Combine ideas, using the words in parentheses.

1. We stayed home. The weather was bad. *(because)*

   → *We stayed home because the weather was bad.* OR
   → *Because the weather was bad, we stayed home.*

2. Emily has never wanted to return to the Yukon to live. The winters are too severe. *(because of)*

3. It is important to wear a hat on cold days. We lose sixty percent of our body heat through our head. *(since)*

4. When I was in my teens and twenties, it was easy for me to get into an argument with my father. Both of us can be stubborn and opinionated. *(for)*

5. A camel can go completely without water for eight to ten days. It is an ideal animal for desert areas. *(due to the fact that)*

6. Bill couldn't pick us up after the concert. His car wouldn't start. *(therefore)*

7. Robert had to ask many of the same questions again the next time he talked to the travel agent. He did not pay close attention to what she said when he went to see her at her office last week. *(so)*

8. A tomato is classified as a fruit, but most people consider it a vegetable. It is often eaten in salads along with lettuce, onions, cucumbers and other vegetables. *(since)*

9. There is consumer demand for ivory. Many African elephants are being slaughtered ruthlessly. Many people who care about saving these animals from extinction refuse to buy any item made from ivory. *(due to, consequently)*

10. Most 15th-century Europeans believed the world was flat and that a ship could conceivably sail off the end of the earth. Many sailors of the time refused to venture forth with explorers into unknown waters. *(because)*

19-4 OTHER WAYS OF EXPRESSING CAUSE AND EFFECT: *SUCH . . . THAT* AND *SO . . . THAT*

(a) Because the weather was nice, we went to the zoo. (b) It was *such nice weather that* we went to the zoo. (c) The weather was *so nice that* we went to the zoo.	Examples (a), (b), and (c) have the same meaning.
(d) It was *such good coffee that* I had another cup. (e) It was *such a foggy day that* we couldn't see the road.	*Such . . . that* encloses a modified noun: *such + adjective + noun + that*
(f) The coffee is *so hot that* I can't drink it. (g) I'm *so hungry that* I could eat a horse.	*So . . . that* encloses an adjective or adverb: $so + \left\{ \begin{array}{c} adjective \\ or \\ adverb \end{array} \right\} + that$
(h) She speaks *so fast that* I can't understand her. (i) He walked *so quickly that* I couldn't keep up with him.	
(j) She made *so many mistakes that* she failed the exam. (k) He has *so few friends that* he is always lonely. (l) She has *so much money that* she can buy whatever she wants. (m) He had *so little trouble* with the test *that* he left twenty minutes early.	*So . . . that* is used with *many*, *few*, *much*, and *little*.
(n) It was *such a good book* (that) I couldn't put it down. (o) I was *so hungry* (that) I didn't wait for dinner to eat something.	Sometimes, primarily in speaking, *that* is omitted.

□ **EXERCISE 9. Using SUCH . . . THAT and SO . . . THAT. (Chart 19-4)**
Directions: Combine the sentences by using *so . . . that* or *such . . . that*.

1. This tea is good. I think I'll have another cup.
   → *This tea is so good that I think I'll have another cup.*

2. This is good tea. I think I'll have another cup.
   → *This is such good tea that I think I'll have another cup.*

3. It was an expensive car. We couldn't afford to buy it.

4. The car was expensive. We couldn't afford to buy it.

5. The weather was hot. You could fry an egg on the sidewalk.

6. During the summer, we had hot and humid weather. It was uncomfortable just sitting in a chair doing nothing.

7. I don't feel like going to work. We're having beautiful weather.

8. Ivan takes everything in life too seriously. He is unable to experience the small joys and pleasures of daily living.

9. I've met too many people in the last few days. I can't possibly remember all of their names.

10. Tommy ate too much candy. He got a stomachache.

11. It took us only ten minutes to get there. There was little traffic.

12. In some countries, few students are accepted by the universities. As a result, admission is virtually a guarantee of a good job upon graduation.

☐ EXERCISE 10. Using SUCH . . . THAT and SO . . . THAT. (Chart 19-4)
Directions: Make sentences using **such** or **so** by combining the ideas in Column A and Column B.

Example: The wind was strong. → *The wind was so strong that it blew my hat off my head.*

Column A

1. The wind was strong.
2. Karen is a good pianist.
3. The radio was too loud.
4. Small animals in the forest move about quickly.
5. Olga did poor work.
6. The food was too hot.
7. There are many leaves on a single tree.
8. The tornado struck with great force.
9. Grandpa held me tightly when he hugged me.
10. Few students showed up for class.
11. Sally used too much paper when she was writing her report.

Column B

A. It burned my tongue.
B. She was fired from her job.
✓ C. It blew my hat off my head.
D. The teacher postponed the test.
E. It is impossible to count them.
F. It lifted automobiles off the ground.
G. I couldn't hear what Michael was saying.
H. I'm surprised she didn't go into music professionally.
I. The wastepaper basket overflowed.
J. One can barely catch a glimpse of them.
K. I couldn't breathe for a moment.

☐ EXERCISE 11. Using SO . . . THAT. (Chart 19-4)
Directions: Work in pairs, in groups, or as a class.
Speaker A: Your book is open. Give the cue and engage Speaker B in conversation.
Speaker B: Your book is closed. Answer the *how*-question using **so . . . that**.

Example: Think of a time you were tired. How tired were you?
SPEAKER A: Think of a time you were very tired. Can you remember one particular time?
SPEAKER B: There was one time when I'd stayed up all night writing a paper.
SPEAKER A: And you were very tired the next morning, right? How tired were you?
SPEAKER B: I was so tired that I almost fell asleep in my morning classes.

Think of a time you were

1. . . . nervous. How nervous were you?
2. . . . angry. How angry were you?
3. . . . happy. How happy were you?
4. . . . surprised. How surprised were you?
5. . . . exhausted. How exhausted were you?
6. . . . unhappy/embarrassed/glad/sick/sad/ frightened/excited/disappointed/etc.

19-5 EXPRESSING PURPOSE: USING *SO THAT*

(a) I turned off the TV *in order to* enable my roommate to study in peace and quiet.	***In order to*** expresses *purpose.* (See Chart 15-1, p. 326.) In (a): I turned off the TV for a purpose. The purpose was to make it possible for my roommate to study in peace and quiet.
(b) I turned off the TV *so (that)* my roommate could study in peace and quiet.	***So that*** also expresses *purpose.** It expresses the same meaning as ***in order to***. The word "that" is often omitted, especially in speaking.
SO THAT + *CAN* or *COULD* (c) I'm going to cash a check *so that I can* buy my textbooks. (d) I cashed a check *so that I could* buy my textbooks.	***So that*** is often used instead of ***in order to*** when the idea of ability is being expressed. ***Can*** is used in the adverb clause for a present/future meaning. In (c): *so that I can buy = in order to be able to buy*. ***Could*** is used after ***so that*** in past sentences.**
SO THAT + *WILL* / SIMPLE PRESENT or *WOULD* (e) I'll take my umbrella *so that I won't* get wet. (f) I'll take my umbrella *so that I don't* get wet. (g) Yesterday I took my umbrella *so that I wouldn't* get wet.	In (e): *so that I won't get wet = in order to make sure that I won't get wet.* In (f): It is sometimes possible to use the simple present after ***so that*** in place of ***will***; the simple present expresses a future meaning. ***Would*** is used in past sentences; as in (g).

*NOTE: ***In order that*** has the same meaning as ***so that*** but is less commonly used.
   Example: *I turned off the TV **in order that** my roommate could study in peace and quiet.*
   Both ***so that*** and ***in order that*** introduce adverb clauses. It is unusual, but possible, to put these adverb clauses at the beginning of a sentence: ***So that*** *my roommate could study in peace and quiet, I turned off the TV.*

Also possible but less common: the use of ***may* or ***might*** in place of ***can*** or ***could***: e.g., *I cashed a check **so that I might** buy my textbooks.*

□ EXERCISE 13. Using SO THAT. (Chart 19-5)
   Directions: Combine the ideas by using ***so (that)***.

1. Please turn down the radio. I want to be able to get to sleep.
   → *Please turn down the radio so (that) I can get to sleep.*

2. My wife turned down the radio. I wanted to be able to get to sleep.
   → *My wife turned down the radio so (that) I could get to sleep.*

3. Put the milk in the refrigerator. We want to make sure it won't (OR doesn't) spoil.
   → *Put the milk in the refrigerator so (that) it won't (OR doesn't) spoil.*

4. I put the milk in the refrigerator. I wanted to make sure it didn't spoil.
   → *I put the milk in the refrigerator so (that) it wouldn't spoil.*

5. Please be quiet. I want to be able to hear what Sharon is saying.

6. I asked the children to be quiet. I wanted to be able to hear what Sharon was saying.

7. I'm going to cash a check. I want to make sure that I have enough money to go to the market.

8. I cashed a check yesterday. I wanted to make sure that I had enough money to go to the market.

9. Ann and Larry have a six-year-old child. Tonight they're going to hire a babysitter. They want to be able to go out with some friends.

10. Last week Ann and Larry hired a babysitter. They wanted to be able to go to a dinner party at the home of Larry's boss.

11. Be sure to put the meat in the oven at 5:00. You want to be sure that it will be (OR is) ready to eat by 6:30.

12. Yesterday I put the meat in the oven at 5:00. I wanted it to be ready to eat by 6:30.

13. I'm going to leave the party early. I want to be able to get a good night's sleep tonight.

14. When it started to rain, Harry opened his umbrella. He wanted to be sure he didn't get wet.

15. The little boy pretended to be sick. He wanted to stay home from school.

16. A lot of people were standing in front of me. I stood on tiptoes. I wanted to see the parade better.

☐ EXERCISE 14. Using SO THAT. (Chart 19-5)
Directions: Complete the sentences in Column A with the ideas in Column B. Pay special attention to the verb forms following *so that*.

Example: Ali borrowed an eraser so that . . . .
→ *Ali borrowed an eraser so that he could erase a mistake in his composition.*

Column A

1. Ali borrowed an eraser so that . . . .
2. I turned on the radio so that . . . .
3. I need to buy some detergent so that . . . .
4. Roberto fixed the leak in the boat so that . . . .
5. Mr. Kwan is studying the history and government of Canada so that . . . .
6. Ms. Gow put on her reading glasses so that . . . .
7. Jane is taking a course in auto mechanics so that . . . .
8. Omar is working hard to impress his supervisor so that . . . .
9. Po is saving his money so that . . . .
10. During the parade, Toshi lifted his daughter to his shoulder so that . . . .

Column B

A. wash my clothes
B. read the fine print at the bottom of the contract
C. not sink
✔ D. erase a mistake in his composition
E. travel in Europe next summer
F. listen to the news
G. see the dancers in the street
H. fix her own car
I. become a Canadian citizen
J. be considered for a promotion at his company

☐ EXERCISE 15. Using SO THAT. (Chart 19-5)
Directions: Complete the sentences with your own words.

Examples: Sam took lots of pictures on his vacation so (that) . . . .
→ *Sam took lots of pictures on his vacation so (that) he could show us where he'd been.*

. . . so (that) I could see better.
→ *I moved to the front of the room so (that) I could see better.*

1. I need a pen so (that) . . . .
2. . . . so (that) he can improve his English.
3. I turned on the TV so (that) . . . .
4. Mary hurried to get the child out of the road so (that) . . . .
5. . . . so (that) he wouldn't miss his important appointment.
6. I'm taking a bus instead of flying so (that) . . . .
7. . . . so (that) I could tell him the news in person.

8. . . . so (that) his children will have a better life.

9. Martina is trying to improve her English so (that) . . . .

10. . . . so (that) the celebration would be a great success.

11. Tarek borrowed some money from his friend so (that) . . . .

12. . . . so (that) you can be ready to leave on time.

☐ EXERCISE 16. Summary: cause and effect. (Charts 19-2 → 19-5)
Directions: Using the given words, make sentences about yourself, your friends, your family, your classes, today's weather, current events in the world, etc.

1. now that
2. therefore
3. for (meaning *because*)
4. consequently
5. so (meaning *therefore*)
6. since (meaning *because*)
7. in order to
8. so that
9. so . . . that
10. such . . . that
11. because
12. because of
13. due to
14. due to the fact that

19-6 SHOWING CONTRAST (UNEXPECTED RESULT)

All these sentences have the same meaning. The idea of cold weather is contrasted with the idea of going swimming. Usually if the weather is cold, one does not go swimming, so going swimming in cold weather is an "unexpected result." It is surprising that the speaker went swimming in cold weather.

ADVERB CLAUSES	*even though* *although* *though*	(a) *Even though it was cold*, I went swimming. (b) *Although it was cold*, I went swimming. (c) *Though it was cold*, I went swimming.
CONJUNCTIONS	*but . . . anyway* *but . . . still* *yet . . . still*	(d) It was cold, *but* I went swimming *anyway*. (e) It was cold, *but* I *still* went swimming. (f) It was cold, *yet* I *still* went swimming.
TRANSITIONS	*nevertheless* *nonetheless* *however . . . still*	(g) It was cold. *Nevertheless*, I went swimming. (h) It was cold; *nonetheless*, I went swimming. (i) It was cold. *However*, I *still* went swimming.
PREPOSITIONS	*despite* *in spite of* *despite the fact that* *in spite of the fact that*	(j) I went swimming *despite* the cold weather. (k) I went swimming *in spite of* the cold weather. (l) I went swimming *despite the fact that* the weather was cold. (m) I went swimming *in spite of the fact that* the weather was cold.

☐ EXERCISE 17. Showing contrast (unexpected result). (Chart 19-6)
Directions: Complete the sentences with the given words. Pay close attention to the given punctuation and capitalization.

PART I. Complete the sentences with *but*, *even though*, or *nevertheless*.

1. Bob ate a large dinner. _____Nevertheless_____, he is still hungry.

2. Bob ate a large dinner, _____but_____ he is still hungry.

3. Bob is still hungry _____ even though _____ he ate a large dinner.

4. I had a lot of studying to do, _____ I went to a movie anyway.

5. I had a lot of studying to do. _____, I went to a movie.

6. _____ I had a lot of studying to do, I went to a movie.

7. I finished all of my work _____ I was very sleepy.

8. I was very sleepy, _____ I finished all of my work anyway.

9. I was very sleepy. _____, I finished all of my work.

PART II. Complete the sentences with *yet, although,* or *however*.

10. I washed my hands. _____, they still looked dirty.

11. I washed my hands, _____ they still looked dirty.

12. _____ I washed my hands, they still looked dirty.

13. Diana didn't know how to swim, _____ she jumped into the swimming pool.

14. _____ Diana didn't know how to swim, she jumped into the swimming pool.

15. Diana didn't know how to swim. _____, she jumped into the swimming pool.

☐ EXERCISE 18. Showing contrast (unexpected result). (Chart 19-6)
Directions: Add commas, periods, and capital letters as necessary. Do not add, omit, or change any words.

1. Anna's father gave her some good advice nevertheless she did not follow it.

→ *Anna's father gave her some good advice. Nevertheless, she did not follow it.*

2. Anna's father gave her some good advice but she didn't follow it.

3. Even though Anna's father gave her some good advice she didn't follow it.

4. Anna's father gave her some good advice she did not follow it however.

5. Thomas was thirsty I offered him some water he refused it.

6. Thomas refused the water although he was thirsty.

7. Thomas was thirsty nevertheless he refused the glass of water I brought him.

8. Thomas was thirsty yet he refused to drink the water that I offered him.

□ EXERCISE 19. Showing contrast (unexpected result). (Chart 19-6)
    Directions: Combine the ideas in the two sentences, using the given words. Discuss correct punctuation. Use the negative if necessary to make a logical statement.

    1. *We went for a walk. It was raining.*
       even though
       but . . . anyway
       nevertheless
       in spite of
       because

    2. *His grades were low. He was admitted to the university.*
       although
       yet . . . still
       nonetheless
       despite
       because of

□ EXERCISE 20. Showing opposition (unexpected result). (Chart 19-6)
    Directions: Complete the sentences with your own words. Add commas where appropriate.

    1. I had a cold but I _____ anyway.

    2. Even though I had a cold I _____

    3. Although I didn't study _____

    4. I didn't study but _____ anyway.

    5. I got an "A" on the test even though _____

    6. Even though Howard is a careful driver _____

    7. Even though the food they served for dinner tasted terrible _____

    8. My shirt still has coffee stains on it even though _____

    9. I still trust him even though _____

    10. Even though he was drowning no one _____

    11. Although I tried to be very careful _____

    12. Even though Ruth is one of my best friends _____

    13. It's still hot in here even though _____

    14. Even though I had a big breakfast _____

☐ EXERCISE 21. Showing contrast (unexpected result). (Chart 19-6)
  Directions: Create sentences with the same meaning by using ***in spite of*** or ***despite***.

  1. Even though her grades were low, she was admitted to the university.
     → *In spite of her low grades,*
     → *Despite her low grades,*
     → *In spite of the fact that her grades were low,* } *she was admitted to the university.*
     → *Despite the fact that her grades were low,*
  2. I like living in the dorm even though it is noisy.
  3. Even though the work was hard, they enjoyed themselves.
  4. They wanted to climb the mountain even though it was dangerous.
  5. Although the weather was extremely hot, they went jogging in the park.
  6. He is unhappy even though he has a vast fortune.

☐ EXERCISE 22. Showing contrast (unexpected result). (Chart 19-6)
  Directions: Complete the sentences, punctuating carefully. (Correct punctuation is not indicated in the given cues.) Capitalize as necessary.

  1. I didn't . . . but . . . anyway.

  2. He is very old yet he still . . . .

  3. . . . nevertheless we arrived on schedule.

  4. Even though she wanted . . . .

  5. I wanted . . . however I . . . because . . . .

  6. The teacher . . . even though . . . .

  7. Although . . . only . . . years old . . . .

  8. She never went to school however she . . . despite her lack of education.

  9. Despite the fact that my . . . .

  10. I have decided to . . . even though . . . .

19-7 SHOWING DIRECT CONTRAST

All of the sentences have the same meaning.

ADVERB CLAUSES	*while*	(a) Mary is rich, *while John is poor.*
		(b) John is poor, *while Mary is rich.*
	whereas	(c) Mary is rich, *whereas John is poor.*
		(d) *Whereas Mary is rich,* John is poor.
CONJUNCTION	*but*	(e) Mary is rich, *but* John is poor.
		(f) John is poor, *but* Mary is rich.
TRANSITIONS	*however*	(g) Mary is rich; *however,* John is poor.
		(h) John is poor; Mary is rich, *however.*
	on the other hand	(i) Mary is rich. John, *on the other hand,* is poor.
		(j) John is poor. Mary, *on the other hand,* is rich.

□ EXERCISE 23. Showing direct contrast. (Chart 19-7)
    Directions: Create sentences with the same meaning by using **however** or **on the other hand**. Punctuate carefully.

    1. Florida has a warm climate, whereas Alaska has a cold climate.
    2. While Fred is a good student, his brother is lazy.
    3. In the United States, gambling casinos are not legal in most places, while in my country it is possible to gamble in any city or town.
    4. Sue and Ron are expecting a child. Sue is hoping for a boy, whereas Ron is hoping for a girl.
    5. Old people in my country usually live with their children, whereas the old in the United States often live by themselves.

□ EXERCISE 24. Showing direct contrast. (Chart 19-7)
    Directions: Complete the sentences with your own words.

    1. Some people really enjoy swimming, while others . . . *are afraid of water.*

    2. In the United States, people drive on the right-hand side of the road. However, people in . . . .

    3. While my apartment always seems to be a mess, my . . . .

    4. Marge keeps to herself and has few friends. Carol, on the other hand, ...

    5. People who grew up on farms are accustomed to dealing with various kinds of animals. However, city people like myself . . . .

    6. Teak is a hard wood that is difficult to cut. Balsa, on the other hand, ...

    7. My oldest son is shy, while my youngest son . . . .

    8. I'm right-handed. That means that I can accomplish difficult manipulations with my right hand. However, ...

□ EXERCISE 25. Activity: expressing direct contrast. (Chart 19-7)
    Directions: What aspects of your country and the United States or Canada are in contrast? Use **while, whereas, however, on the other hand**.

    1. Size?
    2. Population?
    3. Food?
    4. Time of meals?
    5. Climate?
    6. Political system?
    7. Economic system?
    8. Educational system?
    9. Religion?
    10. Student life?
    11. Coffee/tea?
    12. Role of women?
    13. Language?
    14. Educational costs?
    15. Medical care?
    16. Family relationships?
    17. Public transportation?
    18. Length of history?
    19. Dating customs?
    20. Predictability of the weather?

☐ EXERCISE 26. Showing cause and effect and contrast.
(Charts 19-1, 19-2, 19-7, and 19-8)

Directions: Complete the sentences, using the words and phrases below. There may be more than one possible completion. Add any necessary punctuation and capitalization.

although	*despite the fact that*	*nevertheless*
because	*even though*	*now that*
because of	*however*	*therefore*
but		

1. It was cold and wet ___. Nevertheless,___ Bob put on his swimming suit and went to the beach.

2. I can't ride my bicycle _____ there isn't any air in one of the tires.

3. I got to class on time _____ I had missed my bus.

4. Brian used to be an active person, but now he has to limit his activities _____ problems with his health.

5. It should be easy for Bob to find more time to spend with his children _____ he no longer has to work in the evenings and on weekends.

6. Jake is a very good student of languages. His brother Michael _____ has never been able to master another language.

7. The ancient Aztecs of Mexico had no technology for making tools from metal _____ they had sharp knives and spears. They made them from a stone called obsidian.

8. Garlic was believed in ancient Rome to make people courageous _____ Roman soldiers ate large quantities of it before a battle.

9. I usually enjoy attending amateur productions in small community theaters. The play we attended last night _____ was so bad that I wanted to leave after the first act.

10. Some snakes are poisonous _____ others are harmless.

11. Roberta missed the meeting without a good reason _____ she had been told that it was critical that she be there. I wouldn't want to be in her shoes at work tomorrow.

19-8 EXPRESSING CONDITIONS: USING *OTHERWISE* AND *OR (ELSE)*

ADVERB CLAUSE	(a) *If I don't eat breakfast,* I get hungry. (b) You'll be late *if you don't hurry.* (c) You'll get wet *unless you take your umbrella.*	*If* and *unless* state conditions that produce certain results. (See Charts 17-5 and 17-8, pp. 367 and 370.)
TRANSITION	(d) I always eat breakfast. *Otherwise,* I get hungry during class. (e) You'd better hurry. *Otherwise,* you'll be late. (f) Take your umbrella. *Otherwise,* you'll get wet.	*Otherwise* expresses the idea "if the opposite is true, then there will be a certain result." In (d): *otherwise* = *if I don't eat breakfast.*
CONJUNCTION	(g) I always eat breakfast, *or (else)* I get hungry during class. (h) You'd better hurry, *or (else)* you'll be late. (i) Take your umbrella, *or (else)* you'll get wet.	*Or else* and *otherwise* have the same meaning.

☐ EXERCISE 27. Using OTHERWISE and OR (ELSE). (Chart 19-8)
Directions: Create sentences with the same meaning by using *otherwise.*

1. If I don't call my mother, she'll start worrying about me.

   → *I am going to / should / had better / have to / must call my mother. Otherwise, she'll start worrying about me.*

2. If you don't leave now, you'll be late for class.

3. If you don't go to bed, your cold will get worse.

4. Unless you have a ticket, you can't get into the theater.

5. You can't enter that country unless you have a passport.

6. If Tom doesn't get a job soon, his family won't have enough money for food.

7. Only if you speak both Japanese and Chinese fluently will you be considered for that job.*

8. Mary can go to school only if she gets a scholarship.

9. If I don't wash my clothes tonight, I won't have any clean clothes to wear tomorrow.

---

*Notice that the subject and verb in the main clause are inverted because the sentence begins with *only if.*
See Chart 17-9, pp. 371.

☐ EXERCISE 28. Using OTHERWISE and OR (ELSE). (Chart 19-8)
   Directions: Complete the sentences, punctuating correctly. Use capital letters where appropriate.

1. I am going to . . . even if . . . .
2. We have no choice we have to . . . whether . . . .
3. I will go to . . . only if . . . .
4. . . . is very inconsiderate he plays his record player even if . . . .

5. I can't . . . unless . . . .
6. Tomorrow I'd better . . . otherwise . . . .
7. You should . . . in case . . . .
8. I will . . . only if . . . .
9. I will . . . unless . . . .
10. . . . must . . . otherwise . . . .

19-9 SUMMARY OF CONNECTIVES: CAUSE AND EFFECT, CONTRAST, CONDITION

	ADVERB CLAUSE WORDS		TRANSITIONS	CONJUNCTIONS	PREPOSITIONS
CAUSE AND EFFECT	*because* *since* *now that*	*so (that)*	*therefore* *consequently*	*so* *for*	*because of* *due to*
CONTRAST	*even though* *although* *though*	*whereas* *while*	*however* *nevertheless* *nonetheless* *on the other hand*	*but (. . . anyway)* *yet (. . . still)*	*despite* *in spite of*
CONDITION	*if* *unless* *only if* *even if* *whether or not*	*in case* *in the event that*	*otherwise*	*or (else)*	

☐ EXERCISE 29. Summary of connectives. (Chart 19-9)
   Directions: Using the two ideas of *to study* and *to pass or fail the exam*, complete the sentences. Punctuate and capitalize correctly.

1. Because I did not study _____ *, I failed the exam.* _____

2. I failed the exam because _____

3. Although I studied _____

4. I did not study   therefore _____

5. I did not study   however _____

6. I studied   nevertheless _____

7. Even though I did not study _____

8. I did not study   so _____

9. Since I did not study _____

10. If I study for the test _____

11. Unless I study for the test _____

12. I must study   otherwise _____

13. Even if I study _____

14. I did not study   consequently _____

15. I did not study   nonetheless _____

16. I will probably fail the test whether _____

17. I failed the exam   for _____

18. I have to study so that _____

19. Only if I study _____

20. I studied hard   yet _____

21. You'd better study   or else _____

☐ EXERCISE 30. Summary of connectives. (Chart 19-9)
Directions: Using the ideas of to be hungry (or not to be hungry) and to eat breakfast (or not to eat breakfast), complete the following. Punctuate and capitalize correctly.

1. Because I was not hungry this morning _____

2. Because I ate breakfast this morning _____ now.

3. Because I was hungry this morning _____

4. I did not eat breakfast this morning even though _____

5. Although I was hungry this morning _____

6. I was hungry this morning   therefore _____

7. I was hungry this morning   nevertheless _____

8. I was so hungry this morning _____

9. I was not hungry this morning   but _____

10. I ate breakfast this morning even though _____

11. Since I did not eat breakfast this morning _____

12. I ate breakfast this morning   nonetheless _____

13. I was not hungry   so _____

14. Even though I did not eat breakfast this morning _____

15. I never eat breakfast unless _____

16. I always eat breakfast whether or not _____

17. I eat breakfast even if _____

18. Now that I have eaten breakfast _____

19. I eat breakfast only if _____

20. I ate breakfast this morning   yet _____

21. Even if I am hungry _____

22. I was not hungry   however _____

☐ EXERCISE 31. Summary of connectives.   (Chart 19-9)
   Directions: Using the given words, combine the following two ideas. The time is now, so use present and future tenses.

   (a) **to go (or not to go) to the beach**   (b) **hot, cold, nice weather**

   1. because → *Because the weather is cold, we aren't going to go to the beach.*
                 → *We're going to go to the beach because the weather is hot.*

   2. so . . . that   9. because of   16. therefore
   3. so   10. consequently   17. only if
   4. nevertheless   11. as soon as   18. nonetheless
   5. despite   12. such . . . that   19. in spite of
   6. now that   13. since   20. even if
   7. once   14. but . . . anyway   21. yet . . . still
   8. although   15. unless   22. whether . . . or not

☐ EXERCISE 32. Summary of connectives.   (Chart 19-9)
   Directions: Complete the sentences, adding punctuation and capitalization.

   1. While some people are optimists . . . .

   2. Even though he drank a glass of water . . . still . . . .

   3. Even if she invites me to her party . . . .

   4. I have never been to Hawaii my parents however . . . .

   5. I couldn't . . . for my arms were full of packages.

   6. I need to borrow some money so that . . . .

   7. The airport was closed due to fog therefore . . . .

   8. . . . therefore the airport was closed.

   9. As soon as the violinist played the last note at the concert . . . .

10. Since neither my roommate nor I know how to cook . . . .

11. I am not a superstitious person nevertheless . . . .

12. The crops will fail unless . . . .

13. Just as I was getting ready to eat dinner last night . . . .

14. We must work quickly otherwise . . . .

15. Some children are noisy and wild my brother's children on the other hand . . . .

16. According to the newspaper, now that . . . .

17. Ever since I can remember . . . .

18. Although my . . . .

19. The United States . . . whereas . . . .

20. I was tired however I . . . because . . . .

21. You must . . . whether . . . .

22. . . . nevertheless I could not understand what the person who . . . because . . . .

☐ EXERCISE 33. Error analysis: general review. (Chapters 16 → 19)
Directions: Correct the errors.

1. Unless I study very hard, I will pass all of my exams.

2. My shoes and pants got muddy. Even though I walked carefully through the wet streets.

3. My neighborhood is quiet and safe however I always lock my doors.

4. Although I usually don't like Mexican food, but I liked the food I had at the Mexican restaurant last night.

5. Although my room in the dormitory is very small, but I like it. Because it is a place where I can be by myself and studying in peace and quiet.

6. Despite I prefer to be a history teacher, I am studying in the Business School in order for I can get a job in industry.

7. A little girl approached the cage however when the tiger shows its teeth and growls she run to her mother. Because she was frightened.

8. Many of the people working to save our environment think that they are fighting a losing battle. Because big business, and the government have not joined together to eliminate pollution.

9. The weather was so cold that I don't like to leave my apartment.

10. I have to study four hour every day because of my courses are difficult.

11. On the third day of our voyage, we sailed across a rough sea before to reach the shore.

12. I can't understand the lectures in my psychology class therefore my roommate lets me borrow her notes.

13. According to this legend, a man went in search of a hidden village, he finally found it after walk two hundred mile.

14. Because my country it is located in a subtropical area, so the weather is hot.

15. I will stay at the united state for two more year. Because I want finish my degree before go home.

☐ **EXERCISE 34. Activity: connectives.** (Chart 19-9)
Directions: Form a group of four people. One of you will begin a "chain sentence" by speaking the given words plus one, two, or three additional words. Each of the others should add one, two, or three words until the sentence is completed. The maximum number of words a person can add is three. When you complete your sentence, one person in the group should write it down (with correct punctuation, spelling, and capitalization).

Example: Although education is . . . .
SPEAKER A: Although education is **important,** . . . .
SPEAKER B: Although education is important, **some students** . . . .
SPEAKER C: Although education is important, some students **would rather** . . . .
SPEAKER D: Although education is important, some students would rather **fly a kite** . . . .
SPEAKER A: Although education is important, some students would rather fly a kite **than** . . . .
SPEAKER B: Although education is important, some students would rather fly a kite than **go to class**.
FINAL SENTENCE: → *Although education is important, some students would rather fly a kite than go to class.*

1. Because we are . . . .
2. Unless you . . . .
3. Students have to study. Otherwise, ...
4. In spite of the fact that students . . . .
5. Even if we . . . .
6. Only if . . . .
7. An educated populace is important to a nation's future. Therefore, ...
8. I was so confused when the teacher . . . .
9. Now that we . . . .
10. Even though students who . . . .

☐ EXERCISE 35. Review: punctuation and capitalization. (Chapters 13 and 16 → 19)

Directions: Add appropriate punctuation and capitalization. Notice how these clarify meaning in written English.

1. I did not expect to get a pay raise nevertheless I accepted when my boss offered it.
   → *I did not expect to get a pay raise. Nevertheless, I accepted when my boss offered it.*

2. Although a computer has tremendous power and speed it cannot think for itself a human operator is needed to give a computer instructions for it cannot initially tell itself what to do.

3. Being a lawyer in private practice I work hard but I do not go into my office on either Saturday or Sunday if clients insist upon seeing me on those days they have to come to my home.

4. Whenever the weather is nice I walk to school but when it is cold or wet I either take the bus or get a ride with one of my friends even though my brother has a car I never ask him to take me to school because he is very busy he has a new job and has recently gotten married so he doesn't have time to drive me to and from school anymore I know he would give me a ride if I asked him to but I don't want to bother him.

5. The common cold which is the most widespread of all diseases continues to plague humanity despite the efforts of scientists to find its prevention and cure even though colds are minor illnesses they are one of the principal causes of absence from school and work people of all ages get colds but children and adults who live with children get them the most colds can be dangerous for elderly people because they can lead to other infections I have had three colds so far this year I eat the right kinds of food get enough rest and exercise regularly nevertheless I still get at least one cold a year.

6. Whenever my father goes fishing we know we will have fish to eat for dinner for even if he doesn't catch any he stops at the fish market on his way home and buys some.

□ **EXERCISE 36. Review: showing relationships. (Chapters 5 and 16 → 19)**
Directions: Using the words in parentheses, combine the sentences to show relationships between the ideas. Punctuate and capitalize correctly.

1. a. Jack hates going to the dentist.
   b. He should see his dentist soon.
   c. He has a very bad toothache.
   (even though, because)
   → *Even though Jack hates going to the dentist, he should see his dentist soon because he has a very bad toothache.*

2. a. You may really mean what you say.
   b. I'll give you one more chance.
   c. You have to give me your best effort.
   d. You'll lose your job.
   (if, but, otherwise)

3. a. The weather is bad.
   b. I'm going to stay home.
   c. The weather may change.
   d. I don't want to go to the picnic.
   (due to, even if)

4. a. The children had eaten lunch.
   b. They got hungry in the middle of the afternoon.
   c. I took them to the market.
   d. They wanted to get some fruit for a snack.
   e. We went home for dinner.
   (even though, therefore, so that, before)

5. a. Robert is totally exhausted after playing tennis.
   b. Marge isn't even tired.
   c. She ran around a lot more during the game.
   (whereas, in spite of the fact that)

6. a. Many animals are most vulnerable to predators when they are grazing.
   b. Giraffes are most vulnerable when they are drinking.
   c. They must spread their legs awkwardly in order to lower their long necks to the water in front of them.
   d. It is difficult and time-consuming for them to stand up straight again to escape a predator.
   e. Once they are up and running, they are faster than most of their predators.
   (while, consequently, however)

7. a. My boss promised me that I could have two full weeks.
   b. It seems that I can't take my vacation after all.
   c. I have to train the new personnel this summer.
   d. I may not get a vacation in the fall either.
   e. I will be angry.
   (even though, because, if)

8. a. Education, business, and government are all dependent on computers.
   b. It is advisable for all students to have basic computer skills.
   c. They graduate from high school and enter the work force or college.
   d. A course called "Computer Literacy" has recently become a requirement for graduation from Westside High School.
   e. Maybe you will want more information about this course.
   f. You can call the academic counselor at the high school.
   (since, before, therefore, if)

□ EXERCISE 37. Review: showing relationships. (Chapters 5 and 13 → 19)
   Directions: Write out the sentences on another piece of paper, completing them with your own words. Some punctuation is given; add other punctuation as necessary. (NOTE: Some of your sentences will have to get a little complicated.)

   Examples: I have trouble _____ , so I _____ when I _____

   → *I have trouble **remembering people's names,** so I **concentrate** when I **first meet someone.***

   I wanted to _____. Nevertheless, I _____ because _____

   → *I wanted to **go to Chicago.** Nevertheless, I **stayed home** because **I had to study for final exams.***

   1. _____ sore throat. Nevertheless, _____ .

   2. I _____ . My _____, on the other hand, _____ .

   3. When a small, black insect _____ , I _____ because _____ .

   4. I _____ because _____ . However, _____ .

   5. Even though I told _____ that _____ , _____ .

   6. According to the newspaper, now that _____ . Therefore, _____ .

   7. Since neither the man who _____ nor _____ , I _____ .

   8. When people who _____ , _____ because _____ .

   9. Since I didn't know whose _____ , I _____ .

   10. Even though the book which _____ , I _____ .

   11. What did the woman who _____ when you _____ ?

   12. If what he said _____ .

   13. Because the man who _____ .

14. Even though she didn't understand what the man who _____.

15. Now that all of the students who _____.

16. Since the restaurant where we _____.

☐ EXERCISE 38. Error analysis: general review. (Chapters 1 → 19)
   Directions: These passages are taken from student writing. You are the editor for these students. Rewrite the passages, correcting errors and making whatever revisions in phrasing or vocabulary you feel will help the writers say what they intended to say.

   Example: My idea of the most important thing in life. It is to be healthy. Because a person can't enjoy life without health.
   → *In my opinion, the most important thing in life is good health, for a person cannot enjoy life fully without it.*

1. We went shopping after ate dinner. But the stores were closed. We had to go back home even we hadn't found what were we looking for.

2. I want explain that I know alot of grammers but is my problem I haven't enough vocabularies.

3. When I got lost in the bus station a kind man helped me, he explained how to read the huge bus schedule on the wall. Took me to the window to buy a ticket and showed me where was my bus, I will always appreciate his kindness.

4. I had never understand the important of know English language. Until I worked at a large international company.

5. Since I was young my father found an American woman to teach me and my brothers English, but when we move to other town my father wasn't able to find other teacher for other five years.

6. I was surprised to see the room that I was given at the dormitory. Because there aren't any furniture, and dirty.

7. When I meet Mr. Lee for the first time, we played ping pong at the student center even though we can't communicate very well, but we had a good time.

8. Because the United States is a large and also big country. It means that they're various kinds of people live there and it has a diverse population.

9. My grammar class was start at 10:35. When the teacher was coming to class, she returned the last quiz to my classmates and I. After we have had another quiz.

10. If a wife has a work, her husband should share the houseworks with her. If both of them help, the houseworks can be finish much faster.

11. The first time I went skiing. I was afraid to go down the hill. But somewhere from a little corner of my head kept shouting, "Why not! Give it a try. You'll make it!" After stand around for ten minutes without moving. Finally, I decided go down that hill.

12. This is a story about a man. He had a big garden. One day he was sleeping in his garden. Then he woke up. He ate some fruit. Then he picked some apples and he walked to a small river and he saw a beautiful woman was on the other side. And he gave her some apples and then she gave him a loaf of bread. The two of them walked back to the garden. Then some children came and were playing games with him. Everyone was laughing and smiling. Then one child destroyed a flower and the man became angry and he said to them, "Get out of here." Then the children left and the beautiful woman left. Then the man built a wall around his garden and would not let anyone in. He stayed in his garden all alone for the rest of his life.

☐ **EXERCISE 40. Activity: general review. (Chapters 1 → 19)**
Directions: Read and discuss.

In prehistoric times, humans probably spoke between 10,000 and 15,000 languages. Today about 6,000 languages are spoken around the world. Experts predict that up to 50 percent of these languages will probably become extinct during the 21st century.

Question for discussion and/or writing:
What do you think accounts for the decrease in the number of languages in the world?

CHAPTER 20
Conditional Sentences and Wishes

A **conditional sentence** typically consists of an *if*-clause (which presents a condition) and a result clause.* Example: *If it rains, the streets get wet.*

*See Charts 17-1 (p. 359) and 17-5 (p. 367) for the basic structure of adverb clauses of condition.

☐ **EXERCISE 1. Preview: conditional sentences. (Charts 20-1 → 20-4)**
   Directions: Answer the questions with "yes" or "no."

1. *If the weather had been good yesterday, our picnic would not have been canceled.*

   a. Was the picnic canceled? ___yes___

   b. Was the weather good? ___no___

2. *If I had an envelope and a stamp, I would mail this letter right now.*

   a. Do I have an envelope and a stamp right now? _____

   b. Do I want to mail this letter right now? _____

   c. Am I going to mail this letter right now? _____

3. *Ann would have made it to class on time this morning if the bus hadn't been late.*

   a. Did Ann try to make it to class on time? _____

   b. Did Ann make it to class on time? _____

   c. Was the bus late? _____

4. *If the hotel had been built to withstand an earthquake, it would not have collapsed.*

   a. Was the hotel built to withstand an earthquake? _____

   b. Did the hotel collapse? _____

5. *If I were a carpenter, I would build my own house.*

    a. Do I want to build my own house? _____

    b. Am I going to build my own house? _____

    c. Am I a carpenter? _____

6. *If I didn't have any friends, I would be lonely.*

    a. Am I lonely? _____

    b. Do I have friends? _____

7. *If Bob had asked me to keep the news a secret, I wouldn't have told anybody.*

    a. Did I tell anybody the news? _____

    b. Did Bob ask me to keep it a secret? _____

8. *If Ann and Jan, who are twins, dressed alike and had the same hairstyle, I wouldn't be able to tell them apart.*

    a. Do Ann and Jan dress alike? _____

    b. Do they have the same hairstyle? _____

    c. Can I tell them apart? _____

20-1 OVERVIEW OF BASIC VERB FORMS USED IN CONDITIONAL SENTENCES

SITUATION	*IF*-CLAUSE	RESULT CLAUSE	EXAMPLES
True in the present/future	simple present	simple present *will* + simple form	If I *have* enough time, I *watch* TV every evening. If I *have* enough time, I *will watch* TV later on tonight.
Untrue in the present/future	simple past	*would* + simple form	If I *had* enough time, I *would watch* TV now or later on.
Untrue in the past	past perfect	*would have* + past participle	If I *had had* enough time, I *would have watched* TV yesterday.

☐ EXERCISE 2. Basic verb forms in conditional sentences. (Chart 20-1)
    Directions: Complete the sentences with the verbs in parentheses.

    1. SITUATION: *I usually write my parents a letter every week. That is a true fact. In other words:*

        If I *(have)* ____**have**____ enough time, I *(write)* ____**write**____ my parents a letter **every week**.

2. SITUATION: *I may have enough time to write my parents a letter later tonight. I want to write them a letter tonight. Both of those things are true. In other words:*

   If I *(have)* _____ enough time, I *(write)* _____ my parents a letter **later tonight**.

3. SITUATION: *I don't have enough time right now, so I won't write my parents a letter. I'll try to do it later. I want to write them, but the truth is that I just don't have enough time right now. In other words:*

   If I *(have)* _____ enough time **right now**, I *(write)* _____ my parents a letter.

4. SITUATION: *I won't have enough time tonight, so I won't write my parents a letter. I'll try to do it tomorrow. I want to write them, but the truth is that I just won't have enough time. In other words:*

   If I *(have)* _____ enough time **later tonight**, I *(write)* _____ my parents a letter.

5. SITUATION: *I wanted to write my parents a letter last night, but I didn't have enough time. In other words:*

   If I *(have)* _____ enough time, I *(write)* _____ my parents a letter **last night**.

20-2 TRUE IN THE PRESENT OR FUTURE

(a) If I *don't eat* breakfast, I always *get* hungry during class.	In conditional sentences that express true, factual ideas in the present/future, the *simple present* (not the simple future) is used in the *if*-clause.
(b) Water *freezes* OR *will freeze* if the temperature *reaches* 32°F/0°C.	The result clause has various possible verb forms. A result clause verb can be:
(c) If I *don't eat* breakfast tomorrow morning, I *will get* hungry during class.	1. the *simple present*, to express a habitual activity or situation, as in (a). 2. either the *simple present* or the *simple future*, to express an established, predictable fact or general truth, as in (b).
(d) If it *rains*, we *should stay* home. If it *rains*, I *might decide* to stay home. If it *rains*, we *can't go*. If it *rains*, we*'re going to stay* home.	3. the *simple future*, to express a particular activity or situation in the future, as in (c). 4. *modals* and *phrasal modals* such as ***should***, ***might***, ***can***, ***be going to***, as in (d).* 5. an imperative verb, as in (e).
(e) If anyone *calls*, please *take* a message.	
(f) If anyone ***should call***, please take a message.	Sometimes ***should*** is used in an *if*-clause. It indicates a little more uncertainty than the use of the simple present, but basically the meaning of examples (e) and (f) is the same.

*See Chart 9-1, p. 151, for a list of modals and phrasal modals.

□ EXERCISE 3. True in the present or future. (Chart 20-2)
Directions: Answer the questions. Pay special attention to the verb forms in the result clauses. Work in pairs, in groups, or as a class.

    1. If it rains, what always happens?*
    2. If it rains tomorrow, what will happen?
    3. If it should rain tomorrow, what will you do or not do?
    4. If it's cold tomorrow, what are you going to wear to class?
    5. Fish can't live out of water. If you take a fish out of water, what will happen? / If you take a fish out of water, what happens?
    6. If I want to learn English faster, what should I do?
    7. If you run up a hill, what does/will your heart do?**
    8. Tell me what to do, where to go, and what to expect if I visit your hometown as a tourist.

20-3 UNTRUE (CONTRARY TO FACT) IN THE PRESENT OR FUTURE

(a) If I *taught* this class, I *wouldn't give* tests.	In (a): In truth, I don't teach this class.
(b) If he *were* here right now, he *would help* us.	In (b): In truth, he is not here right now.
(c) If I *were* you, I *would accept* their invitation.	In (c): In truth, I am not you.
	Note: *Were* is used for both singular and plural subjects. *Was* (with *I, he, she, it*) is sometimes used in informal speech: *If I was you, I'd accept their invitation.*
COMPARE	In (d): The speaker wants a car, but doesn't have enough money. *Would* expresses desired or predictable results.
(d) If I had enough money, I *would* buy a car.	In (e): The speaker is expressing one possible result. *Could* = *would be able to.* *Could* expresses possible options.
(e) If I had enough money, I *could* buy a car.	

□ EXERCISE 4. Present or future conditional sentences. (Charts 20-2 and 20-3)
Directions: Complete the sentences with the verbs in parentheses.

    1. If I have enough apples, I *(bake)* _____will bake_____ an apple pie this afternoon.

    2. If I had enough apples, I *(bake)* _____ an apple pie this afternoon.

    3. I will fix your bicycle if I *(have)* _____ a screwdriver of the proper size.

    4. I would fix your bicycle if I *(have)* _____ a screwdriver of the proper size.

    5. Sally always answers the phone if she *(be)* _____ in her office.

    6. Sally would answer the phone if she *(be)* _____ in her office right now.

_____

*In true conditional sentences that express a habitual activity or general truth, *if* is very close in meaning to *when* or *whenever*. These sentences have essentially the same meaning:
    If it rains, the streeets get wet.
    When it rains, the streets get wet.
    Whenever it rains, the streets get wet.

**In this sentence, *you* is an impersonal pronoun. Begin the response to this question with "*If you run . . . .*"

7. I (be, not) _____ a student in this class if English (be) _____

my native language.

8. Most people know that oil floats on water. If you pour oil on water, it (float)

_____.

9. If there (be) _____ no oxygen on earth, life as we know it (exist, not)

_____.

10. My evening newspaper has been late every day this week. If the paper (arrive, not)

_____ on time today, I'm going to cancel my subscription.

11. If I (be) _____ a bird, I (want, not)

_____ to live my whole

life in a cage.

12. How old (human beings, live) _____

_____ to be

if all diseases in the world (be) _____

completely eradicated?

13. If you boil water, it (disappear) _____

_____ into the

atmosphere as vapor.

14. If people (have) _____ paws instead of hands with fingers and

opposable thumbs, the machines we use in everyday life (have to) _____

_____ be constructed very differently. We (be, not) _____

_____ able to turn knobs, push small buttons, or hold tools and

utensils securely.

☐ **EXERCISE 5. Activity: present or future untrue conditions. (Chart 20-3)**
   Directions: In small groups or as a class, discuss the questions.

   Under what conditions, if any, would you . . .
   1. exceed the speed limit while driving?
   2. lie to your best friend?
   3. disobey an order from your boss?
   4. steal food?
   5. carry a friend on your back for a long distance?
   6. not pay your rent?
   7. *(Make up other conditions for your classmates to discuss.)*

☐ EXERCISE 6. Activity: present conditionals. (Chart 20-3)

Directions: Use the statistics in *PART I* to answer the question in *PART II*. Work in pairs, in groups, or as a class.

PART I. POPULATION STATISTICS

1. 51% of the world's population is female.
2. 57% of the people in the world are from Asia, the Middle East, and the South Pacific.
3. 21% are Europeans.
4. 14% are from the Western Hemisphere.
5. 8% are from Africa.
6. 50% of the world's population suffers from malnutrition.
7. 30% of the world's population is illiterate. 60% of the people who are illiterate are women.
8. 1% of the world's population has a college education.
9. 6% of the people in the world own half of the world's wealth.
10. One person in three is below 15 years of age. One person in ten is over 65 years old.

PART II. QUESTION

If there were only one village on earth and it had exactly 100 people, who would it consist of? Assuming that the village would reflect global population statistics, describe the people in this imaginary village. Use the illustration to point out the number of people who fit each description you make.

→ *If there were only one village on earth and it had exactly 100 people, 51 of them would be women and 49 of them would be men. More than half of the people in the village (57 of them) would . . .* (continue describing the village).

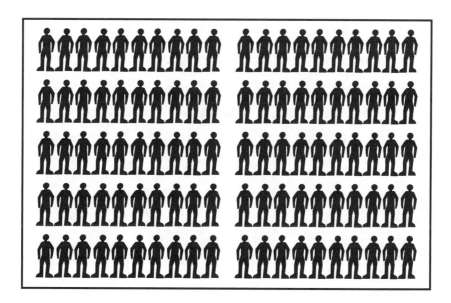

A village of 100 people

20-4 UNTRUE (CONTRARY TO FACT) IN THE PAST

(a) If you **had told** me about the problem, I **would have helped** you. (b) If they **had studied**, they **would have passed** the exam. (c) If I **hadn't slipped** on the stairs, I **wouldn't have broken** my arm.	In (a): In truth, you did not tell me about it. In (b): In truth, they did not study. Therefore, they failed the exam. In (c): In truth, I slipped on the stairs. I broke my arm. Note: The auxiliary verbs are almost always contracted in speech. "If you'd told me, I would've helped you (OR I'd've helped you)."*
COMPARE (d) If I had had enough money, I **would** have bought a car. (e) If I had had enough money, I **could** have bought a car.	In (d): **would** expresses a desired or predictable result. In (e): **could** expresses a possible option; *could have bought = would have been able to buy.*

*In casual, informal speech, some native speakers sometimes use **would have** in an *if*-clause: *If you **would've told** me about the problem, I would've helped you.* This verb form usage is generally considered not to be grammatically correct standard English, but it occurs fairly commonly.

☐ **EXERCISE 7. Conditional sentences. (Charts 20-1 → 20-4)**
Directions: Complete the sentences with the verbs in parentheses.

1. If I *(have)* _____ enough money, I will go with you.

2. If I *(have)* _____ enough money, I would go with you.

3. If I *(have)* _____ enough money, I would have gone with you.

4. If the weather is nice tomorrow, we *(go)* _____ to the zoo.

5. If the weather were nice today, we *(go)* _____ to the zoo.

6. If the weather had been nice yesterday, we *(go)* _____ to the zoo.

7. If Sally *(be)* _____ at home tomorrow, I am going to visit her.

8. Jim isn't home right now. If he *(be)* _____ at home right now, I *(visit)* _____ him.

9. Linda wasn't at home yesterday. If she *(be)* _____ at home yesterday, I *(visit)* _____ her.

10. A: Shh! Your father is taking a nap. Uh-oh. You woke him up.

    B: Gee, I'm sorry, Mom. If I *(realize)* _____ he was sleeping, I *(make, not)* _____ so much noise when I came in. But how was I supposed to know?

10. Last night Alex ruined his sweater when he washed it. If he *(read)* _____ the label, he *(wash, not)* _____ it in hot water.

12. A: Ever since I broke my foot, I haven't been able to get down to the basement to wash my clothes.

   B: Why didn't you say something? I *(come)* _____ over and *(wash)* _____ them for you if you *(tell)* _____ me.

   A: I know you *(come)* _____ right away if I *(call)* _____ you. I guess I didn't want to bother you.

   B: Nonsense! What are good neighbors for?

☐ EXERCISE 8. Untrue in the past. (Chart 20-4)
   Directions: Work in pairs.
   Speaker A: Your book is open. Give the cue.
   Speaker B: Your book is closed. Begin your response with "But if I had known . . . ."

   Example:
   SPEAKER A *(book open):*   There was a test yesterday. You didn't know that, so you didn't study.
   SPEAKER B *(book closed):*   But if I had known (that there was a test yesterday), I would have studied.

   1. Your friend was in the hospital. You didn't know that, so you didn't visit her.
   2. I've never met your friend. You didn't know that, so you didn't introduce me.
   3. There was a meeting last night. You didn't know that, so you didn't go.
   4. Your friend's parents are in town. You didn't know that, so you didn't invite them to dinner.

   Switch roles.
   5. I wanted to go to the soccer game. You didn't know that, so you didn't buy a ticket for me.
   6. I was at home last night. You didn't know that, so you didn't visit me.
   7. Your sister wanted a gold necklace for her birthday. You didn't know that, so you didn't buy her one.
   8. I had a problem. You didn't know that, so you didn't offer to help.

☐ **EXERCISE 9. Untrue conditionals. (Charts 20-3 and 20-4)**
   Directions: Change the statements into conditional sentences.

1. Roberto came, so I wasn't disappointed. But . . . .
   → *But if he hadn't come, I would have been disappointed.*

2. There are so many bugs in the room because there isn't a screen on the window. But . . . .

3. I didn't buy a bicycle because I didn't have enough money. But . . . .

4. I won't buy a bicycle because I don't have enough money. But . . . .

5. You got into so much trouble because you didn't listen to me. But . . . .

6. The woman didn't die because she received immediate medical attention. But . . . .

7. Nadia didn't pass the entrance examination, so she wasn't admitted to the university. But . . . .

8. We ran out of gas because we didn't stop at the service station. But . . .

☐ **EXERCISE 10. Untrue conditional sentences. (Charts 20-3 and 20-4)**
   Directions: Make an *if*-clause from the given information and then supply a result clause using your own words.

   Examples: I wasn't late to work yesterday.
   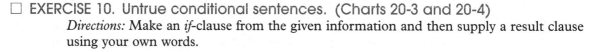
   → *If I had been late to work yesterday, I would have missed the regular morning meeting.*
   Tom asked my permission before he took my bicycle.
   → *If Tom hadn't asked my permission before he took my bicycle, I would have been angry.*

1. I wasn't absent from class yesterday.

2. I don't have enough energy today.

3. Ocean water is salty.

4. Our teacher likes his/her job.

5. People don't have wings.

6. You didn't ask for my opinion.

7. Water is heavier than air.

8. Most nations support world trade agreements.

☐ EXERCISE 11. Review: conditional sentences. (Charts 20-1 → 20-4)
   Directions: Complete the sentences with the verbs in parentheses.

1. You should tell your father exactly what happened. If I *(be)* _____ you, I
   (tell) _____ him the truth as soon as possible.

2. If I *(have)* _____ my camera with me yesterday, I *(take)* _____
   _____ a picture of Alex standing on his head.

3. I'm almost ready to plant my garden. I have a lot of seeds. Maybe I have more than I
   need. If I *(have)* _____ more seeds than I need, I *(give)* _____
   _____ some to my neighbor.

4. George has only two pairs of socks. If he *(have)* _____ more than two pairs
   of socks, he *(have to, not)* _____ wash his socks so
   often.

5. The cowboy pulled his gun to shoot at the rattlesnake, but he was
   too late. If he *(be)* _____
   quicker to pull the trigger, the snake *(bite, not)*
   _____ him on
   the foot. It's a good thing he was wearing
   heavy leather boots.

6. What *(we, use)* _____
   to look at ourselves when we comb our hair
   if we *(have, not)* _____
   mirrors?

7. It's been a long drought. It hasn't rained for over a month. If it *(rain, not)*
   _____ soon, a lot of crops *(die)* _____. If the
   crops *(die)* _____, many people *(go)* _____ hungry this
   coming winter.

8. According to one scientific theory, an asteroid collided with the earth millions of years
   ago, causing great changes in the earth's climate. Some scientists believe that if this
   asteroid *(collide, not)* _____ with the earth, the dinosaurs
   (become, not) _____ extinct. Can you imagine what the
   world *(be)* _____ like today if dinosaurs *(exist, still)* _____
   _____ ? Do you think it *(be)* _____ possible for
   dinosaurs and human beings to coexist on the same planet?

□ **EXERCISE 12. Untrue conditionals. (Charts 20-3 and 20-4)**

Directions: Make a true statement about the given topic. Then make a contrary-to-fact conditional sentence about that statement. Work in pairs, in groups, or as a class.

Examples: yourself
    → *I am twenty years old. If I were seventy years old, I would already have lived most of my life.*

    ice
    → *Ice doesn't sink. If the polar ice caps sank, the level of the oceans would rise and flood coastal cities.*

Topics:

1. yourself	5. peace	9. a famous person
2. fire	6. your activities right now	10. your activities last night
3. space travel	7. air	11. dinosaurs
4. vegetables	8. a member of this class	12. a member of your family

□ **EXERCISE 13. Conditional sentences. (Charts 20-1 → 20-4)**

Directions: Complete each sentence with an appropriate auxiliary verb.

1. I don't have a pen, but if I _____*did*_____, I would lend it to you.

2. He is busy right now, but if he _____*weren't*_____, he would help us.

3. I didn't vote in the last election, but if I _____*had*_____, I would have voted for Senator Anderson.

4. I don't have enough money, but if I _____, I would buy that book.

5. The weather is cold today, but if it _____, I would go swimming.

6. She didn't come, but if she _____, she would have met my brother.

7. I'm not a good cook, but if I _____, I would make all of my own meals.

8. I have to go to class this afternoon, but if I _____, I would go downtown with you.

9. He didn't go to a doctor, but if he _____, the cut on his hand wouldn't have gotten infected.

10. I always pay my bills. If I _____, I would get in a lot of trouble.

11. Helium is lighter than air. If it _____, a helium-filled balloon wouldn't float upward.

12. I called my husband to tell him I would be late. If I _____, he would have gotten worried about me.

☐ EXERCISE 14. Conditional sentences. (Charts 20-1 → 20-4)
Directions: Work in pairs.
Speaker A: Your book is open. Ask the questions.
Speaker B: Your book is closed. Begin your answers with "No, but . . . ."

Example:
SPEAKER A *(book open):* Do you have a dollar?
SPEAKER B *(book closed):* No, but if I did (No, but if I had a dollar), I would lend it to you.

Switch roles.

1. Are you rich?
2. Do you have a car?
3. Are you a bird?
4. Are you in *(student's country/ hometown)?*
5. Do you live in a hotel?
6. Are you the teacher of this class?
7. Do you have your own airplane?
8. Did you watch TV last night?
9. Did you grow up in *(another country)?*

10. Are you tired?
11. Are you at home right now?
12. Are you married/single?
13. Do you speak *(another language)?*
14. Is the weather hot/cold today?
15. Are you hungry?
16. Do you live in *(a different city)?*
17. Did we eat dinner together last night?
18. Did you forget to bring your grammar book to class today?

20-5 USING PROGRESSIVE VERB FORMS IN CONDITIONAL SENTENCES

Notice the use of progressive verb forms in these examples. Even in conditional sentences, progressive verb forms are used in progressive situations. (See Chart 1-2, p. 3, for a discussion of progressive verbs.)

(a) TRUE:	It *is raining* right now, so I *will not go for* a walk.	
(b) CONDITIONAL:	If it *were not raining* right now, I *would go* for a walk.	
(c) TRUE:	I *am not living* in Chile. I *am not working* at a bank.	
(d) CONDITIONAL:	If I *were living* in Chile, I *would be working* at a bank.	
(e) TRUE:	It *was raining* yesterday afternoon, so I *did not go* for a walk.	
(f) CONDITIONAL:	If it *had not been raining*, I *would have gone* for a walk.	
(g) TRUE:	I *was not living* in Chile last year. I *was not working* at a bank.	
(h) CONDITIONAL:	If I *had been living* in Chile last year, I *would have been working* at a bank.	

☐ EXERCISE 15. Using progressive verb forms in conditional sentences. (Chart 20-5)
Directions: Change the statements into conditional sentences.

1. It is snowing, so I won't go with you. But . . . .
   → *But if it weren't snowing, I would go with you.*
2. The child is crying because his mother isn't here. But . . . .
3. You weren't listening, so you didn't understand the directions. But . . . .
4. Joe got a ticket because he was driving too fast. But . . . .

5. I was listening to the radio, so I heard the news bulletin. But . . . .
6. Grandpa is not wearing his hearing aid because it's broken. But . . . .
7. You were sleeping, so I didn't tell you the news as soon as I heard it. But . . . .
8. I'm enjoying myself, so I won't leave. But . . . .

20-6 USING "MIXED TIME" IN CONDITIONAL SENTENCES

Frequently the time in the *if*-clause and the time in the result clause are different: one clause may be in the present and the other in the past. Notice that past and present times are mixed in these sentences.

(a)	TRUE:	I *did not eat* breakfast several hours ago, so I *am* hungry now.
(b)	CONDITIONAL:	If I *had eaten* breakfast several hours ago, I *would not be* hungry now.
		(past) *(present)*
(c)	TRUE:	He *is not* a good student. He *did not study* for the test yesterday.
(d)	CONDITIONAL:	If he *were* a good student, he *would have studied* for the test yesterday.
		(present) *(past)*

☐ **EXERCISE 16. Using "mixed time" in conditional sentences. (Chart 20-6)**
Directions: Change the statements into conditional sentences.

1. I'm hungry now because I didn't eat dinner. But . . . .
   → *But if I'd eaten dinner, I wouldn't be hungry now.*
2. The room is full of flies because you left the door open. But . . . .
3. You are tired this morning because you didn't go to bed at a reasonable hour last night. But . . . .
4. I didn't finish my report yesterday, so I can't begin a new project today. But . . . .
5. Anita is sick because she didn't follow the doctor's orders. But . . . .
6. I'm not you, so I didn't tell him the truth. But . . . .
7. I don't know anything about plumbing, so I didn't fix the leak in the sink myself. But . . . .
8. I received a good job offer from the oil company, so I won't seriously consider taking the job with the electronics firm. But . . . .

20-7 OMITTING *IF*

(a) *Were I* you, I wouldn't do that. (b) *Had I known*, I would have told you. (c) *Should anyone call*, please take a message.	With *were, had* (past perfect), and *should*, sometimes *if* is omitted and the subject and verb are inverted. In (a): *Were I you* = *if I were you.* In (b): *Had I known* = *if I had known.* In (c): *Should anyone call* = *if anyone should call.*

☐ EXERCISE 17. Omitting IF. (Chart 20-7)
   Directions: Create sentences with the same meaning by omitting *if*.

1. If you should need more money, go to the bank before six o'clock.
   → *Should you need more money, go to the bank before six o'clock.*
2. If I were you, I wouldn't do that.
3. If they had realized the danger, they would have done it differently.
4. If I were your teacher, I would insist you do better work.
5. If you should change your mind, please let me know immediately.
6. She would have gotten the job if she had been better prepared.
7. Your boss sounds like a real tyrant. If I were you, I would look for another job.
8. I'll be out of the country until June 12. If you should need to reach me, I'll be at the Hilton Hotel in Seoul.
9. The artists and creative thinkers throughout the history of the world have changed all of our lives. If they had not dared to be different, the history of civilization would have to be rewritten.
10. If there should be a global nuclear war, life on earth as we know it would end forever.

20-8 IMPLIED CONDITIONS

(a) I *would have gone* with you, *but I had to study.* (b) I never *would have succeeded* *without your help.*	Often the *if*-clause is implied, not stated. Conditional verbs are still used in the result clause. In (a): the implied condition = *if I hadn't had to study.* In (b): the implied condition = *if you hadn't helped me.*
(c) She ran; *otherwise*, she *would have missed* her bus.	Conditional verbs are frequently used following ***otherwise***. In (c), the implied *if*-clause = *if she had not run.*

☐ EXERCISE 18. Implied conditions. (Chart 20-8)
   Directions: Identify the implied conditions by creating sentences using *if*-clauses.

1. I would have visited you, but I didn't know that you were at home.
   → *I would have visited you if I had known you were at home.*
2. It wouldn't have been a good meeting without Rosa.
   → *It wouldn't have been a good meeting if Rosa hadn't been there.*
3. I would have answered the phone, but I didn't hear it ring.
4. I couldn't have finished the work without your help.
5. I like to travel. I would have gone to Nepal last summer, but I didn't have enough money.
6. I stepped on the brakes. Otherwise, I would have hit the child on the bicycle.
7. Olga turned down the volume on the tape player. Otherwise, the neighbors probably would have called to complain about the noise.
8. Tarek would have finished his education, but he had to quit school and find a job in order to support his family.

☐ EXERCISE 19. Implied conditions. (Chart 20-8)
   Directions: Complete the sentences with your own words.

   1. I would have . . . , but I didn't have enough time.
   2. I couldn't have . . . without my parents' help.
   3. I would . . . , but I don't have enough money.
   4. I ran out of time. Otherwise, I would have . . . .
   5. I could . . . , but I don't want to.
   6. I would have . . . , but I didn't know about it.
   7. Without water, all life on earth would . . . .
   8. I set my alarm for six every day. Otherwise, I would . . . .
   9. I set my alarm for six this morning. Otherwise, I would have . . . .
  10. I would have . . . , but I didn't . . . .

☐ EXERCISE 20. Review: conditional sentences. (Charts 20-1 → 20-8)
   Directions: Complete the sentences with the verbs in parentheses. Some of the verbs are passive.

   1. If I could speak Japanese, I *(spend)* _____ next year studying in Japan.

   2. Had I known Mr. Jung was in the hospital, I *(send)* _____ him a note and some flowers.

   3. We will move into our new house next month if it *(complete)* _____ _____ by then.

   4. It's too bad that it's snowing. If it *(snow, not)* _____ , we could go for a drive.

   5. I was very tired. Otherwise, I *(go)* _____ to the party with you last night.

   6. I'm glad I have so many friends and such a wonderful family. Life without friends or family *(be)* _____ lonely for me.

   7. My grandfather is no longer alive, but if he *(be)* _____ , I'm sure he *(be)* _____ proud of me.

   8. If you *(sleep, not)* _____ last night when we arrived, I would have asked you to go with us, but I didn't want to wake you up.

   9. Bill has such a bad memory that he *(forget)* _____ his head if it *(be, not)* _____ attached to his body.

10. According to one report, the average hen lays 247 eggs a year, and the average person eats 255 eggs a year. If hens *(outnumber, not)* _____ people, the average person *(eat, not)* _____ 255 eggs a year.

11. A: What would you be doing right now if you *(be, not)* _____ in class?

    B: I *(sleep)* _____ .

12. A: Boy, is it ever hot today!

    B: You said it! If there *(be)* _____ only a breeze, it *(be, not)* _____ quite so unbearable.

13. A: Why isn't Peggy Anderson in class today?

    B: I don't know, but I'm sure she *(be, not)* _____ absent unless * she *(have)* _____ a good reason.

14. A: Hi. Sorry I'm late.

    B: That's okay.

    A: I *(be)* _____ here sooner, but I had car trouble.

15. A: Want to ride on the roller coaster?

    B: No way! I *(ride, not)* _____ on the roller coaster even if you paid me a million dollars!

16. A: Hi, Pat. Come on in.

    B: Oh, I didn't know you had company. I *(come, not)* _____ if *(I, know)* _____ someone was here.

    A: That's okay. Come in and let me introduce you to my friends.

17. A: Are you coming to the party?

    B: I don't think so, but if I change my mind, I *(tell)* _____ you.

☐ EXERCISE 21. Review: conditional sentences. (Charts 20-1 → 20-8)
   Directions: Complete the sentences. Add commas where necessary.

   1. If it hadn't rained . . . .
   2. If it weren't raining . . . .
   3. You would have passed the test had . . . .

———————
unless = if not (See Chart 17-8, p. 370.)

4. It's a good thing we took a map with us. Otherwise . . . .

5. Without electricity modern life . . . .

6. If you hadn't reminded me about the meeting tonight . . . .

7. Should you need any help . . . .

8. If I could choose any profession I wanted . . . .

9. If I were at home right now . . . .

10. Without your help yesterday . . . .

11. Were I you . . . .

12. What would you do if . . . .

13. If I had the chance to live my childhood over again . . . .

14. Had I known . . . .

15. Can you imagine what life would be like if . . . .

☐ **EXERCISE 22. Activity: conditional sentences. (Charts 20-1 → 20-8)**

Directions: Explain what you would do in these situations. Work in pairs, in groups, or as a class.

Example:

SPEAKER A *(book open):* Suppose the student sitting next to you drops her pen. What would you do?

SPEAKER B *(book closed):* I would pick it up for her.

1. Suppose (pretend) there is a fire in this building right now. What would you do?

2. Suppose there is a fire in your room or apartment or house. You have time to save only one thing. What would you save?

3. Suppose you go to the bank to cash a check for (twenty dollars). The bank teller cashes your check and you leave, but when you count the money, you find she gave you (thirty dollars) instead of (twenty). What would you do?

4. Same situation, but she gave you only (fifteen dollars) instead of (twenty).

5. John was cheating during an examination. Suppose you were the teacher and you saw him. What would you have done?

6. You are at a party. A man starts talking to you, but he is speaking so fast that you can't catch what he is saying. What would you do?

7. Late at night you're driving your car down a deserted street. You're all alone. In an attempt to avoid a dog in the road, you swerve and hit a parked car. You know that no one saw you. What would you do?

8. (. . .) goes to a friend's house for dinner. Her/His friend serves a dish that (. . .) can't stand, doesn't like at all. What if you were (. . .)?

9. My friend borrowed (ten dollars) from me and told me he would repay it in a couple of days, but it's been three weeks. I think he has forgotten about it. I really need the money, but I don't want to ask him for it. Give me some advice.

10. John was driving over the speed limit. A police car began to chase him, with lights flashing. John stepped on the accelerator and tried to escape the police car. Put yourself in his position.

11. Suppose you are walking down the street at night all by yourself. A man suddenly appears in front of you. He has a gun. He says, "Give me your money!" Would you try to take his gun away?

12. Suppose you go to (Chicago) to visit a friend. You have never been there before. Your friend said he would meet you at the airport, but he's not there. You wait a long time, but he never shows up. You try to call him, but nobody answers the phone. Now what?

☐ EXERCISE 23. Activity: conditional sentences. (Charts 20-1 → 20-8)
Directions: Discuss the situations. Use the given information to make conditional sentences.

Example:
　Jan is working for a law firm, but she has been trying to find a different job for a long time. She doesn't like her job at the law firm. Recently she was offered a job with a computer company closer to her home. She wanted to accept it, but the salary was too low.
→ *If Jan liked her job at the law firm, she wouldn't be trying to find a different job.*
→ *Jan would have accepted the job at the computer company if the salary hadn't been too low.*
→ Etc.

1. Jim:　Why don't we go to the ball game after work tonight?
　Ron:　I'd like to, but I can't.
　Jim:　Why not?
　Ron:　I have a dinner meeting with a client.
　Jim:　Well, maybe some other time.

2. Tommy had a pet mouse. He took it to school. His friend Jimmy put the mouse in the teacher's desk drawer. When the teacher found the mouse, she jumped in surprise and tried to kill it with a book. Tommy ran to the front of the room and saved his pet mouse. Tommy and Jimmy got into a lot of trouble with their teacher.

3. Ivan's axe was broken, and he wanted to borrow his neighbor Dan's axe so that he could chop some wood. Then Ivan remembered that he had already borrowed Dan's saw and had never returned it. He has since lost the saw, and he's too embarrassed to tell Dan. Because of that, Ivan decided not to ask Dan for his axe.

□ **EXERCISE 24. Activity: conditional sentences. (Charts 20-1 → 20-8)**
Directions: Discuss and/or write about one or more of the topics.

1. If, beginning tomorrow, you had a two-week holiday and unlimited funds, what would you do? Why?
2. If you had to teach your language to a person who knew nothing at all about your language, how would you begin? What would you do so that this person could learn your language as quickly and easily as possible?
3. If you were Philosopher-King of the world, how would you govern? What would you do? What changes would you make? (A "Philosopher-King" may be defined as a person who has ideal wisdom and unlimited power to shape the world as s/he wishes.)
4. Suppose you had only one year to live. What would you do?
5. Describe your activities if you were in some other place (in this country or in the world) at present. Describe your probable activities today, yesterday, and tomorrow. Include the activities of other people you would be with if you were in that place.

20-9   USING *AS IF/AS THOUGH*

(a) It looks *like rain.* (b) It looks *as if it is going to rain.* (c) It looks *as though it is going to rain.* (d) It looks *like it is going to rain. (informal)*	Notice in (a): *like* is followed by a noun object. Notice in (b) and (c): *as if* and *as though* are followed by a clause. Notice in (d): *like* is followed by a clause. This use of *like* is common in informal English, but is not generally considered appropriate in formal English; *as if* or *as though* is preferred. (a), (b), (c), and (d) all have the same meaning.

"TRUE" STATEMENT (FACT)	VERB FORM AFTER *AS IF/AS THOUGH*	
(e) He *is not* a child.	She talked to him *as if* he *were* a child.	Usually the idea following *as if/as though* is "untrue." In this case, verb usage is similar to that in conditional sentences.
(f) She *did not take* a shower with her clothes on.	When she came in from the rainstorm, she looked *as if* she *had taken* a shower with her clothes on.	
(g) He *has met* her.	He acted *as though* he *had never met* her.	
(h) She *will be* here.	She spoke *as if* she *wouldn't be* here.	

□ **EXERCISE 25. Using AS IF/AS THOUGH. (Chart 20-9)**
Directions: Using the given idea, complete each sentence with *as if/as though*.

1. *I wasn't run over by a ten-ton truck.*

   I feel terrible. I feel <u>as if (as though) I had been run over by a ten-ton truck.</u>

2. *English is not her native tongue.*

   She speaks English _____

3. *You didn't see a ghost.*

   What's the matter? You look _____

2. *His animals aren't people.*

   I know a farmer who talks to his animals

   _____

   _____

5. *His father is not a general in the army.*

   Sometimes his father gives orders _____

   _____

6. *I didn't climb Mt. Everest.*

   When I reached the fourth floor, I was

   winded. I felt _____

   instead of just three flights of stairs.

7. *He does have a brain in his head.*

   Sometimes he acts _____

8. *We haven't known each other all of our lives.*

   We became good friends almost immediately. After talking to each other for only a

   short time, we felt _____

9. *A giant bulldozer didn't drive down Main Street.*

   After the tornado, the town looked _____

10. *I don't have wings and can't fly.*

    I was so happy that I felt _____

11. *The child won't burst.*

    The child was so excited that he looked _____

12. NOTE: The following sentiments were expressed by Helen Keller, a woman who was
    both blind and deaf but who learned to speak and to read (Braille⋆). Complete these
    sentences.

    Use your eyes as if tomorrow you _____ become blind. Hear the music

    of voices, the song of a bird, as if you _____ become deaf tomorrow. Touch

    each object as if tomorrow you _____ never be able to feel anything again.

    Smell the perfume of the flowers and taste with true enjoyment each bite of food as if

    tomorrow you _____ never be able to smell and taste again.

_____

⋆A system of writing for the blind devised by the Frenchman Louis Braille. Blind people read Braille by
placing the tips of their fingers on raised dots that represent letters, punctuation, etc.

20-10 VERB FORMS FOLLOWING *WISH*

Wish is used when the speaker wants reality to be different, to be exactly the opposite.

	"TRUE" STATEMENT	VERB FORM FOLLOWING *WISH*	*Wish* is followed by a noun clause. (See Chart 12-5, p. 248.) Past verb forms, similar to those in conditional sentences, are used in the noun clause. For example, in (a): *would*, the past form of *will*, is used to make a wish about the future. In (d): the simple past *(knew)* is used to make a wish about the present. In (g): the past perfect *(had come)* is used to make a wish about the past.
A wish about the future	(a) She *will not tell* me. (b) He *isn't going to be* here. (c) She *can't come* tomorrow.	I *wish* (that) she *would tell* me. I *wish* he *were going to be* here. I *wish* she *could come* tomorrow.	
A wish about the present	(d) I *don't know* French. (e) It *is raining* right now. (f) I *can't speak* Japanese.	I *wish* I *knew* French. I *wish* it *weren't raining* right now. I *wish* I *could speak* Japanese.	
A wish about the past	(g) John *didn't come*. (h) Mary *couldn't come*.	I *wish* John *had come*.* I *wish* Mary *could have come*.	

*Sometimes in very informal speaking: *I wish John **would have come**.*

☐ EXERCISE 26. Verb forms following WISH. (Chart 20-10)
Directions: Complete the sentences with an appropriate verb form.

1. Our classroom doesn't have any windows. I wish our classroom _____had_____ windows.

2. The sun isn't shining. I wish the sun _____ right now.

3. I didn't go shopping. I wish I _____ shopping.

4. I don't know how to dance. I wish I _____ how to dance.

5. You didn't tell them about it. I wish you _____ them about it.

6. It's cold today. I'm not wearing a coat. I wish I _____ a coat.

7. I don't have enough money to buy that book. I wish I _____ enough money.

8. Elena is tired because she went to bed late last night. She wishes she _____ _____ to bed earlier last night.

9. I can't go with you tomorrow, but I wish I _____ .

10. My friend won't ever lend me his car. I wish he _____ me his car for my date tomorrow night.

11. Mrs. Takasawa isn't coming to dinner with us tonight. I wish she _____ _____ to dinner with us.

12. The teacher is going to give an exam tomorrow. I wish he _____

    _____ us an exam tomorrow.

13. You can't meet my parents. I wish you _____ them.

14. Khalid didn't come to the meeting. I wish he _____ to the meeting.

15. I am not lying on a beach in Hawaii. I wish I _____ on a beach in

    Hawaii.

☐ EXERCISE 27. Activity: verb forms following WISH. (Chart 20-10)
    Directions: Discuss the questions.

1. What is something you can't do, but you wish you could do?
2. What do you wish you were doing right now?
3. What is something you don't have but wish you had?
4. What is something that didn't happen yesterday, but that you wish had happened?
5. What is something that has never happened in your life, but that you wish would happen?
6. What is something that happened in your life, but that you wish had not happened?
7. What is something you have to do but wish you didn't have to do?
8. What is something that will not happen tomorrow, but that you wish would happen?
9. What is something you don't know but wish you knew?
10. What is something you were unable to do yesterday, but you wish you could have done?

☐ EXERCISE 28. Verb forms following WISH. (Chart 20-10)
    Directions: Complete the sentences with an appropriate auxiliary verb.

1. I'm not at home, but I wish I _____were_____.

2. I don't know her, but I wish I _____did_____.

3. I can't sing well, but I wish I _____could_____.

4. I didn't go, but I wish I _____had_____.

5. He won't talk about it, but I wish he _____would_____.

6. I didn't read that book, but I wish I _____.

7. I want to go, but I can't. I wish I _____.

8. I don't have a bicycle, but I wish I _____.

9. He didn't buy a ticket to the game, but he wishes he _____.

10. She can't speak English, but she wishes she _____.

11. It probably won't happen, but I wish it _____.

12. He isn't old enough to drive a car, but he wishes he _____.

13. They didn't go to the movie, but they wish they _____.

14. I don't have a driver's license, but I wish I _____.

15. I'm not living in an apartment, but I wish I _____.

20-11 USING *WOULD* TO MAKE WISHES ABOUT THE FUTURE

(a) It is raining. I *wish* it **would stop**. (*I want it to stop raining.*) (b) I'm expecting a call. I *wish* the phone **would ring**. (*I want the phone to ring.*)	**Would** is usually used to indicate that the speaker wants something to happen or someone other than the speaker to do something in the future. The wish may or may not come true (be realized).
(c) It's going to be a good party. I *wish* you **would come**. (d) We're going to be late. I *wish* you **would hurry**.	In (c) and (d): **I wish you would** . . . is often used to make a request.

☐ **EXERCISE 29. Using WOULD to make wishes. (Chart 20-10 and 20-11)**
   Directions: Use the given information to answer the questions.

   Example:
   TOM: *Why are you watching the telephone?*
   SUE: *I'm waiting to hear from Sam. I want him to call me. I need to talk to him right now. We had an argument. I need to make sure everything's okay.*
   TOM: *Watching the phone won't make it ring, you know.*

   (a) What does Sue want to happen in the near future? (Use *wish + would*.)
       → She wishes the phone **would** ring.
   (b) What else does Sue wish?
       → She wishes Sam would call her. She wishes she could talk to Sam right now.
         She probably wishes she and Sam hadn't had an argument.

   1. RITA: *It's raining. I want to go for a walk, but not in the rain.*
      YOKO: *I want the rain to stop, too.*

      (a) What does Rita want to happen in the near future? (Use *wish + would*.)
      (b) What does Yoko wish?

   2. ANNA: *Can't you come to the concert? Please change your mind. I'd really like you to come.*
      YOKO: *No, I can't. I have to work.*

      (a) What does Anna want Yoko to do? (Use *wish + would*.)
      (b) What else does Anna wish?

   3. BOB'S MOTHER: *Do you really like how you look with a beard?*
               BOB: *Yes.*
      BOB'S MOTHER: *Don't you want to shave it off?*
               BOB: *Nope.*

      (a) What does Bob's mother want Bob to do? (Use *wish + would*.)
      (b) What does Bob probably wish?

4. *Helen is a neat and orderly person. Judy, her roommate, is messy. Judy never picks up after herself. She leaves dirty dishes in the sink. She drops her clothes all over the apartment. She clutters the apartment with her stuff everywhere. She never makes her bed. Helen nags Judy to pick up after herself.*

   (a) What does Helen want Judy to do? (Use *wish + would*.)
   (b) What does Judy probably wish?

☐ EXERCISE 30. Using WISH. (Charts 20-10 and 20-11)
   Directions: Complete the sentences with an appropriate form of the verbs in parentheses.

1. We need some help. I wish Alfred *(be)* _____ here now. If he *(be)* _____, we could finish this work very quickly.

2. We had a good time in Houston over vacation. I wish you *(come)* _____ with us. If you *(come)* _____ with us, you *(have)* _____ _____ a good time.

3. I wish it *(be, not)* _____ so cold today. If it *(be, not)* _____ so cold, I *(go)* _____ swimming.

4. I missed part of the lecture because I was daydreaming, and now my notes are incomplete. I wish I *(pay)* _____ more attention to the lecturer.

5. A: Did you study for that test?
   B: No, but now I wish I *(have)* _____ because I flunked it.

6. A: Is the noise from the TV in the next apartment bothering you?
   B: Yes. I'm trying to study. I wish he *(turn)* _____ it down.

7. A: What a beautiful day! I wish I *(lie)* _____ in the sun by a swimming pool instead of sitting in a classroom.
   B: I wish I *(be)* _____ anywhere but here!

8. A: I wish we *(have, not)* _____ to go to work today.
   B: So do I. I wish it *(be)* _____ a holiday.

9. A: He couldn't have said that! That's impossible. You must have misunderstood him.
   B: I only wish I *(have, not)* _____, but I'm sure I heard him correctly.

10. Alice doesn't like her job as a nurse. She wishes she *(go, not)* _____ to nursing school.

11. A: I know that something's bothering you. I wish you *(tell)* _____ me what it is. Maybe I can help.
    B: I appreciate it, but I can't discuss it now.

12. A: My feet are killing me! I wish I *(wear)* _____ more

comfortable shoes.

B: Yeah, me too. I wish I *(know)* _____ that we were going to

have to walk this much.

☐ EXERCISE 31. Using WISH. (Charts 20-10 and 20-11)
Directions: Answer the questions. Use **wish**. Work in pairs, in groups, or as a class.

1. Where do you wish you were right now? What do you wish you were doing?

2. Are you pleased with the weather today, or do you wish it were different?

3. Look around this room. What do you wish were different?

4. Is there anything you wish were different about the place you are living?

5. What do you wish were different about this city/town?

6. What do you wish were different about this country?

7. What do you wish were different about a student's life? about a worker's life?

8. Where do you wish you could go on your next vacation?

9. Your friend gave you his phone number, but you didn't write it down because you thought you would remember it. Now you have forgotten the number. What do you wish?

10. (. . .) kept all of his money in his wallet instead of putting it in the bank. Then he lost his wallet. What does he probably wish?

11. You didn't eat breakfast/lunch/dinner before you came to class. Now you are hungry. What do you wish?

12. (. . .) stayed up very late last night. Today she is tired and sleepy. What does she probably wish?

☐ EXERCISE 32. Using WISH. (Charts 20-10 and 20-11)
Directions: Using the given ideas, create sentences with **wish**. Add something that explains why you are making that wish.

Examples: be different
→ *I wish my name were different. I've never liked having "Daffodil" as my first name.*

go to the moon
→ *I wish I could go to the moon for a vacation. It would be fun to be able to leap long distances in the moon's lighter gravity.*

1. be different
2. know several world leaders personally
3. speak every language in the world
4. be more patient and understanding
5. interview some great people in history

6. travel by instant teleportation
7. remember everything I read
8. be a big movie star
9. read people's minds
10. be born in the last century

□ **EXERCISE 33. Activity: conditionals and wishes. (Chapter 20)**
Directions: Answer the questions. Work in pairs, in groups, or as a class.

1. If you could have free service for the rest of your life from a chauffeur, cook, housekeeper, or gardener, which would you choose? Why?

2. If you had to leave your country and build a new life elsewhere, where would you go? Why?

3. If you had control of all medical research in the world and, by concentrating funds and efforts, could find the cure for only one disease in the next 25 years, which disease would you select? Why?

4. If you could stay one particular age for a span of 50 years, what age would you choose? Why? (At the end of the 50 years, you would suddenly turn 50 years older.)

5. You have promised to spend an evening with your best friend. Then you discover you have the chance to spend the evening with *(supply the name of a famous person)*. Your friend is not invited. What would you do? Why?

6. Assume that you have a good job. If your boss told you to do something that you think is wrong, would you do it? Why or why not? (You understand that if you don't do it, you will lose your job.)

7. If you had to choose among perfect health, a loving family, and wealth (and you could have only one of the three during the rest of your life), which would you choose? Why?

8. Just for fun, what do you wish were or could be different in the world? What about animals being able to speak? people being able to fly? there being only one language in the world? being able to take a vacation on the moon? speed of transportation?

9. Is there anything in your past life that you would change? What do you wish you had or had not done? Why?

10. Suppose you were offered the opportunity to be a crew member on a spaceship that would travel to far points in the universe. There would be no guarantee that you would ever return to earth. Would you go? Why or why not?

APPENDIX
Supplementary Grammar Units

CONTENTS

UNIT A: Basic Grammar Terminology

A-1   SUBJECTS, VERBS, AND OBJECTS

S **V** (a) *Birds* *fly*. (NOUN) (VERB)	Almost all English sentences contain a subject (**s**) and a verb (**v**). The verb may or may not be followed by an object (**o**).

S   **V**
 (b) The *baby*   *cried*.
       (NOUN)   (VERB)
	VERBS: Verbs that are not followed by an object, as in (a) and (b), are called "intransitive verbs." Common intransitive verbs: *agree, arrive, come, cry, exist, go, happen, live, occur, rain, rise, sleep, stay, walk*.
	 Verbs that are followed by an object, as in (c) and (d), are called "transitive verbs." Common transitive verbs: *build, cut, find, like, make, need, send, use, want*.
	 Some verbs can be either intransitive or transitive.
	     intransitive: *A student studies.*
	     transitive: *A student studies books.*

S **V** **O** (c) The *student needs* a *pen*. (NOUN) (VERB) (NOUN)	
S **V** **O** (d) My *friend enjoyed* the *party*. (NOUN) (VERB) (NOUN)	SUBJECTS AND OBJECTS: The subjects and objects of verbs are nouns (or pronouns). Examples of nouns: *person, place, thing, John, Asia, pen, information, appearance, amusement.*

□ **EXERCISE 1. Subjects, verbs, and objects. (Chart A-1)**
   Directions: <u>Underline</u> the subject (**s**), verb (**v**), and object of the verb (**o**) in each sentence.

             S   V   O
   1. The <u>politician</u> <u>supported</u> new <u>taxes</u>.
   2. The <u>mechanic</u> <u>repaired</u> the <u>engine</u>.
   3. Those <u>boxes</u> <u>contain</u> old <u>photographs</u>.
   4. The <u>teacher</u> <u>canceled</u> the <u>test</u>.
   5. An <u>earthquake</u> <u>destroyed</u> the <u>village</u>.
   6. All <u>birds</u> <u>have</u> <u>feathers</u>.

   List all of the nouns in the above sentences.

   <u>politician, taxes</u>

□ **EXERCISE 2. Transitive vs. intransitive verbs. (Chart A-1)**
   Directions: <u>Underline</u> each verb in the sentences. Write **vt** if it is transitive. Write **vi** if it is intransitive.

                VT
   1. Mr. West <u>repeated</u> his question.

              VI
   2. Smoke <u>rises</u>.

   3. The children divided the candy.

   4. I sneezed.

   5. A strange thing happened.

   6. The customer bought some butter.

   7. Our team won the game.

   8. Our team won yesterday.

   9. The fog disappeared, and the sun shone.

   10. Omar boiled some water. We made tea and drank it.

A-2 PREPOSITIONS AND PREPOSITIONAL PHRASES

COMMON PREPOSITIONS

about	*at*	*beyond*	*into*	*since*	*up*
above	*before*	*by*	*like*	*through*	*upon*
across	*behind*	*despite*	*near*	*throughout*	*with*
after	*below*	*down*	*of*	*till*	*within*
against	*beneath*	*during*	*off*	*to*	*without*
along	*beside*	*for*	*on*	*toward(s)*	
among	*besides*	*from*	*out*	*under*	
around	*between*	*in*	*over*	*until*	

(a) The <u>student</u> <u>studies</u> <u>*in* the</u> <u>*library*</u>. S V PREP O of PREP (NOUN)	An important element of English sentences is the prepositional phrase. It consists of a preposition (**PREP**) and its object (**O**). The object of a preposition is a noun or pronoun. In (a): ***in the library*** is a prepositional phrase.
(b) <u>We</u> <u>enjoyed</u> <u>the party</u> <u>*at*</u> <u>*your*</u> <u>*house*</u>. S V O PREP O of PREP (NOUN)	
(c) We went *to the zoo* *in the afternoon*. (place) (time)	In (c): In most English sentences, "place" comes before "time."
(d) ***In the afternoon***, we went to the zoo.	In (d): Sometimes a prepositional phrase comes at the beginning of a sentence.

☐ EXERCISE 3. Identifying prepositions. (Chart A-2)

Directions: <u>Underline</u> the prepositional phrases in the following. Identify the preposition (**P**) and the noun that is used as the object of the preposition (**O of P**).

                                P   O of P

1. Grasshoppers destroyed the wheat <u>in the field</u>.

2. The waiter cleared the dirty dishes from our table.

3. I parked my car in the garage.

4. Trees fell during the violent storm.

5. Cowboys depended on horses for transportation.

6. We walked to the park after class.

☐ EXERCISE 4. Sentence elements. (Charts A-1 and A-2)

Directions: <u>Underline</u> the subjects (**S**), verbs (**VT** or **VI**), objects of verbs (**O**), and prepositional phrases (**PP**) in the following sentences.

           S   VT   O   PP

1. <u>Alex</u> <u>needs</u> new <u>batteries</u> <u>for his camera</u>.

           S   VI   PP

2. A <u>bomb</u> <u>exploded</u> <u>in the road</u>.

3. <u>Sally</u> <u>wore</u> her blue suit <u>to the meeting</u>.

4. Beethoven wrote nine symphonies.

5. Bells originated in Asia.

6. Plants need a reliable supply of water.

7. We enjoyed the view of snowy mountains from the window of our hotel room.

8. The child sat between her parents on the sandy beach. Above her, an eagle flew across the cloudless sky.

A-3 ADJECTIVES

(a) Ann is an *intelligent student*.
        (ADJECTIVE) (NOUN)
(b) The *hungry child* ate fruit.
        (ADJECTIVE) (NOUN)
	Adjectives describe nouns. In grammar, we say that adjectives modify nouns. The word "modify" means "change a little." Adjectives give a little different meaning to a noun: *intelligent student, lazy student, good student*. Examples of adjectives: *young, old, rich, beautiful, brown, French, modern*.

(c) I saw some *beautiful pictures*. *INCORRECT*: *beautifuls pictures*	An adjective is neither singular nor plural. A final *-s* is never added to an adjective.

A-4 ADVERBS

(a) He walks *quickly*.
        (ADVERB)
(b) She opened the door *quietly*.
        (ADVERB)
	Adverbs modify verbs. Often they answer the question *"How?"* In (a): *How does he walk?* Answer: *Quickly*.
	Adverbs are often formed by adding *-ly* to an adjective.
	    adjective: **quick**
	    adverb: **quickly**

(c) I am *extremely happy*. (ADVERB) (ADJECTIVE)	Adverbs are also used to modify adjectives, i.e., to give information about adjectives, as in (c).
(d) Ann will come *tomorrow*. (ADVERB)	Adverbs are also used to express time or frequency. Examples: *tomorrow, today, yesterday, soon, never, usually, always, yet*.

MIDSENTENCE ADVERBS
(e) Ann *always comes* on time.
(f) Ann *is always* on time.
(g) Ann *has always come* on time.
(h) *Does she always come* on time?
	Some adverbs may occur in the middle of a sentence. Midsentence adverbs have usual positions; they
	    (1) come in front of simple present and simple past verbs (except **be**), as in (e);
	    (2) follow **be** (simple present and simple past), as in (f);
	    (3) come between a helping verb and a main verb, as in (g).
	In a question, a midsentence adverb comes directly after the subject, as in (h).

COMMON MIDSENTENCE ADVERBS					
ever	*usually*	*generally*	*seldom*	*never*	*already*
always	*often*	*sometimes*	*rarely*	*not ever*	*finally*
	frequently	*occasionally*	*hardly ever*		*just*
					probably

□ EXERCISE 5. Nouns, verbs, adjectives, adverbs. (Charts A-1 → A-4)

Directions: <u>Underline</u> the adjectives (**ADJ**) and adverbs (**ADV**) in the sentences.

      ADJ   ADV   ADJ

1. A <u>terrible</u> fire spread <u>rapidly</u> through the <u>old</u> house.

2. A <u>small</u> child cried <u>noisily</u> in the third row of the theater. *(adj)* *(adv)*

3. The <u>eager</u> player waited <u>impatiently</u> for the <u>start</u> of the game. *(adj)* *(adv)* *(adj)*

4. An <u>unusually</u> <u>large</u> crowd came to the concert. *(adv)* *(adj)*

5. Arthur <u>carefully</u> repaired the <u>antique</u> vase with <u>special</u> glue. *(adv)* *(adj)* *(adj)*

6. On especially <u>busy</u> days, the telephone in the <u>main</u> office rings <u>constantly.</u> *(adv)* *(adj)* *(adj)* *(adv)*

The above six sentences have 10 adjectives and 7 adverbs.

Count the total number of nouns in the above six sentences: _____

Count the total number of verbs in the above six sentences: _____

□ EXERCISE 6. Adjectives and adverbs. (Charts A-3 and A-4)

Directions: Choose the correct adjective or adverb in parentheses.

1. George is a *(careless, carelessly)* writer. He writes *(careless, carelessly)*.
2. Frank asked me an *(easy, easily)* question. I answered it *(easy, easily)*.
3. Sally speaks *(soft, softly)*. She has a *(soft, softly)* voice.
4. I entered the classroom *(quiet, quietly)* because I was late. *adj*
5. Ali speaks English very *(good, well)*. He has very *(good, well)* pronunciation.* *adv*

□ EXERCISE 7. Midsentence adverbs. (Chart A-4)

Directions: Put each adverb in parentheses in its usual midsentence position.

1. *(never)*   Erica has seen snow. → *Erica has never seen snow.*
2. *(often)*   Ted studies at the library in the evening. *often*
3. *(often)*   Ann is at the library in the evening, too. *often*
4. *(already)*   Fred has finished studying for tomorrow's test. *already*
5. *(seldom)*   Jack is at home. *seldom*
6. *(always)*   Does he stay there? *always*
7. *(often)*   He goes into town to hang around with his buddies. *often*
8. *(always)*   You should tell the truth. *always*

---

*The word **well** can be either an adverb or an adjective.

   *Ron writes **well**. **well** =* an adverb meaning "in a good manner." It describes how Ron writes.

   *Mary was sick, but now she **is well**. **well** =* an adjective meaning "healthy, not sick." It follows the verb ***be*** and describes the subject "she"; i.e., Mary is a *well person*, not a sick person.

NOTE: After the linking verb ***feel***, either ***good*** or ***well*** may be used:

   *I feel **good*** and *I feel **well*** have essentially the same meaning. However, ***well*** usually refers specifically to health, whereas ***good*** can refer to one's physical and/or emotional condition.

A-5 THE VERB BE

(a) John *is* **a student**.
  (BE) (NOUN)
(b) John *is* **intelligent**.
  (BE) (ADJ)
(c) John *was* **at the library**.
  (BE) (PREP. PHRASE)
	A sentence with *be* as the main verb has three basic patterns:
	In (a): *be* + *a noun*
	In (b): *be* + *an adjective*
	In (c): *be* + *a prepositional phrase*

(d) Mary *is* *writing* a letter. (e) They ***were*** *listening* to some music. (f) That letter ***was*** *written* by Alice.	*Be* is also used as an auxiliary verb in progressive verb tenses and in the passive. In (d): *is* = *auxiliary*; ***writing*** = *main verb*

TENSE FORMS OF *BE*

	SIMPLE PRESENT	SIMPLE PAST	PRESENT PERFECT
SINGULAR	*I am* *you are* *he, she, it is*	*I was* *you were* *he, she, it was*	*I have been* *you have been* *he, she, it has been*
PLURAL	*we, you, they are*	*we, you, they were*	*we, you, they have been*

A-6 LINKING VERBS

(a) The soup *smells* **good**. (LINKING VERB) (ADJECTIVE) (b) This food *tastes delicious*. (c) The children *feel happy*. (d) The weather *became cold*.	Other verbs like *be* that may be followed immediately by an adjective are called "linking verbs." An adjective following a linking verb describes the subject of a sentence.* Common verbs that may be followed by an adjective: • *feel, look, smell, sound, taste* • *appear, seem* • *become* (and *get, turn, grow* when they mean "become")

*COMPARE:
> (1) *The man looks angry.* → An adjective *(angry)* follows **look**. The adjective describes the subject *(the man)*. **Look** has the meaning of "appear."
> (2) *The man looked at me angrily.* → An adverb *(angrily)* follows **look at**. The adverb describes the action of the verb. **Look at** has the meaning of "regard, watch."

☐ **EXERCISE 8. Linking verbs. (Charts A-3 → A-6)**
  Directions: Choose the correct adjective or adverb in parentheses.

1. This math problem looks *(easy, easily)*. I'm sure I can do it *(easy, easily)*.
2. That chair looks *(comfortable, comfortably)*.
3. I looked at the problem *(careful, carefully)* and then solved it.
4. I felt *(sad, sadly)* when I heard the news.
5. Susan smiled *(cheerful, cheerfully)*. She seemed *(cheerful, cheerfully)*.
6. I tasted the soup *(careful, carefully)* because it was hot. The soup tasted *(good, well)*.
7. The room got *(quiet, quietly)* when the professor entered. The students sat *(quiet, quietly)* at their desks.
8. The sky grew *(dark, darkly)* as the storm approached.

☐ EXERCISE 9. Nouns, verbs, adjectives, adverbs, prepositions. (Charts A-1 → A-6)
   Directions: Identify each underlined word as a noun, verb, adjective, adverb, or preposition.

1. *PREP* Through the centuries, many people have confused *NOUN* whales with fish.

2. *N* Whales are *adj* mammals, not fish. They *V* breathe *N* air and give birth to live young.

3. Some species of whales *V* dive *adv* deeply *adj* beneath the *N* surface of the ocean in order to feed
   and can stay *adj* under the *N* water for more than an hour. All whales, however, must come
   to the surface *PREP* for air.

4. Whales make the longest *V* migrations known *adj* among mammals. Gray whales *V* swim *PREP* from the
   Pacific coast of Mexico, where they give birth in winter, *PREP* to the *adj* icy Arctic for the summer.

5. Orca whales, which are black and white, are *adv* highly *adj* trainable. They are also called
   "killer whales," but trainers tell us that these whales are *adj* intelligent and *adj* sensitive. One
   time, a newly captured male orca *V* refused to eat for a long time. *adv* Finally, he took a fish
   from the trainer. However, he didn't eat the fish *adv* immediately; he *V* took it to another
   recently captured whale, a female who had also refused to eat, and *V* shared it with her.

6. Whales have no sense of *V* smell and *adj* poor eyesight. Their senses of touch and hearing,
   however, are highly developed. They can hear an *adv* extremely *adj* wide *adj* range *V* of sounds and
   adj use *N* sound to locate objects.

7. Whales do not have vocal chords, but they can communicate with^{PREP} each other. They have a wide range of <u>clicks</u>, <u>whistles</u>, and <u>songs</u>. When a whale is captured in a net, other whales <u>gather</u> <u>around</u> it and <u>communicate</u> <u>through</u> the net. They follow the captured whale for long distances.

UNIT B: Questions

B-1 FORMS OF YES/NO AND INFORMATION QUESTIONS

<table>
<tr><td colspan="7">A yes/no question = a question that may be answered by yes or no.
A: Does he live in Chicago?
B: Yes, he does. OR No, he doesn't.</td></tr>
<tr><td colspan="7">An information question = a question that asks for information by using a question word.
A: Where does he live?
B: In Chicago.</td></tr>
<tr><td colspan="7">Question word order = (Question word) + helping verb + subject + main verb
Notice that the same subject-verb order is used in both yes/no and information questions.</td></tr>
<tr>
<th>(QUESTION WORD)</th>
<th>HELPING VERB</th>
<th>SUBJECT</th>
<th>MAIN VERB</th>
<th>(REST OF SENTENCE)</th>
<th colspan="2"></th>
</tr>
<tr>
<td>(a)
(b) Where</td>
<td>Does
does</td>
<td>she
she</td>
<td>live
live?</td>
<td>there?
</td>
<td colspan="2" rowspan="6">If the verb is in the simple present, use does (with he, she, it) or do (with I, you, we, they) in the question. If the verb is simple past, use did.
Notice: The main verb in the question is in its simple form; there is no final -s or -ed.</td>
</tr>
<tr>
<td>(c)
(d) Where</td>
<td>Do
do</td>
<td>they
they</td>
<td>live
live?</td>
<td>there?
</td>
</tr>
<tr>
<td>(e)
(f) Where</td>
<td>Did
did</td>
<td>he
he</td>
<td>live
live?</td>
<td>there?
</td>
</tr>
<tr>
<td>(g)
(h) Where</td>
<td>Is
is</td>
<td>he
he</td>
<td>living
living?</td>
<td>there?
</td>
<td colspan="2" rowspan="4">If the verb has an auxiliary (a helping verb), the same auxiliary is used in the question. There is no change in the form of the main verb. If the verb has more than one auxiliary, only the first auxiliary precedes the subject, as in (m) and (n).</td>
</tr>
<tr>
<td>(i)
(j) Where</td>
<td>Have
have</td>
<td>they
they</td>
<td>lived
lived?</td>
<td>there?
</td>
</tr>
<tr>
<td>(k)
(l) Where</td>
<td>Can
can</td>
<td>Mary
Mary</td>
<td>live
live?</td>
<td>there?
</td>
</tr>
<tr>
<td>(m)
(n) Where</td>
<td>Will
will</td>
<td>he
he</td>
<td>be living
be living?</td>
<td>there?
</td>
</tr>
<tr>
<td>(o) Who
(p) Who</td>
<td>Ø
can</td>
<td>Ø
Ø</td>
<td>lives
come?</td>
<td>there?
</td>
<td colspan="2">If the question word is the subject, usual question word order is not used; does, do, and did are not used. The verb is in the same form in a question as it is in a statement.
Statement: Tom came.
Question: Who came?</td>
</tr>
<tr>
<td>(q)
(r) Where
(s)
(t) Where</td>
<td>Are
are
Was
was</td>
<td>they
they?
Jim
Jim?</td>
<td>Ø
Ø
Ø
Ø</td>
<td>there?

there?
</td>
<td colspan="2">Main verb be in the simple present (am, is, are) and simple past (was, were) precedes the subject. It has the same position as a helping verb.</td>
</tr>
</table>

□ EXERCISE 10. Forms of yes/no and information questions. (Chart B-1)
   Directions: For each of the following, first make a yes/no question. Then make an information question using ***where***.

   Example: They can stay there.
   Yes/no question: Can they stay there?
   Information question: Where can they stay?

   1. She stays there.
   2. She is staying there.
   3. She will stay there.
   4. She is going to stay there.
   5. They stayed there.
   6. They will be staying there.
   7. They should stay there.
   8. He has stayed there.
   9. He has been staying there.
   10. John is there.
   11. John will be there.
   12. John has been there.
   13. Judy will have been there.
   14. Ann and Tom were married there.
   15. This package should have been taken there.

B-2 QUESTION WORDS

	QUESTION	ANSWER	
WHEN	(a) *When* did they arrive? *When* will you come?	Yesterday. Next Monday.	***When*** is used to ask questions about *time*.
WHERE	(b) *Where* is she? *Where* can I find a pen?	At home. In that drawer.	***Where*** is used to ask questions about *place*.
WHY	(c) *Why* did he leave early? *Why* aren't you coming with us?	Because he's ill. I'm tired.	***Why*** is used to ask questions about *reason*.
HOW	(d) *How* did you come to school? *How* does he drive?	By bus. Carefully.	***How*** generally asks about *manner*.
	(e) *How much* money does it cost? *How many* people came?	Ten dollars. Fifteen.	***How*** is used with ***much*** and ***many***.
	(f) *How old* are you? *How cold* is it? *How soon* can you get here? *How fast* were you driving?	Twelve. Ten below zero. In ten minutes. 50 miles an hour.	***How*** is also used with adjectives and adverbs.
	(g) *How long* has he been here? *How often* do you write home? *How far* is it to Miami from here?	Two years. Every week. 500 miles.	***How long*** asks about *length of time*. ***How often*** asks about *frequency*. ***How far*** asks about *distance*.

WHO	(h) *Who* can answer that question? *Who* came to visit you?	I can. Jane and Eric.	*Who* is used as the subject of a question. It refers to people.
	(i) *Who* is coming to dinner tonight? *Who* wants to come with me?	Ann, Bob, and Al. We do.	*Who* is usually followed by a singular verb even if the speaker is asking about more than one person.
WHOM	(j) *Who(m)* did you see? *Who(m)* are you visiting? (k) *Who(m)* should I talk *to*? *To whom* should I talk? *(formal)*	I saw George. My relatives. The secretary.	*Whom* is used as the object of a verb or preposition. In everyday spoken English, *whom* is rarely used; *who* is used instead. *Whom* is used only in formal questions. Note: *Whom*, not *who*, is used if preceded by a preposition.
WHOSE	(1) *Whose* book did you borrow? *Whose* key is this? (*Whose* is this?)	David's. It's mine.	*Whose* asks questions about *possession*.
WHAT	(m) *What* made you angry? *What* went wrong?	His rudeness. Everything.	*What* is used as the subject of a question. It refers to things.
	(n) *What* do you need? *What* did Alice buy? (o) *What* did he talk *about*? *About what* did he talk? *(formal)*	I need a pencil. A book. His vacation.	*What* is also used as an object.
	(p) *What kind of* soup is that? *What kind of* shoes did he buy?	It's bean soup. Sandals.	*What kind of* asks about the particular variety or type of something.
	(q) *What did* you *do* last night? *What is* Mary *doing*?	I studied. Reading a book.	*What + a form of do* is used to ask questions about activities.
	(r) *What countries* did you visit? *What time* did she come? *What color* is his hair?	Italy and Spain. Seven o'clock. Dark brown.	*What* may accompany a noun.
	(s) *What is* Ed *like*? (t) *What is* the weather *like*?	He's kind and friendly. Hot and humid.	*What + be like* asks for a general description of qualities.
	(u) *What does* Ed *look like*? (v) *What does* her house *look like*?	He's tall and has dark hair. It's a two-story,★ red brick house.	*What + look like* asks for a physical description.
WHICH	(w) I have two pens. *Which pen* do you want? *Which one* do you want? *Which do* you want? (x) *Which book* should I buy?	The blue one. That one.	*Which* is used instead of *what* when a question concerns choosing from a definite, known quantity or group.
	(y) *Which countries* did he visit? *What countries* did he visit? (z) *Which class* are you in? *What class* are you in?	Peru and Chile. This class.	In some cases, there is little difference in meaning between *which* and *what* when they accompany a noun, as in (y) and (z).

★American English: *a two-story house.*
 British English: *a two-storey house.*

☐ EXERCISE 11. Information questions. (Charts B-1 and B-2)

Directions: Work in pairs, in groups, or as a class.

Speaker A: Give the cues in the text. The first of the two cues is the answer to the question you want Speaker B to form. Your book is open.

Speaker B: Make an appropriate question for the answer Speaker A gives you. Your book is closed.

Examples:

SPEAKER A *(book open):* The teacher. The teacher opened the door.

SPEAKER B *(book closed):* Who opened the door?

SPEAKER A *(book open):* Opening the door. The teacher is opening the door.

SPEAKER B *(book closed):* What is the teacher doing?

1. My friend. That letter is from my friend.
2. Maria. Maria wrote that letter.
3. My mother's. That is my mother's coat.
4. In August. Alice and John are going to get married in August.
5. Gray. Her eyes are gray.
6. Black. Her hair is black.
7. Herb tea. I'd like some herb tea.
8. Coffee. I usually drink coffee with my breakfast.
9. The soap bubbles. The soap bubbles made her sneeze.
10. Ten minutes. It usually takes me ten minutes to eat breakfast.
11. By taxi. I got to the airport by taxi.
12. A ball. The boy has a ball in his pocket.★
13. Four. I have four brothers and sisters.
14. Florida. I grew up in Florida.
15. Five hours. It takes five hours to get there by plane.
16. Historical novels. I like to read historical novels.
17. Chapters 2 and 3. The test will cover Chapters 2 and 3.
18. I was late. I was late because the traffic was heavy.★★
19. For three days. She's been sick for three days.
20. Twenty. I'm going to invite twenty people to my party.
21. This one. You should buy this camera, not that one.
22. Marie Curie. Marie Curie discovered radium.
23. Practicing asking questions. We're practicing asking questions.
24. Great. Everything's going great.

★A form of *do* is usually used in questions when the main verb is *have* (especially in American English but also commonly in British English); e.g. *Do you have a car?* Using *have* without a form of *do* is also possible but less common; e.g., *Have you a car?*

  NOTE: Especially in British English but also in American English, the idiom *have got* is used to indicate possession instead of *have* alone; e.g., Bob *has got* a car. *Have* you *got* a car?

★★In informal spoken English, another way of asking *why* is *how come*. Usual question word order is not used with *how come*; instead, the subject comes in front of the verb.

  Example: John isn't here *(because he is sick).* → *Why isn't John here?* OR

  How come John isn't here?

□ **EXERCISE 12. Activity: asking questions. (Charts B-1 and B-2)**
Directions: Pair up with another student. Together create a dialogue for one or more of the situations. One of you is Speaker A, and the other is Speaker B. If you don't have a partner, write a dialogue as you would imagine the conversation to go. The beginning of each dialogue is given.

1. *This conversation takes place after class is over.*
   Speaker A: You are a student. You have a problem.
   Speaker B: You are a teacher. You try to solve the problem.

   SPEAKER A: Excuse me, _____. Do you have a few minutes?
   SPEAKER B: Certainly.
   SPEAKER A: I'd like to talk to you about _____.
   SPEAKER B: _____.
   Etc.

2. *This conversation takes place on the telephone.*
   Speaker A: You work for a travel agency.
   Speaker B: You want to take a trip.

   SPEAKER A: Hello. Worldwide Travel Agency. May I help you?
   SPEAKER B: Yes. I need to make arrangements to go to _____.
   Etc.

3. *This conversation takes place at a job interview.*
   Speaker A: You are the interviewer.
   Speaker B: You are the interviewee.

   SPEAKER A: Mr./Ms. _____, isn't it?
   SPEAKER B: Yes.
   SPEAKER A: I'm Mr./Ms. _____. It's nice to meet you. Come in
             and have a seat.
   Etc.

4. *Choose a situation that involves one person asking another person a series of questions. Assign yourselves roles and make up a conversation.*

B-3 SHORTENED YES/NO QUESTIONS

(a) ***Going** to bed now?* = ***Are you going** to bed now?* (b) ***Finish** your work?* = ***Did you finish** your work?* (c) ***Want** to go to the movie with us?* = ***Do you want** to go to the movie with us?*	Sometimes in spoken English, the auxiliary and the subject **you** are dropped from a yes/no question, as in (a), (b), and (c).

□ **EXERCISE 13. Shortened yes/no questions. (Chart B-3)**
Directions: Find the shortened questions, then give the complete question form.

1. A: Need some help? → *Do you need some help?*
   B: Thanks.

2. A: Why do you keep looking out of the window? Expecting someone?
   B: I'm waiting for the mail to come.

3. A: You look tired.
   B: I am.
   A: Stay up late last night?
   B: Yup.

4. A: I'm looking forward to going to Colorado over spring vacation.
   B: Ever been there before?

5. A: Why are you pacing the floor? Nervous?
   B: Who me?

6. A: Want a cup of coffee?
   B: Only if it's already made.

7. A: Heard any news about your scholarship?
   B: Not yet.

8. A: Hungry?
   B: Yeah. You?

B-4 NEGATIVE QUESTIONS

(a) *Doesn't she live* in the dormitory? (b) *Does she not live* in the dormitory? *(very formal)*	In a yes/no question in which the verb is negative, usually a contraction (e.g., *does + not = doesn't*) is used, as in (a). Example (b) is very formal and is usually not used in everyday speech. Negative questions are used to indicate the speaker's idea (i.e., what s/he believes is or is not true) or attitude (e.g., surprise, shock, annoyance, anger).
(c) Bob returns to his dorm room after his nine o'clock class. Matt, his roommate, is there. Bob is surprised. Bob says, *"What are you doing here? Aren't you supposed to be in class now?"*	In (c): Bob believes that Matt is supposed to be in class now. *Expected answer:* **Yes.**
(d) Alice and Mary are at home. Mary is about to leave on a trip, and Alice is going to take her to the airport. Alice says, *"It's already two o'clock. We'd better leave for the airport. Doesn't your plane leave at three?"*	In (d): Alice believes that Mary's plane leaves at three. She is asking the negative question to make sure that her information is correct. *Expected answer:* **Yes.**
(e) The teacher is talking to Jim about a test he failed. The teacher is surprised that Jim failed the test because he usually does very well. The teacher says: *"What happened? Didn't you study?"*	In (e): The teacher believes that Jim did not study. *Expected answer:* **No.**
(f) Barb and Ron are riding in a car. Ron is driving. He comes to a corner where there is a stop sign, but he does not stop the car. Barb is shocked. Barb says, *"What's the matter with you? Didn't you see that stop sign?"*	In (f): Barb believes that Ron did not see the stop sign. *Expected answer:* **No.**

☐ EXERCISE 14. Negative questions. (Chart B-4)

Directions: Sometimes the expected answer to a negative question is "yes" and sometimes "no." In the following dialogues, make negative questions from the words in parentheses and determine the expected response.

1. A: Why didn't you come too lunch with us? *(be hungry)* <u>Weren't you hungry</u> ?

   B: _____ . I had a late breakfast.

2. A: It's almost dinner time, and you haven't eaten since breakfast.

   (you, be) _____ hungry?

   B: _____ . I'm starving. Let's go eat.

3. A: You look tired this morning. *(you, sleep)* _____ well?

   B: _____ . I tossed and turned all night.

4. A: Daddy, Tommy said that the sun rises in the west. *(it, rise)* _____

   in the east?

   B: _____ , Annie. You're right. Tommy is a little mixed up.

5. A: See that man over there, the one in the green shirt?

   B: Yes. Who is he?

   A: *(you, recognize)* _____ him?

   B: _____ . Am I supposed to?

6. A: I can't understand why David isn't here yet. *(he, say, not)* _____

   _____ he would be here by 4:00?

   B: _____ . Something must have delayed him. I'm sure he'll be here soon.

7. A: What's the matter? Everyone else at the party seems to be having fun, but you look

   bored. *(you, have, not)* _____ a good time?

   B: _____ . I'm thinking about going home pretty soon.

8. A: Did you know that the Missouri River is the longest river in the United States?

   B: Are you sure? *(the Mississippi, be, not)* _____

   the longest?

   A: _____ . The Missouri is
   around 2,565 miles
   (4,130 kilometers) long.
   The Mississippi is around
   2,350 miles (3,800 kilometers).

B-5 TAG QUESTIONS

(a) Jack *can* come, *can't* he? (b) Fred *can't* come, *can* he?	A tag question is a question added at the end of a sentence. Speakers use tag questions chiefly to make sure their information is correct or to seek agreement.*

AFFIRMATIVE SENTENCE + NEGATIVE TAG → AFFIRMATIVE ANSWER EXPECTED	
Mary *is* here, *isn't* she?	Yes, she is.
You *like* tea, *don't* you?	Yes, I do.
They *have left*, *haven't* they?	Yes, they have.

NEGATIVE SENTENCE + AFFIRMATIVE TAG → NEGATIVE ANSWER EXPECTED	
Mary *isn't* here, *is* she?	No, she isn't.
You *don't like* tea, *do* you?	No, I don't.
They *haven't left*, *have* they?	No, they haven't.

(c) *This/That* is your book, isn't *it*? *These/Those* are yours, aren't *they*?	The tag pronoun for *this/that* = *it*. The tag pronoun for *these/those* = *they*.
(d) *There is* a meeting tonight, *isn't there*?	In sentences with *there + be*, *there* is used in the tag.
(e) *Everything* is okay, isn't *it*? (f) *Everyone* took the test, didn't *they*?	Personal pronouns are used to refer to indefinite pronouns. *They* is usually used in a tag to refer to *everyone, everybody, someone, somebody, no one, nobody.*
(g) *Nothing is* wrong, *is* it? (h) *Nobody called* on the phone, *did* they? (i) You*'ve never been* there, *have* you?	Sentences with negative words take affirmative tags.
(j) *I am* supposed to be here, *am I not*? (k) *I am* supposed to be here, *aren't I*?	In (j): *am I not?* is formal English. In (k): *aren't I?* is common in spoken English.

*A tag question may be spoken:
 (1) with a rising intonation if the speaker is truly seeking to ascertain that his/her information, idea, belief is correct (e.g., *Ann lives in an apartment, doesn't she?*); OR
 (2) with a falling intonation if the speaker is expressing an idea with which s/he is almost certain the listener will agree (e.g., *It's a nice day today, isn't it?*).

□ EXERCISE 15. Tag questions. (Chart B-5)
    Directions: Add tag questions.

  1. They want to come, ___don't they___?

  2. Elizabeth is a dentist, _____?

  3. They won't be there, _____?

  4. You'll be there, _____?

  5. There aren't any problems, _____?

  6. That's your umbrella, _____?

  7. George is a student, _____?

  8. He's learned a lot in the last couple of years, _____?

9. Larry has* a bicycle, _____?

10. Monkeys can't swim, _____?

11. Tina will help us later, _____?

12. Peggy would like to come with us to the party, _____?

13. Those aren't Tony's books, _____?

14. You've never been to Paris, _____?

15. Something is wrong with Jane today, _____?

16. Everyone can learn how to swim, _____?

17. Nobody cheated on the exam, _____?

18. Nothing went wrong while I was gone, _____?

19. I am invited, _____?

20. This grammar is easy, _____?

☐ EXERCISE 16. Tag questions. (Chart B-5)
Directions: Add tag questions. Work in pairs, in groups, or as a class.

Example: *(Carlos)* is a student . . . .
SPEAKER A *(book open):* (Carlos) is a student . . . .
SPEAKER B *(book closed):* . . . isn't he?

1. That's (. . .)'s pen . . . .
2. (. . .) is living in an apartment . . . .
3. (. . .) lives on (Main Street) . . . .
4. There isn't a test tomorrow . . . .
5. (. . .) has his/her book . . . .
6. You had a good time . . . .
7. (. . .) has been invited to the party . . . .
8. You didn't forget your key . . . .
9. Your parents haven't arrived yet . . . .
10. Turtles lay eggs . . . .
11. (. . .) can't speak (Arabic) . . . .
12. (. . .) is never late to class . . . .
13. Something will be done about that problem right away . . . .
14. These keys don't belong to you . . . .
15. You used to live in New York . . . .
16. There's a better way to solve that problem . . . .
17. (. . .) is going to come to class tomorrow . . . .
18. You should leave for the airport by six . . . .
19. (. . .) doesn't have a car . . . .
20. (. . .) sat next to (. . .) yesterday . . . .
21. We have class tomorrow . . . .
22. You've already seen that movie . . . .
23. (. . .) will help us . . . .
24. Nobody has told you the secret . . . .
25. I am right . . . .
26. Class ends at (ten) . . . .

---

*A form of *do* is usually used in the tag when *have* is the main verb: *Tom *has* a car, *doesn't* he?* Also possible, but less common: *Tom *has* a car, *hasn't* he?*

UNIT C: Contractions

C CONTRACTIONS

IN SPEAKING: In everyday spoken English, certain forms of *be* and auxiliary verbs are usually contracted with pronouns, nouns, and question words.

IN WRITING: (1) In written English, contractions with pronouns are common in informal writing, but not generally acceptable in formal writing.

(2) Contractions with nouns and question words are, for the most part, rarely used in writing. A few of these contractions may be found in quoted dialogue in stories or in very informal writing, such as a chatty letter to a good friend, but most of them are rarely if ever written.

In the following, quotation marks indicate that the contraction is frequently spoken, but rarely if ever written.

	WITH PRONOUNS	WITH NOUNS	WITH QUESTION WORDS
am	*I'm* reading a book.	Ø	*"What'm"* I supposed to do?
is	*She's* studying. *It's* going to rain.	My *"book's"* on the table. *Mary's* at home.	*Where's* Sally? *Who's* that man?
are	*You're* working hard. *They're* waiting for us.	My *"books're"* on the table. The *"teachers're"* at a meeting.	*"What're"* you doing? *"Where're"* they going?
has	*She's* been here for a year. *It's* been cold lately.	My *"book's"* been stolen! *Sally's* never met him.	*Where's* Sally been living? *What's* been going on?
have	*I've* finished my work. *They've* never met you.	The *"books've"* been sold. The *"students've"* finished the test.	*"Where've"* they been? *"How've"* you been?
had	*He'd* been waiting for us. *We'd* forgotten about it.	The *"books'd"* been sold. *"Mary'd"* never met him before.	*"Where'd"* you been before that? *"Who'd"* been there before you?
did	Ø	Ø	*"What'd"* you do last night? *"How'd"* you do on the test?
will	*I'll* come later. *She'll* help us.	The *"weather'll"* be nice tomorrow. *"John'll"* be coming soon.	*"Who'll"* be at the meeting? *"Where'll"* you be at ten?
would	*He'd* like to go there. *They'd* come if they could.	My *"friends'd"* come if they could. *"Mary'd"* like to go there, too.	*"Where'd"* you like to go?

☐ EXERCISE 17. Contractions. (Chart C)

Directions: Read the sentences aloud. Practice usual contracted speech.

Example: The streets are wet. → "The streets're wet."

PART I. CONTRACTIONS WITH NOUNS

1. My friend is here.
2. My friends are here.
3. Tom has been here since two.
4. The students have been here since one.
5. Bob had already left.
6. Bob would like to come with us.
7. Ron will be here soon.
8. The window is open.
9. The windows are open.
10. Jane has never seen a ghost.
11. The boys have been there before.
12. Sally had forgotten her book.
13. Sally would forget her book if I didn't remind her to take it.

14. Who is that woman?
15. Who are those people?
16. Who has been taking care of your house?
17. What have you been doing?
18. What had you been doing before that?
19. What would you like to do?

20. What did you do yesterday?
21. Why did you stay home?
22. When will I see you again?
23. How long will you be away?
24. Where am I supposed to go?
25. Where did you stay?

UNIT D: Negatives

D-1 USING *NOT* AND OTHER NEGATIVE WORDS

(a) AFFIRMATIVE: The earth is round. (b) NEGATIVE: The earth is *not* flat.	*Not* expresses a *negative* idea.

AUX + *NOT* + MAIN VERB
(c) I   *will*   *not*   *go*   there.
   I   *have* *not*   *gone* there.
   I   *am*   *not*   *going* there.
   I   *was*   *not*   there.
   I   *do*   *not*   *go*   there.
  He *does* *not*   *go*   there.
   I   *did*   *not*   *go*   there.
	Not immediately follows an auxiliary verb or *be*. (Note: If there is more than one auxiliary, *not* comes immediately after the first auxiliary: *I will not be* going there.)
	Do or *does* is used with *not* to make a simple present verb (except *be*) negative.
	Did is used with *not* to make a simple past verb (except *be*) negative.

CONTRACTIONS OF AUXILIARY VERBS WITH *NOT*		
are not = aren't* cannot = can't could not = couldn't did not = didn't does not = doesn't do not = don't	has not = hasn't have not = haven't had not = hadn't is not = isn't must not = mustn't should not = shouldn't	was not = wasn't were not = weren't will not = won't would not = wouldn't

(d) I almost *never* go there.
    I have *hardly ever* gone there.
 	
(e) There's *no* chalk in the drawer.
	In addition to *not*, the following are negative adverbs:
	   never, rarely, seldom
	   hardly (ever), scarcely (ever), barely (ever)
	No also expresses a negative idea.

COMPARE: *NOT* VS. *NO* (f) I *do not have* any money. (g) I have *no money*.	*Not* is used to make a verb negative, as in (f). *No* is used as an adjective in front of a noun (e.g., *money*), as in (g). Note: (f) and (g) have the same meaning.

*Sometimes in spoken English you will hear "ain't." It means "am not," "isn't," or "aren't." *Ain't* is not considered proper English, but many people use *ain't* regularly, and it is also frequently used for humor.

☐ EXERCISE 18. Using NOT and NO. (Chart D-1)
    Directions: Complete the sentences with *not* or *no*.

1. There are ___no___ mountains in Iowa. You will ___not___ see any mountains in Iowa.

2. Fish have _____ eyelids. They are _____ able to shut their eyes, and although

   they rest, they do _____ actually go to sleep in the same way mammals do.

3. _____ automobiles are permitted in the park on Sundays.

4. I can do it by myself. I need _____ help.

5. The operation was _____ successful. The patient did _____ survive.

6. When I became ill, I had _____ choice but to cancel my trip.

7. The opera *Rigoletto* was _____ composed by Mozart; it was composed by Verdi.

8. I have _____ patience with cheaters.

9. Ask me _____ questions, and I'll tell you _____ lies.

10. You should _____ ask people embarrassing questions about their personal lives.

11. "Colour" is spelled with a "u" in British English, but there is _____ "u" in the American English spelling ("color").

12. I excitedly reeled in my fishing line, but the big fish I had expected to find did _____ appear. Instead, I pulled up an old rubber boot.

D-2 AVOIDING DOUBLE NEGATIVES

(a) *INCORRECT:* I *don't* have *no* money. (b) *CORRECT:* I *don't* have **any** *money*. *CORRECT:* I have **no** *money*.	(a) is an example of a "double negative," i.e., a confusing and grammatically incorrect sentence that contains two negatives in the same clause. One clause should contain only one negative.★

★NOTE: Negatives in two different clauses in the same sentence cause no problems; for example:
> *A person who **doesn't** have love **can't** be truly happy.*
> *I **don't** know why he **isn't** here.*

☐ **EXERCISE 19. Error analysis: double negatives. (Chart D-2)**
   Directions: Correct the sentences, all of which contain double negatives.

1. I don't need no help. → *I don't need any help.* OR *I need no help.*

2. I didn't see nobody.

3. I can't never understand him.

4. He doesn't like neither coffee nor tea.

5. I didn't do nothing.

6. I can't hardly hear the radio. Would you please turn it up?

7. The beach was deserted. We couldn't see nothing but sand.

8. Methods of horse training haven't barely changed at all in the last eight centuries.

D-3 BEGINNING A SENTENCE WITH A NEGATIVE WORD

(a) *Never will I do* that again! (b) *Rarely have I eaten* better food. (c) *Hardly ever does he come* to class on time.	When a negative word begins a sentence, the subject and verb are inverted (i.e., question word order is used).★

★Beginning a sentence with a negative word is relatively uncommon in everyday usage, but is used when the speaker/writer wishes to emphasize the negative element of the sentence and be expressive.

☐ **EXERCISE 20. Negative words. (Chart D-3)**
   Directions: Change each sentence so that it begins with a negative word.

1. We rarely go to movies. → *Rarely do we go to movies.*
2. I seldom sleep past seven o'clock.
3. I hardly ever agree with her.
4. I will never forget the wonderful people I have met here.
5. I have never known Rosa to be dishonest.
6. The mail scarcely ever arrives before noon.

UNIT E: Preposition Combinations

E PREPOSITION COMBINATIONS WITH ADJECTIVES AND VERBS

A
be absent from
be accused of
be accustomed to
be acquainted with
be addicted to
be afraid of
   agree with
be angry at, with
be annoyed with, by
   apologize for
   apply to, for
   approve of
   argue with, about
   arrive in, at
be associated with
be aware of

B
   believe in
   blame for
be blessed with
be bored with, by

C
be capable of
   care about, for
be cluttered with
be committed to
   compare to, with
   complain about, of
be composed of
be concerned about
be connected to
   consist of
be content with
   contribute to
be convinced of
be coordinated with
   count (up)on
be covered with
be crowded with

D
   decide (up)on
be dedicated to
   depend (up)on
be devoted to
be disappointed in, with
be discriminated against
   distinguish from
be divorced from

be done with
   dream of, about
be dressed in

E
be engaged in, to
be envious of
be equipped with
   escape from
   excel in
be excited about
be exhausted from
   excuse for
be exposed to

F
be faithful to
be familiar with
   feel like
   fight for
be filled with
be finished with
be fond of
   forget about
   forgive for
be friendly to, with
be frightened of, by
be furnished with

G
be gone from
be grateful to, for
be guilty of

H
   hide from
   hope for

I
be innocent of
   insist (up)on
be interested in
   introduce to
be involved in

J
be jealous of

K
   keep from
be known for

L
be limited to
be located in
   look forward to

M
be made of, from
be married to

O
   object to
be opposed to

P
   participate in
be patient with
be pleased with
be polite to
   pray for
be prepared for
   prevent from
   prohibit from
be protected from
be proud of
   provide with

Q
be qualified for

R
   recover from
be related to
be relevant to
   rely (up)on
be remembered for
   rescue from
   respond to
be responsible for

S
be satisfied with
be scared of, by
   stare at
   stop from
   subscribe to
   substitute for
   succeed in

T
   take advantage of
   take care of
   talk about, of
be terrified of, by
   thank for
   think about, of
be tired of, from

U
be upset with
be used to

V
   vote for

W
be worried about

☐ EXERCISE 21. Prepositions. (Chart E)

Directions: Complete the sentences with appropriate prepositions.

1. Do you believe ———— *in* ———— ghosts?

2. Anthony is engaged _____ my cousin.

3. Ms. Ballas substituted _____ our regular teacher.

4. I can't distinguish one twin _____ the other.

5. Did you forgive him _____ lying to you?

6. Children rely _____ their parents for food and shelter.

7. Tim wore sunglasses to protect his eyes _____ the sun.

8. Chris excels _____ sports.

9. Andrea contributed her ideas _____ the discussion.

10. I hope you succeed _____ your new job.

11. I'm very fond _____ their children.

12. The firefighters rescued many people _____ the burning building.

13. I don't care _____ spaghetti. I'd rather eat something else.

14. Charles doesn't seem to care _____ his bad grades.

15. Sometimes Bobby seems to be jealous _____ his brother.

☐ EXERCISE 22. Prepositions. (Chart E)

Directions: Complete the sentences with appropriate prepositions.

1. Max is known _____ his honesty.

2. Mr. and Mrs. Jones have always been faithful _____ each other.

3. Do you promise to come? I'm counting _____ you to be here.

4. Trucks are prohibited _____ using residential streets.

5. The little girl is afraid _____ an imaginary
   bear that lives in her closet.

6. Do you take good care _____ your health?

7. I'm worried _____ this problem.

8. I don't agree _____ you.

9. We decided _____ eight o'clock as the
   time we should meet.

10. Who did you vote _____ in the last election?

11. How many students were absent _____ class yesterday?

12. It is important to be polite _____ other people.

13. The farmers are hoping _____ rain.

14. Jason was late because he wasn't aware _____ the time.

15. We will fight _____ our rights.

☐ EXERCISE 23. Prepositions. (Chart E)
Directions: Complete the sentences with appropriate prepositions.

1. I am not familiar _____ that author's works.

2. He doesn't approve _____ smoking.

3. I subscribe _____ several magazines.

4. Water consists _____ oxygen and hydrogen.

5. I became uncomfortable because she was staring _____ me.

6. She hid the candy _____ the children.

7. He never argues _____ his wife.

8. I arrived _____ this country two weeks ago.

9. We arrived _____ the airport ten minutes late.

10. Has Mary recovered _____ her illness?

11. I pray _____ peace.

12. I am envious _____ people who can speak three or four languages fluently.

13. Why are you angry _____ me? Did I do something wrong?

14. They are very patient _____ their children.

15. The students responded _____ the questions.

☐ EXERCISE 24. Prepositions. (Chart E)
Directions: Supply appropriate prepositions.

1. I am grateful _____ you _____ your assistance.

2. The criminal escaped _____ prison.

3. Elizabeth is not content _____ the progress she is making.

4. Paul's comments were not relevant _____ the topic under discussion.

5. Have you decided _____ a date for your wedding yet?

6. My boots are made _____ leather.

7. I'm depending _____ you to finish this work for me.

8. Patricia applied _____ admission _____ the university.

9. Daniel dreamed _____ some of his childhood friends last night.

10. Mr. Miller dreams _____ owning his own business someday.

11. The accused woman was innocent _____ the crime with which she was charged.

12. Ms. Sanders is friendly _____ everyone.

13. Benjamin was proud _____ himself for winning the prize.

14. The secretary provided me _____ a great deal of information.

15. Ivan compared the wedding customs in his country _____ those in the United States.

UNIT F: Connectives to Give Examples and to Continue an Idea

F-1 CONNECTIVES TO GIVE EXAMPLES

(a) There are many interesting places to visit in the city. *For example*, the botanical garden has numerous displays of plants from all over the world. (b) There are many interesting places to visit in the city. The art museum, *for instance*, has an excellent collection of modern paintings.	*For example* and *for instance* have the same meaning. They are often used as transitions. (See Chart 19-3, p. 389.)
(c) There are many interesting places to visit in the city, *e.g.*, the botanical garden and the art museum. (d) There are many interesting places to visit in the city, *for example*, the botanical garden or the art museum.	*e.g.* = *for example* (*e.g.* is an abbreviation of the Latin phrase *exempli gratia*.)* (c) and (d) have the same meaning.
(e) I prefer to wear casual clothes, *such as* jeans and a sweatshirt. (f) Some countries, *such as* Brazil and Canada, are big. (g) Countries *such as* Brazil and Canada are big. (h) *Such* countries *as* Brazil and Canada are big.	*such as* = *for example* (f), (g), and (h) have essentially the same meaning even though the pattern varies.**

*Punctuation note: Periods are used with *e.g.* in American English. Periods are generally not used with *eg* in British English.

**Punctuation note:
  (1) When the "*such as* phrase" can be omitted without substantially changing the meaning of the sentence, commas are used.
      Example: Some words, such as *know* and *see*, are verbs. *(Commas are used.)*
  (2) No commas are used when the "*such as* phrase" gives essential information about the noun to which it refers.
      Example: Words such as *know* and *see* are verbs. *(No commas are used.)*

☐ EXERCISE 25. Giving examples. (Chart F-1)
Directions: Add examples to the given sentences.

1. There are many simple kinds of exercise you could include in your life to improve your health. For example . . . .
   → *For example, you could walk briskly for half an hour three times a week.*

2. Some rock stars have international fame, for example, ...

3. The names of some newspapers are internationally known, e.g., ...

4. Some English words have the same pronunciation but different spelling, e.g., ...

5. Many English words have more than one meaning. For example, ...

6. If you are working too hard and not making time for pleasurable activities in your life, you should consciously schedule in relaxation time. For example, ...

7. Some natural phenomena, such as spring showers or moonlight, do not endanger human life. Other natural phenomena, however, have the potential to be life-threatening to humans, for example, ...

☐ EXERCISE 26. Using SUCH AS. (Chart F-1)
Directions: Complete the sentences with your own words. Use ***such as***.

1. You need a hobby. There are many hobbies you might enjoy, ___such as___ ___ceramics or stamp collecting.___

2. There are certain products that almost everyone buys regularly, _____ _____

3. You should buy a small, economical car, _____

4. Medical science has made many advances, yet there are still serious diseases that have not been conquered, _____

5. Some countries, _____ and _____, are rich in oil.

6. I enjoy such sports _____

7. Such inventions _____ have contributed greatly to the progress of civilization. However, other inventions, _____ _____, have threatened human existence.

8. There are certain times when I wish to be alone, _____ when _____ or when _____

9. Some subjects have always been easy and enjoyable for me, _____ _____. However, other subjects, _____ _____, _____

10. In certain situations, _____ when _____ _____ or when _____, my English still gives me a little trouble.

11. Numbers _____ are odd numbers, whereas numbers _____ are even numbers.

12. Some languages, _____ and _____, are closely related to English, while others, _____ and _____, are not.

F-2 CONNECTIVES TO CONTINUE THE SAME IDEA

(a) The city provides many cultural opportunities. It has an excellent art museum. *Moreover,* *Furthermore,* } it has a fine symphony orchestra. *In addition,*	*Moreover*, *furthermore*, and *in addition* mean "also." They are *transitions*. (See Chart 19-3, p. 389.)
(b) The city provides many cultural opportunities. *In addition to* } an excellent art museum, it has *Besides* a fine symphony orchestra.	In (b): *In addition to* and *besides*★ are used as prepositions. They are followed by an object *(museum)*, not a clause.

★COMPARE: *Besides* means "in addition to."

Beside means "next to"; e.g., *I sat beside my friend.*

☐ EXERCISE 27. Connectives to continue the same idea. (Chart F-2)
Directions: Combine the ideas in these sentences by using *moreover*, *furthermore*, *in addition (to)*, *besides*, or *also* where appropriate.

1. I like to read that newspaper. One reason is that the news is always reported accurately. It has interesting special features.

2. There are many ways you can work on improving your English outside of class. For example, you should speak English as much as possible, even when you are speaking with friends who speak your native language. You should read as many magazines in English as you have time for. Watching television can be helpful.

3. Along with the increase in population in the city, there has been an increase in the rate of crime. A housing shortage has developed. There are so many automobiles in the city that the expressways are almost always jammed with cars, regardless of the time of day.

4. Good health is perhaps one's most valuable asset. To maintain good health, it is important to eat a balanced diet. The body needs a regular supply of vitamins, minerals, protein, carbohydrates, and other nutrients. Physical exercise is essential. Sleep and rest should not be neglected.

UNIT G: Verb Form Review Exercises

☐ EXERCISE 28. General review of verb forms. (Chapters 1 → 20)
Directions: Complete the sentences with the correct form of the verbs in parentheses.

1. Some of the students *(speak, never)* _____
English before they came here last fall.

2. I wish I *(come, not)* _____ here last year.

3. It is essential that you *(be)* _____ here tomorrow.

4. Had I known Dan wouldn't be here, I *(come, not)* _____.

5. My passport *(stamp)* _____ at the airport when I arrived.

6. My seventy-year-old grandfather, who owns his own business, *(continue, probably)*
_____ to work as long as he *(live)* _____ .

7. I arrived here in August 1999. By August 2009, I *(be)* _____ here for ten years.

8. Before *(go)* _____ to bed, I have to finish my homework.

9. *(Hear)* _____ that story many times before, I got bored when Jim began to tell it again.

10. Do you know that man *(sit)* _____ in the brown leather chair?

11. Many of the goods that *(produce)* _____ since the beginning of the twentieth century are totally machine-made.

12. The instructor said that she *(give)* _____ an exam next Friday.

13. I *(know)* _____ Beth for six years. When I *(meet)* _____ her, she *(work)* _____ in a law office.

14. If you *(be)* _____ here yesterday, you *(meet)* _____ my father and mother.

15. This evening the surface of the lake is completely still. It looks as if it *(make)* _____ of glass.

16. I don't know why the food service has to be so slow. We *(stand)* _____ _____ here in the cafeteria line for over half an hour, and there *(be)* _____ still a lot of people in front of us.

17. Sue says she can't come on the picnic with us. I wish she *(change)* _____ _____ her mind and *(decide)* _____ to come with us.

18. My dog turned her head toward me and looked at me quizzically, almost as if she *(understand)* _____ what I said.

19. *(Be)* _____ an excellent researcher, Dr. Barnes *(respect)* _____ _____ by the entire faculty.

20. Without the sun, life as we know it *(exist, not)* _____ .

☐ EXERCISE 29. General review of verb forms. (Chapters 1 → 20)
   Directions: Fill in the blanks with the correct form of the verbs in parentheses.

1. Since *(come)* _____ to the United States six months ago, Maria *(learn)* _____ a lot of English.

2. Mrs. McKay *(give, already)* _____ birth to the child by the time her husband arrived at the hospital.

3. I recommended that he *(apply)* _____ to at least three universities.

4. Thank you for your help. I never (be) _____ able to finish this work without it.

5. Peggy told me she (be) _____ here at six tomorrow.

6. (Sit) _____ on a park bench and (watch) _____ the brightly colored leaves fall gently to the ground, he felt at peace with the world.

7. Why didn't you tell me about this before? I certainly wish I (inform) _____ _____ earlier.

8. The large dormitory (destroy, completely) _____ by fire last week. Since all of the students (go) _____ home for the holidays, there was no loss of life.

9. James blushed when his friend asked him an (embarrass) _____ question.

10. Anna is grown up now. You shouldn't speak to her as if she (be) _____ a child.

11. I asked all of the people (invite) _____ to the party to RSVP.

12. When the (puzzle) _____ student could not figure out the answer to the (puzzle) _____ problem, she demanded that I (give) _____ her the correct answer, but I insisted that she (figure) _____ it out for herself.

13. Ever since I can remember, mathematics (be) _____ my favorite subject.

14. The people (work) _____ to solve the problems of urban poverty are hopeful that many of these problems (solve) _____ within the next ten years.

15. It's a funny story. I'll tell you the details when I (call) _____ you tomorrow.

☐ EXERCISE 30. General review of verb forms. (Chapters 1 → 20)
Directions: This exercise is based on compositions written by students who were members of a multicultural class. Complete the sentences with the correct forms of the verbs in parentheses.

(1)   Next week, when I _____ _____ my final examinations, I
                             (finish)   *(take)*

(2)   _____ one of the best experiences I _____
             (finish, also)   *(have, ever)*

(3)   in my lifetime. In the last four months, I _____ more about
                                                              (learn)

(4)   foreign cultures than I _____ before _____
                                        (anticipate)   *(come)*

(5)   to the United States. _____ in a foreign country and _____
                                      (Live)   *(go)*

(6) to school with people from various parts of the world _____ me the
(give)

(7) opportunity _____ and _____ with people from
(encounter) (interact)

(8) different cultures. I _____ to share some of my experiences and
(like)

thoughts with you.

(9) When I first _____ , I _____ no one and I
(arrive) (know)

(10) _____ all of my fingers _____ what I was
(need) (communicate)

trying to say in English. All of the international students were in the same situation.

(11) When we _____ the right word, we _____
(can, find, not) (use)

(12) strange movements and gestures _____ our meaning.
(communicate)

(13) _____ some common phrases, such as "How are you?", "Fine, thank
(Know)

(14) you, and you?" and "What country are you from?", _____ enough in the
(be)

(15) beginning for us _____ friends with each other. The TV room in the
(make)

(16) dormitory _____ our common meeting place every evening after dinner.
(become)

(17) _____ _____ our English, many of us tried to
(Hope) (improve)

(18) watch television and _____ what the people _____
(understand) (appear)

(19) on the screen _____ , but for the most part their words were just a
(say)

(20) strange mumble to us. After a while, _____ and a little sad, we slowly
(bore)

(21) began to disappear to our separate rooms. I _____ that all of us
(think)

(22) _____ some homesickness. However, despite my loneliness, I
(experience)

(23) I had a good feeling within myself because I _____ what I
(do)

(24) _____ to do for many years: _____ and
(want) (live)

(25) _____ in a foreign country.
(study)

(26) After a few days, classes _____ and we _____
(begin) (have)

(27) another meeting place: the classroom. _____ quite what
(know, not)

(28) _____ the first day of class, I was a bit nervous, but also
(expect)

(29) _____ . After _____ the right building and the
(excite) (find)

(30) right room, I walked in and _____ an empty seat. I _____
(choose)   (introduce)

(31) myself to the person _____ next to me, and we sat _____ to
(sit)   (talk)

(32) each other for a few minutes. Since we _____ from different countries, we
(be)

(33) _____ in English. At first, I was afraid that the other student
(speak)

(34) _____ what I _____, but I _____
(understand, not)   (say)

(35) _____ when she _____ to my questions easily.
(surprise, pleasantly)   (respond)

(36) Together we _____ the first steps toward _____ a friendship.
(take)   (build)

(37) As the semester _____, I _____ out more and more
(progress)   (find)

about my fellow students. Students from some countries were reticent and shy in class.

(38) They almost never _____ questions and _____ very softly.
(ask)   (speak)

(39) Others of different nationalities _____ just the opposite: they spoke in
(be)

(40) booming voices and never _____ _____ questions,
(hesitate)   (ask)

(41) and sometimes they _____ the teacher. I _____
(interrupt, even)   (be, never)

(42) in a classroom with such a mixture of cultures before. I learned _____
(suprise, not)

(43) by anything my classmates might say or do. The time spent _____ our
(share)

(44) ideas with each other and _____ about each other's customs and beliefs
(learn)

(45) _____ valuable and fun. As we progressed in our English, we slowly
(be)

learned about each other, too.

(46) Now, several months after my arrival in the United States, I _____ able
(be)

to understand not only some English but also something about different cultures. If I

(47) _____ here, I _____ able to attain these insights
(come, not)   (be, not)

(48) into other cultures. I wish everyone in the world _____ the same experience.
(have)

(49) Perhaps if all the people in the world _____ more about cultures different
(know)

(50) from their own and _____ the opportunity _____ friends
(have)   (make)

(51) with people from different countries, peace _____ secure.
(be)

INDEX

Accustomed to, 298 *(Look on page 298.)*	The numbers following the words listed in the index refer to page numbers in the main text.
Be, A6 *(Look in the back part of this book on the sixth page of the Appendix.)*	The index numbers preceded by the letter "A" (e.g., A6) refer to pages in the Appendix, which is found in the last part of the text. The main text ends on page 437, and the appendix immediately follows. Page 438 is followed by page A1.
Correlative conjunctions, 353*fn.* *(Look at the footnote on page 353.)*	Information given in the footnotes to charts and exercises is noted by the page number plus the abbreviation *fn.*